LOVE LIES

A TRUE STORY OF MARRIAGE AND MURDER IN THE SUBURBS

AMANDA LAMB

DIVERSIONBOOKS

Diversion Books
A Division of Diversion Publishing Corp.
443 Park Avenue South, Suite 1008
New York, New York 10016
www.DiversionBooks.com

For more information, email info@diversionbooks.com

First Diversion Books edition September 2015.
Print ISBN: 978-1-68230-197-5
eBook ISBN: 978-1-62681-942-9

For Bella and Katie,

may you always be surrounded by people who love you.

ACKNOWLEDGMENTS

I would like to thank Nancy Cooper's loved ones for sharing their memories of their daughter with me. I would also like to thank them for sharing their candid exploration of how domestic abuse touched their family and forever changed the fabric of their lives.

I would also like to thank WRAL-TV for giving me the time and resources to cover stories like this one in my role as a television reporter and also as an author. In addition, I would like to thank Kelly Gardner for his insight into the story and for helping to format the photographs for the book.

My editor, Shannon Jamieson Vazquez, deserves thanks for returning to this project fresh from maternity leave and shepherding it through the eleventh hour as the trial pushed right up against our deadline.

My thanks also goes to my agent, Sharlene Martin, for always believing in me, supporting me, and working hard on my behalf.

And finally, there are no words for my family who somehow put up with me being an author, a television reporter, a mother and a wife simultaneously. They are the best part of my day.

What God hath joined, let no man tear asunder.

—Matthew 19:5

PROLOGUE

SUNDAY, JULY 13, 2008

The way to love anything is to realize that it may be lost.
—Gilbert K. Chesterton

Sunday, July 13, 2008, was one of those typical North Carolina summer days where it was already hot in the shade at seven thirty in the morning. Parents, eager to cheer on their children at the countywide swim meet, were setting up camp along the hill overlooking the pool. They had coolers, folding chairs, binoculars, sunblock, newspapers, and travel coffee mugs. Unfortunately, I was armed only with a slightly stale blueberry muffin and a single bottle of water. I was wishing I had brought more provisions for what promised to be an epic day of watching my oldest daughter compete.

I headed to the team tent where all of the mothers who had volunteered to help were setting up their gear. I was wrestling to take one of the finicky fold-up camping chairs out of its canvas bag when I heard the buzz. *Someone from the neighborhood was missing.*

As a local television journalist for more than two decades, I had become good at eavesdropping on conversations. It's part of the job. I had also become good at quickly discerning if a conversation was simply personal and had no news value or if it contained important information to which I needed to be paying close attention.

I looked around and noticed clusters of people were starting to gather and speak about something in solemn tones with serious looks on their faces. *Missing. Jogging. Mother.* I caught snippets of conversations as they floated through the air around me and tried to piece them together.

I decided to seek out the director of our swim club, Gail Lewis. Surely, she would know what was going on. She did. She told me that a local young married mother of two was missing, that she had gone running the morning before, and that she had not returned home. Lochmere, the Cary, North Carolina, neighborhood where the woman was from, was not the kind of place where joggers disappeared. Lochmere was a neighborhood lined with meticulously manicured lawns. It was a place where the sidewalk was always crowded with children riding bikes and people walking their dogs. There was virtually no crime in the town of Cary other than petty property crimes, and Lochmere was considered one of the safest places to live in the entire region.

The missing woman's name, Lewis told me, was Nancy Cooper. It didn't register with me. I racked my brain, trying to make a connection between the name and people I had met at the swim club over the years. I immediately called my office, the WRAL-TV newsroom, and asked the women on the assignment desk if we were working the story. They told me a crew had already been assigned to cover it. A big community search was scheduled to take place that day in conjunction with the police search that was already under way. They were using a helicopter, dogs, bikes, boats, anything that would help them scour the woods and lakes in and around the subdivision. Volunteers were already plastering the neighborhood with fliers bearing Nancy Cooper's picture.

I quickly pulled up our website on my BlackBerry to check out Nancy Cooper's picture to see if I recognized her. In the photograph that filled my small screen, I saw a woman wearing a blue baseball hat, with shoulder-length brown hair, brown eyes, and a smile that showed a slight gap in between her two front teeth. She was a pretty woman with an imperfect smile that made her even more real than if she'd had beauty queen teeth. Tears began to well up in my eyes and a lump formed in my throat as I imagined Nancy Cooper's children without a mother.

"She always wore a brown bikini with a skirt bottom at the pool. Her daughter, Bella, has almost white hair," one of the mothers said to me.

That was the trigger my memory needed. Suddenly, Nancy Cooper's image became crystal clear in my head. Our paths had in fact crossed many times, though I never knew her name. Our daughters had swum together in the pool and danced together at a weeklong ballet camp that summer. We had chatted casually in the baby pool on several occasions. I remembered her as tall, thin, and athletic. It was funny, because the gap in her teeth in the photograph had thrown me off. I had never noticed it in person, probably because she was such a strikingly attractive woman.

I drifted away for a moment to a day just a few weeks prior when I had met my best friend, Amy, for coffee at a local restaurant called Java Jive. We sat outside and enjoyed the early summer sun, the kind of sun that warms you without making you sweat. It was a perfect day with a slight breeze and a cloudless sky. A few tables away sat the woman I now knew was Nancy Cooper, with a girlfriend. I didn't know her name at the time, but I had noticed her because she was wearing a pretty green sundress and flip-flops with the casual elegance of a woman who always looked good no matter what she put on. Her brunette hair was pulled back in a low, messy, short ponytail that made her look younger than she probably was. I had made a note to myself that I needed some sundresses like that to wear in the summertime.

As she'd talked with her friend and sipped her coffee, Nancy Cooper had looked like a woman without a care in the world. She'd looked like a woman who had it all together, the kind of woman who made other women envious.

That was the last time I remembered seeing Nancy Cooper. Little did I know at that time that our lives would soon intersect in a very intimate way and that everything about her would soon become very familiar to me. And little did I know that while Nancy Cooper appeared totally carefree on that bright early summer day, her entire world was about to come crashing down on her.

CHAPTER ONE

LOST

SATURDAY, JULY 12, 2008

Tears are the silent language of grief.
—VOLTAIRE

On Saturday, July 12, 2008, Jessica Adam called 911 at 1:50 P.M. to report her close friend Nancy Cooper missing.

"She supposedly went out for a run at seven o'clock this morning in Lochmere, and no one has heard from her," Adam told the dispatcher in a shaky voice.

Adam had been home since 8:00 A.M., waiting for Nancy to show up to help her paint. She tried calling Nancy repeatedly at home and on her cell phone. When she got no response, Adam just knew *something was very wrong.*

"She was supposed to be at my house at eight, and just because of the situation with the divorce, I'm just wondering if you could help—I don't know what I should do," Adam said with growing agitation in her voice.

Everyone who knew Nancy and her husband, Brad Cooper, knew they were headed for divorce. The couple had made no secret of the fact that they were in the process of going through a legal separation and that Nancy was thinking about moving back to their native Canada with the couple's two young daughters. Isabella Nancy

Cooper, nicknamed Bella, was four, and Gabriella Kathryn Cooper, who was called Katie, was almost two.

"Her and her husband were living together, but they were in the middle of a divorce," Adam told the dispatcher with some hesitation.

Adam went on to say that she had spoken with Brad Cooper by phone and that he had told her Nancy had gone out for a jog with a friend around seven that morning and had not yet returned. Adam told the dispatcher she had not been aware that Nancy had made plans to go running with a friend that day.

"According to her husband, when I called this morning around nine o'clock," Adam said, in between several deep breaths, "he said she had left this morning for a run, early, he believed with her friend Carey."

Adam said it was not like Nancy not to show up when she'd made a promise to a friend.

"She would have made contact with me or her other friends by now, who both had expected her today," Adam said, obviously trying hard to keep her emotions in check. "And the fact that her car is still at home and her cell phone is there is a little weird. That would not make sense."

Adam's voice sounded strained. It was as if she knew more than she felt comfortable saying, but hoped that the dispatcher could read between the lines. She stopped on occasion to speak to someone in the background before she answered questions. Adam told the dispatcher that she and Nancy's other close friend, Hannah Prichard, were both growing increasingly concerned about their friend's well-being, especially because Nancy had seemingly disappeared in the middle of having marital problems.

"Her husband, maybe that he's done something, I don't … I mean God forbid," Adam said, stopping short.

The dispatcher asked Adam if she knew whether or not Brad Cooper had ever physically abused his wife. Adam covered the receiver and consulted with people in the background before answering. Muffled talking could be heard before she uncovered the receiver again and responded.

"I don't know that he's been physically violent, but I know

there's been a lot of tension. So I wouldn't be surprised," Adam replied to the dispatcher's question. "I hate to say it, but I'm just not sure what to do."

Adam told the dispatcher that Nancy was an avid runner who had been training for a marathon. She said Nancy sometimes ran the trails through the woods that surrounded the neighborhood but usually never strayed too far from public areas, winding back and forth off the main drag, Lochmere Drive. Adam wondered out loud if maybe something had gone wrong with her friend's health; yet she had already called the local hospital emergency room, and there was no one there who fit Nancy's description.

Adam reiterated her concerns to the dispatcher. "As of right now, I think basically the information we have is that she left the house at seven o'clock, assuming her husband is telling the truth, and she's not returned, which wouldn't make sense."

Jessica Adam wanted to know what the Cary Police Department could do to help them find Nancy. She asked if there was a certain amount of time Nancy needed to be missing before they could file a report, and if it had to be Brad who filed the report instead of Nancy's friends.

Suddenly, another dispatcher broke in on the line, telling Adam that they would have an officer go by the Cooper home to speak with Brad about the situation. She said they would check on Nancy's whereabouts and needed a good description of her in order to begin the search.

"Tall, slender, very pretty, blond brownish hair," Adam said with hopefulness in her voice for the first time in the conversation.

The dispatcher then told Adam there was no time limit they had to wait to file a missing persons report, but that Nancy's husband would have to be the one to officially file it.

"I don't know how he's going to react to this either," Adam said, hesitating.

"You know what, it's okay, it's better to be safe than sorry," the new dispatcher said in a soothing voice. "If you're concerned about her, this is what I would want my true friend to do."

FAMILY TIES

At 3:00 P.M. on Saturday, July 12, 2008, Clea Morwick, another friend and neighbor, called Krista Lister, Nancy Cooper's identical twin sister, to tell her about Nancy's disappearance. Krista was at a baseball game in Toronto with her husband at the time.

"Nancy's missing, have you heard from her?" Morwick asked Krista.

Krista hadn't and was immediately worried. As is the case with many sets of identical twins, Krista and Nancy had a unique bond. Even though Nancy lived in North Carolina and Krista lived in Ontario, Canada, the two kept in close contact, talking by phone several times a day.

While the sisters were identical, they still had many differences. Krista was the quieter, more reserved sister. Nancy was the more outgoing one. One thing they did share, however, was a love for children. But Krista, unfortunately, was unable to have children of her own after a medical condition that led to a hysterectomy. As a result, she bonded deeply with her nieces. It was the closest she would ever come to having her own children. Bella called her "Krista-Mum." The twins were so close that Nancy had even talked at one point about being a surrogate for Krista and carrying a child for her.

So when she got the call from Morwick about Nancy's disappearance, Krista knew something was seriously amiss. "She was gone. She'd never leave her kids. So I knew that she was in danger, and I couldn't feel her anymore … I knew something was really wrong," Krista recalled later.

Immediately, Krista hung up with Morwick and called her sister's husband, Brad Cooper. Krista had never really liked Brad or understood her sister's attraction to him. She found him to be insufferably antisocial and dark compared to Nancy who was always so full of life. Lately, the couple had been going through a messy separation while still living in their Cary, North Carolina, home together. Krista decided to cut to the chase with her brother-in-law.

"Where's Nancy?" Krista asked him.

"I don't know, Kris. She went for a run, and she hasn't come back," Brad replied.

"What happened?" Krista demanded.

"I don't know. She hasn't come back from a run," he said again.

"That's not like Nancy, so where is she?" Krista asked, this time in an accusatory tone.

"She went for a run. I don't know," he answered calmly for the third time. Then she asked him an accusatory question—*what have you done to her?* Brad hung up on her.

Krista was baffled. "He sounded sad. He wasn't defensive. He wasn't anything. You know, just answered my questions like normal Brad," she later recalled.

Krista called the rest of the close-knit family—her parents; younger sister, Jill; and older brother, Jeff, who all still lived on the western side of Canada in Edmonton, Alberta, where they had grown up—to fill them in on what was going on down in North Carolina.

Her parents, Donna and Garry Rentz, were in church attending a funeral that day, but Garry's phone kept vibrating, so he finally excused himself and went outside to listen to the message. He returned to the sanctuary and brought his wife back outside to tell her what had happened. Donna was the more sensitive half of the couple, and he expected her reaction would be highly emotional.

"We knew that afternoon this was not going to have a happy ending," Garry said.

"Garry was a little more certain than I was," Donna clarified. She'd clung to the hope that maybe her daughter's disappearance was a misunderstanding, a mix-up, or a mistake.

The Rentzes started making plans to head to North Carolina to help in the search for their daughter. But even as they were getting ready to head to the United States, they never heard a word from their son-in-law, Brad. This bothered them intensely, as they were very close to Brad and had accepted him lovingly into their large nurturing family.

"He did not call us to tell us she was missing," Donna recalled sadly.

Jill Dean, the youngest of the Rentz children, was out furniture shopping with her husband, Chad, when Krista called to tell her about Nancy's disappearance. Jill received three calls from Krista in a row that went to voice mail because she was distracted. When she finally picked up, Jill was sitting on a couch in the middle of a store when Krista told her the news.

"Something bad has happened to Nancy. She went jogging and no one can find her, and I'm really scared," Krista told her hysterically.

Even though Jill was the youngest, she was considered the most rational, least emotional, of the three sisters, able to look at situations logically—a trait she inherited from her father, Garry.

"My immediate response was to try to figure it out," Jill said. "Maybe she went jogging, and maybe she really did go for coffee because she wanted to get away."

But even for Jill, this explanation was a stretch. She knew how devoted her big sister was to her two little girls, Bella and Katie. She also knew that her sister and her husband, Brad, were having serious problems.

"She would never have left her kids with Brad in the morning like that," Jill said. "She was just not like that. She would call for sure. She would never leave her kids. She would never leave and not tell us where she was going. Immediately, something did not add up."

Nine years younger than her twin sisters, Jill had always felt as though she had two extra mothers. But with Nancy, it was more than just having an older sister to look out for her; Nancy represented everything Jill wanted to be when she grew up. When Nancy moved from Edmonton to Calgary after college, Jill, a teenager at the time, had visited her every weekend.

"She was my entire life growing up. I wanted to be Nancy, I wanted to do everything with her," Jill said. "She was just that girl who not only guys but everyone wanted to be around. My friends wanted her to be their sister. Everybody loved her. She was just perfection to me."

As they grew up, Jill could see that Nancy was an imperfect human being like herself. In a way, it was like finding out Santa Claus wasn't real. It was a letdown for Jill, a death of the fantasy she had had about Nancy.

"We fought a lot. We're exactly alike. We're really strong-willed," Jill said.

While this reality made their relationship more complicated, it also changed the balance of power. Instead of blindly worshipping her older sister, Jill became a source of steady advice and calm strength for Nancy as she faced adversity in her adult life.

The oldest sibling and only brother, Jeff Rentz, also got a call from Krista that afternoon saying that Nancy was missing. Jeff, a police officer, was eighteen months older than Nancy and Krista and naturally protective of all of his little sisters. Yet he, too, had a special bond with Nancy.

"She was just that person to me. She was always the person that was there when you needed her," Jeff said.

Nancy was the one there for Jeff when he and his wife, Shannon, had a miscarriage and when they had their first child. She was always the first one to call and the one who would stay on the line as long as he needed to talk.

"I always thought the world of her," Jeff said of his little sister. "The years I was closest with her and did the most with her were some of the best years of my life."

After Nancy married Brad Cooper and moved to North Carolina, Jeff only saw her when she came home to Canada for visits, but they still maintained a close relationship over the phone. When he got the call from Krista about Nancy's disappearance, his heart sank into a dark place.

"When I first heard, I knew it wasn't going to be good. People just don't go missing," Jeff said, calling on his experience as a police officer.

Jeff knew that his sister and her husband were having issues, but he couldn't imagine mild-mannered, reserved Brad having had anything to do with Nancy's disappearance.

"That wasn't my first impression just because of the Brad I'd gotten to know when he lived here. I didn't think that he had had anything like that in him at all," Jeff said sincerely.

For the next several hours, the Rentz family exchanged calls, sharing their concerns and their thoughts about what they should do. Jill elected to stay behind in Edmonton and run the family business, a job placement company, so that her parents, Garry and Donna, could head to North Carolina.

While they wanted to be hopeful, everyone except Donna had low expectations that Nancy would be all right. Krista and Jill told each other to be strong but at the same time shared their fears.

"Within half an hour, Krista and I were saying to each other on the phone, 'This is not good. She's not coming back,'" Jill recalled.

Sunday morning, July 13, 2008, Krista woke up and called Brad again. Nancy was still missing. She immediately booked a flight to North Carolina, but a storm had grounded all of the planes in nearby Buffalo, New York, so Krista decided to rent a car and drive the seven hundred miles by herself.

The twelve-hour drive gave her plenty of time to think. To keep herself awake, she called friends, like Nancy's friend Hannah Prichard, and talked on the phone while she drove.

"They'll find her," Krista's friend Dominick tried to reassure her.

"She's not here anymore. I can't feel her anymore. She's gone. I know she's gone," Krista replied.

TRUE FRIENDS

By Sunday, everyone in the neighborhood had heard the devastating news. One of their own was missing, and they were determined to find her. The normally quiet subdivision was a frenzy of activity as a small army of people fanned out in every direction, posting yellow fliers with Nancy's picture on every possible space available—street signs, utility poles, even trees. A National Guard helicopter circled overhead as a police boat hugged the edge of Lochmere Lake.

The Cary police were managing the search, but dozens of citizens had joined their efforts. A small shopping center at the entrance to the subdivision had been transformed into a command post. Ironically, the effort was staged directly in front of Java Jive, Nancy's favorite coffee shop. Volunteer searchers met there to get maps and discuss routes. They were combing the trails and the neighborhood golf course on foot and on bikes. Many of the searchers were Nancy's friends and neighbors, but just as many were strangers who had heard the news and felt compelled to help.

Police released a description of Nancy Cooper as a thirty-four-year-old white woman, five feet nine inches tall, weighing about 120 pounds, with hazel eyes and shoulder-length brown hair. According to her husband, she had been wearing a T-shirt, running shorts, and blue sneakers.

Nancy had last been seen in public at a neighborhood dinner party two days earlier, on Friday night, July 11, 2008. The party had been hosted by friends who lived directly across the street, Diana and Craig Duncan. Brad had reportedly left the party early, around eight o'clock, to return home with the children and put them to bed, but Nancy had stayed at the neighbors' house until around midnight.

"She has two beautiful little girls who I love so much," Diana Duncan told WRAL-TV. "We love her so much; we all do. We just have to keep looking."

DAY THREE

Monday, July 14, 2008, dawned with no new developments in the case. It was clear that even in suburbia there were plenty of places to hide. Lochmere had nineteen hundred homes and was known for its heavily wooded lots and winding nature trails.

"I knew for sure that it was just a matter of finding her. I knew that we weren't going to find her alive. It was just a matter of finding her body," Jeff Rentz, Nancy's brother said.

The neighborhood was enveloped in a midsummer canopy of lush greenery. The leaves on the trees, the tall grass, and overflowing bushes and plants overpowered the landscape and made the search that much harder. It was easy to imagine that Nancy Cooper might not be found until winter stripped the area bare of its thick foliage.

That Monday, dozens of people arrived at the command post ready to help again. The new strategy was to look ten to fifteen feet off all of the major trails to see if Nancy had been hurt and stumbled or had been dragged into the woods. Two thousand fliers with Nancy's photograph and description had been posted around the neighborhood and throughout the town of Cary in the hope that someone had seen her and would come forward with information.

Volunteers, alone and in groups, young and old, men and women, packed the parking lot. As they walked up to the command post, they were greeted by one of Nancy's friends and neighbors, Mike Morwick, Clea Morwick's husband, who was heading up the search effort. He handed the volunteers maps with highlighted routes and directed them to their assigned search areas in the Lochmere subdivision and the adjoining Regency Park neighborhood, where Nancy sometimes went on her long runs.

"The police have asked us to look a little bit farther off the trail," Morwick said to WRAL-TV. "Yesterday we covered every trail in the Lochmere/Regency area. We're just going farther. We're looking farther into the brush to see if there's anything that might raise suspicion."

Cars continued to stream into the parking lot throughout the morning. It was a grassroots effort in the purest sense—the whole community had literally come out to find the missing young mother.

"Nancy is one of our dearest friends, and we miss her dearly," Morwick said as he wiped sweat off his brow. His face was red from being outside all morning long in the intense heat. His eyes were worried. "And we just want to find an end to this."

FOR THE LOVE OF NANCY

Krista Lister drove through the night directly to the Cary Police Department, where she gave investigators an in-depth interview about her twin sister, Nancy; her habits; and her marriage. Krista wanted to give authorities every possible piece of information about her sister and her sister's life that might help them solve the case.

Late in the morning, Garry and Donna Rentz also arrived from Canada and were picked up at the airport by Cary police officers. They, too, were eager to share what they knew with investigators.

While Nancy's parents were being interviewed by police, Krista decided she needed to see Nancy's girls, Bella and Katie, and make sure they were all right given the chaos. Brad had dropped them off with Nancy's friend, Hannah Prichard, in Apex, the next town over. When Krista got there, the girls were in a frazzled state, clearly not having slept much the night before. Katie, nearly two, greeted Krista as "Mama." Krista put her down for a nap, while four-year-old Bella clung to her and wouldn't let go. A few minutes later Brad showed up at the Prichards' house and demanded the children.

"I begged him not to take the kids," Krista said, but noted, "Brad took them practically screaming."

Krista and Brad eventually compromised. He allowed her and Jessica Adam to go to lunch with him and the girls, so that she could spend more time with her nieces. But when Krista asked Brad repeatedly to let her take the children to the hotel to be with her and her parents, the answer was consistently no.

POLICE LINES

The Cary Police Department called a press conference for one thirty that afternoon. The media interest had begun to swell from a few local news outlets to a contingent that included representatives from every major television network, including Canadian media since both Nancy and Brad Cooper were Canadian citizens. Word had gotten out that a pretty female jogger, the mother of two young children, was missing in an all-American town where crime was virtually absent. Women weren't supposed to disappear in Cary, North Carolina. This made it headline news.

Cary police chief Pat Bazemore was an attractive middle-aged woman with no-nonsense short blond hair and an anxious expression on her face. Instead of a uniform, Bazemore wore a professional black suit and a single strand of white pearls around her neck. She could have been on her way to church, but instead she was about to answer questions regarding what would turn out to be one of the most difficult cases in her career.

Bazemore started off the press conference by introducing Nancy Cooper's family. Even though she was a police chief, Bazemore was also a polite southern woman who clearly wanted to make Nancy's family feel welcome in the midst of what was shaping up to be their darkest hour. This was a test not only of her police department but of her mettle as a leader.

Nancy's family stood awkwardly next to the podium as the chief referenced each one of them by name. As is the case with most victims' family members, they had not yet settled into what their public roles would be in this unfolding tragedy.

Nancy's mother, Donna Rentz, was a petite gray-haired woman with a youthful face now marred with worry. Beneath her wire-framed glasses, her eyes were red and swollen. Her bottom lip quivered as she stood silently next to her husband and daughter.

Krista Lister, Nancy's identical twin sister, looked weary and shell-shocked as she stood stoically in between her parents dressed in traveling clothes—a blue zip-up sweat suit jacket, black Capri pants, and sneakers. Her brown hair was pulled back into a severe ponytail, and she wore thick, modern rectangular black glasses over her red, puffy eyes. Except for the glasses, Krista was the spitting image of Nancy.

Nancy's father, Garry Rentz, stood directly to the right of the chief. He wore a gray golf shirt and a solemn expression. The bald bespectacled patriarch of the family had agreed to make a statement, but according to the chief, he would not answer any questions afterward.

"My wife, Donna, and our family are very grateful for the search that has been mounted by the town of Cary police. We thank them for a job that has been well and very sensitively done. We thank them for their concern, for their sensitivity and their support of us as a family," Garry said with dignity and grace. "We are overwhelmed by Nancy's friends for their notification of police, for the search effort they have mounted, for their contact with our family, and for the care they have extended to our grandchildren. We have been here today to help find Nancy. We believe that she will be brought home soon, and we thank the community for the support they've given, and we ask that they continue in their effort to help find our daughter. Thank you very much."

Garry left the microphone and took a seat at a table to the right of the podium along with Krista and Donna. The chief resumed her spot at the podium, but all eyes were still firmly planted on the family of the missing girl.

"We've had an extraordinary outpouring of volunteers to help us search for Nancy," Chief Bazemore said as she tried to regain the crowd's attention. "We have not named a suspect or a person of interest in this case. We believe that Nancy is alive, and we will continue to investigate this case as a missing person case until we receive information that would indicate otherwise."

The chief reiterated the facts of the case—that Nancy, who was a regular runner, had reportedly gone for a jog Saturday morning and had not been seen since that time. She had left the house without her keys, cell phone, or identification.

"Our hearts are with Nancy's family and her friends during this very trying time. We are working around the clock to try to do everything we can to bring Nancy home," Bazemore said in a tone that sounded more like a mother's than a police chief's.

"When was the last time Nancy Cooper was seen by anyone other than her husband?" a reporter asked.

"She was seen at a party the evening before by friends," Bazemore said with a little hesitation in her voice. "The last person that reported seeing her alive was her husband."

"Have you had any definitive information that anyone saw her jogging Saturday? Or that anyone was jogging with her?" The reporter eagerly followed up.

"We have not had any definitive information," Bazemore responded.

"Is Nancy Cooper's husband cooperating with the investigation?" the reporter asked, getting to the heart of the matter.

"Nancy Cooper's husband is out searching for her right now," Bazemore said. Another reporter wanted to know how many times the police had spoken to Brad Cooper and if he had retained a lawyer.

"We've been in constant communication with the husband since Saturday, and we're talking directly with him," Bazemore said. "He is answering our questions."

"Did you ask him to participate in the press conference?" The first reporter countered.

"We did not," Bazemore said, starting to look a little ruffled. "What I will say to you again is that we have not named a person of interest, and we have no suspects at this time. We continue to look for Nancy. We consider her to be alive and a missing person at this time. Our goal is to bring her home safe."

Nancy's mother, Donna, who was seated at the table next to the podium, was now crying softly. People were tossing around her missing daughter's name like a basketball. All of the cameras quickly swiveled away from the podium to get tight shots of the grieving parent.

"We believe this is an *isolated* incident and we are investigating it as a missing person, an isolated incident with this case," Bazemore said awkwardly, clearly knowing that her choice of the word "isolated" would point in the direction of Nancy's husband, Brad. While it was common knowledge that the spouse was always the first suspect in such cases, her statement appeared to solidify that belief.

"Chief, if you believed that there was someone in this community that was dangerous, that people needed to be concerned about, would you not put that information out?" the first reporter asked, pointedly honing in on the theory that the crime was "isolated."

"Absolutely, we would put that information out. If we had

any indication that our community was at risk, we would get that information out as quickly as we had it," Bazemore answered.

She wouldn't comment as to whether Nancy had any conflicts with her husband, Brad, or anyone else in her life. She did confirm that the girls were still in their father's care.

"We don't want to do anything that would jeopardize our ability to bring Nancy home safe," Bazemore said as she ended the line of questioning involving Brad Cooper.

When the police chief turned to leave, Nancy's family got up from their seats and followed closely behind her. As the door shut behind them, it was hard not to wonder how these gentle people were going to handle what was likely to come next.

BREAKING SILENCE

A second press conference was scheduled for that evening at six thirty, and just before it began, Brad Cooper brought Bella and Katie to the hotel where his in-laws were staying so they could watch the children while Brad attended the second press conference of the day. When he dropped off the girls, there were no kisses or hugs or words exchanged; he simply handed the children over to their grandparents as he looked down at the ground and told Nancy's family he would be back soon to pick his daughters up.

"That's the only contact we had with him, there [was] virtually no conversation," Garry Rentz said.

At the 6:30 P.M. press conference, Chief Pat Bazemore took to the podium and announced that Nancy Cooper's husband, Brad Cooper, would make a short statement but would not be answering questions.

Brad sat alone at the long table to the right of the podium wearing a rumpled, white long-sleeved button-down shirt and a tan baseball hat. He was a tall, athletic man with olive skin and dark hair peeking out beneath the ball cap. His eyes were sunken and outlined with black circles as though he had not slept in days. The chief introduced him, and Brad reluctantly got up and stood in front of the microphone.

"Thanks. I don't really have a prepared statement," he said, nervously stumbling through his words in a barely audible voice. "I just wanted to thank all of the hundreds of volunteers that came out and are continuing to come out. If anyone knows anything I just want them to contact the police with any information they may have. Again, thank you to everyone that continues to come out and help out. Thanks."

After his brief statement, Brad returned to his seat, and the chief returned to the podium. She gave a carefully crafted statement regarding his cooperation.

"Mr. Cooper has been supportive of our work. He has allowed us to look into the couple's home and into both of their vehicles," said Bazemore. She added that he did so without a search warrant. "We have not named a suspect or a person of interest at this time. We still believe Nancy is alive, and we will continue to search for her as a missing person."

The chief then opened up the floor to questions. Naturally, the reporters wanted to know why Bazemore was so convinced Nancy was alive after days had passed without anyone having seen her.

"There is nothing that indicates one way or another, but we'll continue searching for her as a missing person until we identify something otherwise," the chief said cryptically.

While Bazemore talked, Brad sat at the long table next to the podium all alone, his hands in front of him, his eyes focused downward. With his right hand, he turned his gold wedding band slowly around in circles.

"Chief, why didn't her husband report her missing?" a WRAL reporter asked.

"I don't know why he did not report her missing," Bazemore replied sincerely. She repeated her words from the press conference earlier in the day: "There is nothing right now that indicates this is anything other than an isolated case. If there was any indication that our citizens were at risk of harm, we would be putting information out right away to let our citizens know to be careful and that there is a possibility of danger for them." Reporters continued to pepper the chief with questions about the timeline. They wanted to know more about the neighborhood party the Coopers had attended the night before Nancy's disappearance. They wanted to know if Brad had actually seen his wife leave for a jog Saturday morning.

"The last person who saw her was Brad Cooper. He did see her the night before, and he also saw her before she left to go jogging in the morning," Bazemore said, her words faltering a bit.

"Do you believe she's been the victim of foul play?" a reporter in the back of the room asked.

"There's nothing we have, no indication right now, that there's any foul play," Bazemore said.

A reporter from the local ABC affiliate asked the chief if there was a possibility Nancy had simply run away on her own.

"Anything is possible at this point," the chief said. "But there is no indication that she left on her own."

Bazemore appeared steady and calm, but doubtless she was anxious as her small-town police department took on what was turning out to be one of the most high-profile cases it had ever seen.

"It's frustrating, and it's difficult. We know that there is a family that has a family member missing, and it's very frustrating to us to not be able to solve that case right away," Bazemore said with honest emotion. "With your help, we hope that we are going to be able to bring Nancy home alive and that we're going to be able to do that soon."

CHAPTER TWO

FOUND

MONDAY, JULY 14, 2005

No one ever told me that grief felt so like fear.
—C. S. Lewis

"I'd like to report a body I found. I was out walking my dog," William Boyer calmly told the 911 dispatcher.

Boyer described his location as the Oaks subdivision at Meadowridge, just off Holly Springs Road in Wake County, on the edge of Cary. Holly Springs Road ran right behind Nancy Cooper's neighborhood. Boyer said he would walk back to his house on Fielding Drive and meet the officers there because the body was in an undeveloped section of the subdivision that would be hard for them to find on their own. He would take them to it.

"The reason I noticed it was because of all of the vultures hanging around," Boyer told the dispatcher. He said he had decided not to get too close once he realized what it was.

"Do you think she's beyond any help?" the dispatcher asked.

"I think she's dead," Boyer replied matter-of-factly. "My dog went down and sniffed, and I didn't see any movement."

WAITING GAME

Cary police chief Pat Bazemore visited Nancy Cooper's family Monday night at their hotel to tell them a body had been found and that it might be Nancy.

"I didn't know what to feel," her father, Garry Rentz, recalled sadly.

"We weren't hopeful at that point," her mother, Donna, said, with tears in her eyes.

Nancy's brother, Jeff, an Edmonton police officer, received a phone call from his father that night. Jeff counseled his family that they needed to be prepared, that the body was most likely Nancy, and that they should try to accept this fact now instead of waiting until it was confirmed.

"I knew for sure, and I think in the back of their minds everybody knew," Jeff said. "I think Mom was in a state where she wasn't ready to admit it, but I think in her heart of hearts she knew."

Garry also called his youngest daughter, Jill, who was back in Edmonton anxiously awaiting any news from North Carolina. Being thousands of miles and a time zone away, Jill felt very disconnected from the entire situation, and talking to her family on the phone was the only way that she could cope.

"We knew [the body] was her. We just had to wait for confirmation," Jill said of her conversation with her father that night. "You would rather have closure than be that person who loses your family member forever because you never find them, and you always have that question. We said, maybe if she's not coming back this is the best thing that could happen for us."

SEARCH OVER

"At around seven thirty P.M. this evening a man walking a dog called 911 to report seeing a person floating in a pond just outside of Cary town limits very near Lochmere. While we don't know for sure, and we won't know until a full medical examination is conducted, there is a possibility that this could be our Nancy," Chief Pat Bazemore said, her voice heavy with grief at her third press conference of the day.

The police chief went on to say that because the body was discovered in Wake County, and not within the Cary town limits, the scene was now under the jurisdiction of the Wake County sheriff, Donnie Harrison. "We ask that your thoughts and prayers be with all of them as we face what could be a very sad reality," Bazemore said.

The chief explained that the body was female and had been found in close proximity to Nancy's home.

"We do not know that this is Nancy. We are still very hopeful that it is not. But we are dealing with the possibility that it could be," the chief said. "Regardless of whether it's Nancy or whether it's not, it's someone's family member. It's a very sad and difficult time for all of us in the town of Cary and for these family members."

BLACKEST NIGHT

Fancy columns bordered the entrance to the Oaks at Meadowridge off Holly Springs Road. Fielding Drive itself was lined with large, stately brick homes, some costing well over a million dollars. It was not the kind of neighborhood where anyone would typically expect to find a body.

A mile down the road, however, the subdivision ended, and by nightfall there was nothing but blackness. The sheriff's investigators set up their staging area around a short bend where the darkness was suddenly interrupted by flashing blue police lights and the bright white television lights erected in front of the yellow crime scene tape. But despite the bath of light, the darkness spread out like a black hole beyond the tape. At 11:00 P.M., television reporters lined up in between the cameras and the yellow tape. Barely a foot apart, each camera had a powerful spotlight that illuminated the journalists who spoke solemnly and gestured behind them into the darkness.

Somewhere in the woods, investigators were processing the crime scene, away from the intrusive eyes of the media.

Wake County sheriff Donnie Harrison held an impromptu press conference for the live television cameras. The handsome graying sheriff was always seen in uniform, and he often responded to crime scenes personally despite leading one of the largest law enforcement agencies in the state. He was known on the street as an honest man who was passionately dedicated to his profession and hated sitting behind a desk.

"We have an unidentified female body. We're working very closely with Cary," Harrison said. "Tomorrow morning they'll find out the cause of death and who this person is."

Harrison wouldn't talk about the condition of the body or comment on what she had been found wearing. There had already been rampant speculation in the community that Nancy Cooper had been killed sometime during the early-morning hours and had never actually gone jogging. But Harrison wouldn't budge on any of these topics.

"But you do understand, because you've been working with Cary, that this is very close to where they've been searching for the missing woman?" a reporter asked.

"That's correct, and that's the reason we're working with Cary, and Cary is working with us. If it happens to be the lady from Cary, then Cary will take over," Harrison responded.

Harrison explained that the area where the body had been found comprised a new subdivision under construction. Although the streets had been paved, few homes had actually been built in that particular section. The body had been found in a ditch filled with water at the edge of a small cul-de-sac that did not have any homes on it yet. Investigators, he explained, believed that heavy rains late Monday had swamped the ditch with water and made it look like a small pond to the dog walker who had called 911.

A reporter asked the sheriff whether or not it looked like a place where someone might go jogging. Harrison said it was really too dark to be able to determine too much about the area at that point. However, in order to get to the location from Lochmere, a jogger would have had to cross Holly Springs Road, which was one of the busiest roads in Wake County. He made it sound improbable that Nancy Cooper had been jogging in this remote area, especially when she had miles of trails in her own neighborhood.

Just as the sheriff was finishing with the media's questions, Cary police chief Pat Bazemore got out of her car a few feet away. Sheriff Harrison left the bright lights of the television cameras and moved to consult with Bazemore and the investigators. They stood in a tight circle and talked in hushed tones with their heads close together to keep the reporters from hearing them. The chief's brow furrowed at something the sheriff said to her.

Whoever the body was, she had been discarded like a piece of trash in this dark, muddy place.

PRAYERS

Because almost everyone felt certain that the body would be identified as Nancy Cooper, the search that had been planned for Tuesday morning, July 15, 2008, was called off. Instead, searchers were asked to gather at the local Lutheran Church in Nancy's neighborhood for a small prayer service.

Up until this point, the Rentz family had had little or no contact with Brad except for when he'd dropped off and picked up the girls at their hotel Monday night before the press conference. Even then, there had been no significant words exchanged between them.

Nancy's brother Jeff thought this behavior was bizarre, considering how his family had practically adopted Brad. They had treated him like their own son, taking him on frequent family vacations and spending almost every holiday with Brad and Nancy. Brad was closer to Nancy's large, loving family than he had ever been to his own. It was this lack of contact with Nancy's family after her disappearance that started to turn the tide of Jeff's opinion about Brad.

"It didn't look very good once things started to move along," Jeff said.

On that Tuesday morning, Brad stood in the prayer circle in the church parking lot holding hands with the searchers, his head down, eyes hidden beneath the brim of a baseball hat. Nancy's mother couldn't understand why her son-in-law wasn't coming over to greet her and her family, to allow them to all comfort one another. After a few minutes of playing the silent game, she couldn't take it anymore.

"I looked at him, and I thought, 'What the hell?'" Donna said. "I walked over and I put my hand out to him, and he took my hand and he said nothing. So I put my arms out to give him a hug. He gave me a hug. That was it. He didn't talk. He didn't talk to me. When I gave him that hug he put his head down, and I peeked under the brim of his hat, that's when I knew that he killed Nancy. I looked in his eyes, and that's exactly what I felt."

It was difficult for Nancy's family to be in Brad's presence, especially with the way he was acting, so detached and standoffish from the family who had embraced him and loved him unconditionally for eight years. But they couldn't risk upsetting him. They knew his legal rights trumped theirs and that in Nancy's absence he would control all access to her children.

The family decided collectively at the gathering to approach Brad and ask if it wouldn't be prudent for them to take Bella and Katie back to Canada to get them away from the media spotlight. They felt this was the best thing for the children and hoped that he would make a good decision on their behalf.

"He said, no, he needed them as a distraction," Krista recalled. "It was right after that that we said, You know what, he's not going to allow us to see the kids. He's going to harm the kids, not harm them physically, but harm them mentally. He can't care for them, so we need to get the kids in a place that they can be properly taken care of," she described the family's thinking. "I wanted to throw up, I was so angry, and I despised him. But I had to put another face on of I'm here to support you because of the kids," Krista said.

IDENTIFIED

On Tuesday, July 15, 2008, at 5:00 P.M., the Cary Police Department finally broke its day-long silence and held another press conference to update the news media and the public about the case.

This time, perhaps due to the solemnity of the occasion, Chief Pat Bazemore had ditched the black suit and pearls in favor of her official dark blue uniform and gold badge. She walked into the room alongside the Rentz family, which now also included Nancy's brother, Jeff, and Krista's husband, Jim. They all filed in soberly and took their places at the long table, where they were also accompanied by Wake County sheriff Donnie Harrison. Nancy's friends were in the audience, but Brad Cooper was once again conspicuously absent.

The media had also expanded its ranks. Network television crews had arrived in town and set up shop in the back parking lot of the police station. The national news crews elbowed into the small room and wedged their cameras in between the local photographers. In addition, a growing number of Canadian journalists were now following the case. Several Canadian media outlets had dialed in on a conference call speakerphone so that they could not only hear the press conference but ask questions as well.

"As the chief of the Cary Police Department, it is my sad duty to tell you that the search for our Nancy is over. Earlier today, the state medical examiner in Chapel Hill told us that it is Nancy who was found last night just miles from her home in Lochmere," Chief Bazemore said with profound regret in her voice. "Nancy was murdered, and our investigation is now a homicide."

Bazemore announced that Nancy's brother, Jeff Rentz, would make a statement on behalf of the family. Jeff politely thanked the chief and made his way to the podium. In his short-sleeved plaid button-down shirt with a pen in his pocket and notes in his hands, he looked more like a businessman about to make a presentation than a grieving brother. But as soon as he started speaking, Jeff's expression showed the obvious signs of grief welling up inside him.

"We cannot possibly put into words the thanks to Nancy's many friends and the mass of volunteers both of whom are tireless and tenacious in their efforts, the many sectors of emergency services and law enforcement in Cary and surrounding areas including the Wake County Sheriff's Office, the town of Cary Police Department who have displayed dogged determination and the highest degree of professionalism throughout the investigation. We regret that all we can return for your efforts is our gratitude and our thanks," Jeff said with dignity and poise. "The wheel that is our family is missing a spoke, and while that wheel is now forever changed, it's incumbent upon us to adapt so we continue to spin. Nancy is a mother, a daughter, a sister, and that's how we'll keep her alive in our hearts. Thank you."

The police chief returned to the podium and gave what details she could to the room of hungry reporters.

"As you can imagine this is a terrible blow to all of us who feel we have grown to know and care for Nancy and her family," Bazemore said in a compassionate tone. "We are appalled and outraged by this terrible tragedy. And as the chief of this department, I promise each one of you that nothing will stand in our way of doing our very best to ensure a swift and certain closure to this case."

The chief then told the reporters that she didn't want to say anything that would jeopardize the investigation. As a result, she said, she would be very limited in what she could say publicly from here on out. When asked why Brad Cooper was not in attendance at the press conference, she said, "He was going to be here, but at the last minute he declined."

Once again, a reporter asked the chief to address why Brad had not reported his wife missing.

"He has not explained that," Bazemore said. "We have spoken with Brad. Today he is aware of everything that we've shared with the family. He has cooperated with us today, and we are still working with him."

When asked how Brad reacted to the news of his wife's body being found, the chief said simply, "He was devastated."

Another reporter asked the chief if the investigators were aware that Nancy might have been contemplating leaving her husband. "We have heard there were marital difficulties and that will also be a part of the investigation," Bazemore conceded.

Suddenly, out of nowhere, a voice from CBC radio in Edmonton came over the speakerphone. The journalist said reports had surfaced online that indicated that Brad may have gone to the local Harris Teeter grocery store early Saturday morning and purchased some bleach and possibly other cleaning products. The reporter added that he heard there was surveillance video of the transaction. This rumor had been swirling around, but no one had asked the police about it until now. The chief, in a carefully worded sentence, avoided answering the question, saying she could not "confirm or deny" this report because it had the potential to interfere with the investigation.

"I will tell you we will work this around the clock. We will not stop working this case until we do find the person who committed this crime and bring him to justice," Bazemore said. "I am extremely confident."

WHEELS IN MOTION

When Nancy was first reported missing, her father called his daughter's divorce attorney, Alice Stubbs, to tell her what was going on and to ask for her assistance. At the time, Stubbs asked Garry Rentz on a scale of one to ten what he thought the chances were that Brad was involved in his Nancy's disappearance. Garry's answer was eight.

After talking with Garry, Stubbs started to put together a custody motion that she would use to petition the court to get the girls into the custody of Nancy's family. It was a long shot at best. Grandparents had no special legal standing in North Carolina when it came to child custody or visitation. The fact that Brad had not been charged with a crime would make matters that much harder. It would be a tough sell for a judge to take the children away from a biological parent in this situation.

Nancy's family tried to give Stubbs as much ammunition as possible. Nancy's close friend and neighbor, Diana Duncan, had told them that Brad had called her the day after Nancy's body was discovered, asking her frantically to come to the house. There she'd found an unsettling scene: the children were not dressed, they were hungry, and there was no food in the house. She told Nancy's parents that Brad was disoriented and unable to care for the girls. The Rentzes gave this information to Stubbs to include in the custody petition. They knew that Brad had previously had issues with depression and handling stress, and had even attempted suicide once when he was younger. They also shared these facts with Stubbs.

"Brad had a history of suicidal ideation or actual attempt. It had been discussed by Nancy with us and in front of Brad with no denial," Garry said. He said the suicidal tendencies, along with the pressure of the murder investigation, made for a bad combination, one that didn't bode well for the safety of the girls. Neither Nancy's family nor Stubbs knew if what they had would be enough to convince a judge to give them custody of the children, but they decided to go for it.

CRIME SCENE

That Tuesday evening after the press conference, the Coopers' home in Cary was surrounded by yellow crime scene tape and police cars. Clearly the police were preparing to search the house, fueling speculation that Nancy might have been killed in the home, not out on a remote jogging trail. Chief Pat Bazemore confirmed this at a press conference the following morning.

"Around two A.M. this morning the Cary police obtained a search warrant for the home Nancy and Brad Cooper shared, for both of their vehicles, and for Brad himself," Bazemore said at the top of the Wednesday morning press conference, on July 16, 2008. "The moment we announced this was a murder, it was important that we secured the home as a possible crime scene."

While Brad Cooper had previously allowed investigators to casually look around the home, the warrant allowed them to do a detailed search, as well as to confiscate any items that might be considered evidence. The police were doing the search with crime scene investigators from the City/County Bureau of Identification.

A reporter asked why Brad was not there for the press conference. Garry; Donna; Krista; her husband, Jim; and Jeff were all sitting in their usual spots at the long table next to the podium. Their brightly colored shirts—Donna in pink, Jim in orange, and Jeff in yellow—sharply contrasted with their solemn faces. Garry kept his hand on his wife's leg. Once again, her eyes were red and puffy, carrying the weight of undeniable grief. Krista leaned into her husband for support and held his hand.

Their eyes instinctively turned toward the chief as they waited for her answer.

"He was invited. He's been given an open invitation as the rest of the family has. I do not know why he's not here," Bazemore said sternly.

The chief told the reporters in the audience that Brad Cooper was now staying with friends and would not be back at the house while the search was ongoing.

"Brad continues to be cooperative with us, and we still have not named a suspect or a person of interest," the chief added for what seemed like the one hundredth time. "As you know, an investigation is as important for ruling things out as it is for ruling things in."

The chief's words seemed to imply that the search of the Cooper home was routine. But part of the warrant also required Brad to hand over samples of his DNA. No one else's DNA had been requested at this point. This only added more fuel to the speculation surrounding Brad.

"Cary continues to be one of the safest places to live in the nation, and we will do everything possible to make sure our community stays safe," Bazemore said confidently.

ELUSIVE ANSWERS

The Coopers' modest two-story house sat on a small well-maintained yard wedged in between other similar homes. Lochmere was one of the more expensive neighborhoods in Cary, but unlike some of the newer subdivisions, it had a wide range of home styles and prices. The twenty-eight-hundred-square-foot brick home, while clearly an upper-middle class residence, was one of the lower-priced homes in the area. The home was built in 1993, and the Coopers had purchased it in January of 2001 for $250,000. The tax value of the home had increased to $335,000 since they'd bought it.

Investigators wearing blue latex gloves traipsed in and out of the house carrying large brown paper bags full of items. They strode across the lawn and deposited the bags into waiting dark unmarked sport utility vehicles. Clusters of neighbors gathered in their yards to watch the surreal scene, like an episode of *CSI* unfolding right in front of them.

The investigators also got down on their hands and knees and searched beneath the two BMWs in the driveway. They opened all of the doors on both cars and went through each vehicle, removing more bags of evidence. Brad's car was a white older-model sedan; Nancy's was a silver sport utility vehicle. Investigators appeared to be paying particular attention to the trunk of Brad's car.

Late in the day, an e-mail was sent out to the media by the Raleigh law firm Kurtz and Blum, headed by Howard Kurtz and Seth Blum, young personal injury lawyers not known for handling high-profile murder cases. They said they were now representing Brad Cooper and issued a formal public statement.

"Brad is devastated by the news of Nancy's death," it said. "He has and will continue to assist law enforcement efforts to bring his wife's killer or killers to justice."

CHAPTER THREE

TUG OF WAR

JULY 17, 2008

The probability that we may fail in the struggle ought not to deter us from the support of a cause we believe to be just.
—Abraham Lincoln

At the same time that news reporters were standing in front of the Cooper home delivering the latest information in the developing murder case, another drama was unfolding undetected by the media at the Wake County Courthouse in downtown Raleigh.

Nancy Cooper's divorce attorney, Alice Stubbs, had taken on the representation of the Rentz family in their quest to get custody of Bella and Katie. Stubbs completed the motion for custody of the Cooper children and headed to the courthouse. There she met with Judge Debra Sasser of the Wake County District Court and one of the lead investigators in the criminal case, Detective Jim Young, behind closed doors as Nancy's family waited anxiously for news.

In the formal application from Donna and Garry Rentz and Krista Lister for the emergency custody order, they laid out their case for why they should have the girls. First and foremost, they said that they did not believe Nancy Cooper had ever gone jogging. This added fuel to the argument that Nancy was killed sometime during the night after she left the neighborhood party.

They said that Brad Cooper had "engaged in a pattern of emotional abuse directed towards" Nancy and the children. They also said Brad "frequently yelled at Nancy Cooper and belittled her in the presence of her minor children."

In addition, the application stated that Brad was "unfaithful during his marriage" and "carried on a sexual relationship with a woman." This lent credibility to the rampant rumors around the neighborhood that Brad had cheated on his wife with one of Nancy's close friends.

The Rentzes said in the court documents that Brad had also "withheld funds from Nancy" and "refused to provide adequate financial support" to the point that she'd had to borrow money from her family to pay for things like groceries or other necessities such as gas for her car. Because she was a Canadian citizen with no green card, Nancy had no ability to work and earn her own money in the United States. She was totally dependent upon whatever money Brad gave her.

According to the filing, Brad had initially told Nancy she could move back to Canada with the girls, but then he had retracted his offer. To make sure she couldn't leave, the Rentzes said Brad had taken the children's American passports from Nancy's car, where she had been keeping them, and refused to give them back to her.

It also stated that on March 10, 2008, Nancy had retained Alice Stubbs to draw up a formal separation and child custody agreement between her and Brad.

Judge Sasser was convinced by the application and by her meeting with Stubbs and Detective Young. She granted temporary emergency custody to Nancy's family and set a hearing on the matter for July 25, 2008.

The order also allowed Nancy's family to take the children back to Canada so that they could attend their mother's memorial service there.

While the civil court matter was a completely separate issue from the criminal investigation, there was no doubt that the custody case gave everyone the opportunity to learn far more about Brad

Cooper than would ever normally be revealed by investigators. Neither investigators nor the district attorney would comment on the custody issue, but they didn't have to. In the days and weeks to come, Brad and Nancy's marriage would become an open book.

THE HANDOFF

After what seemed like an eternity, Stubbs came out of the judge's chambers with a broad smile on her face. Donna and Garry Rentz immediately knew they had won, at least this round. They then headed to the Wake County Sheriff's Office to talk about how the warrant allowing them to take custody of the children would be handled.

Nancy's family had already planned to meet Brad Cooper at a restaurant in Cary called Bullwinkle's that evening for dinner with the girls. The sheriff's deputies said that would be as good a place as any to serve Brad with the paperwork and take custody of the children.

They headed in multiple police cars to the restaurant. Garry, Donna, and Krista remained in an unmarked car around the corner about a block away. The exact moment of the transfer was traumatic, as deputies had to forcibly take the children away from Brad. The girls cried and protested, as any children would who were being taken from their parent by strangers in uniforms and put into a waiting patrol car. But they calmed down within seconds once the police car rounded the corner and they were handed off to Nancy's family.

"As soon as the kids got around the corner—" Garry recalled.

"They saw us," Donna said, finishing her husband's sentence. "It wasn't even a minute. It was just around the corner, we opened the door. As soon as they saw us and [the officers] handed them off, they were fine."

That night, at the police department's urging, the family moved to a new, more secure hotel in Cary, one with key card access to the individual floors. Nancy's family now had some very precious cargo to think about.

REMEMBERING NANCY

On Thursday, July 17, 2008, Nancy Cooper's family decided to talk about her at a press conference at the Cary Police Department for the first time since her body was found.

They paraded into the room in a line in the same order they had adopted every day since the tragedy had begun. But on this day, something was different. Each family member appeared to be carrying notes in their hands. Garry held a large brown accordion file folder. Donna held a white folded piece of paper in her small clenched hand. Krista carried a manila file folder under her arm. They took what now seemed like their assigned seats to the right of the podium. Chief Pat Bazemore stood at the podium, again in her dark blue police uniform.

"We will continue to do everything possible to ensure this is a professional investigation. I need to stress again today that investigations are as much about ruling things out as they are about ruling things in. We still have not named a suspect or person of interest. Everyone in this case continues to be cooperative with us," the chief said, dancing around any mention of Brad Cooper.

The chief asked the public for help removing the two thousand or so missing signs posted all over the Lochmere subdivision and surrounding neighborhoods. They were a painful and daily reminder to Nancy's family. To honor Nancy's memory, they asked instead that people tie white ribbons around their mailboxes or around trees in their yards.

Then Bazemore dropped the bombshell.

"Late yesterday, custody of Nancy and Brad's two children, Bella and Katie, was officially transferred to Garry, Donna, and Krista," the chief said as gasps could be heard in the audience. "I want to stress that this custody issue is a private civil matter between Nancy's family and Brad. It was not initiated by the town of Cary Police Department, and it was not a part of the investigation into Nancy's murder." However, she stressed, "That said, any information that comes from this civil matter will be considered by our investigators as we move forward in this case."

Nancy's family had agreed to speak with the media on this day, not about the investigation, not about Brad, but about Nancy. To a hungry press corps feeding on every new detail in the case, this was enough to satiate them for at least another day.

"We've heard so much about Nancy as a mother, and what a great mother she was, and what an inspiration she was to her friends, can you expand upon that?" A female reporter asked from a seat at the front table, just a few feet from the family.

"Nancy took very naturally to motherhood. I know no one who was more dedicated to their [children's] needs than Nancy," Garry said with a large smile. "She was a good mom."

Krista abruptly jumped in. She obviously had something she wanted to say before she lost her nerve.

"I am one of the luckiest people in the world. I am a twin," Krista said, breaking down in tears. She paused for a moment and then continued. "Sorry. I have a bond with Nancy that no one in the world has. All I have to do to remember her is to look in the mirror. I will continue to talk to her every morning as I always have. She's my biggest supporter, and she's my biggest fan. She's my best friend and my soul mate. She's my sister; she's my everything. She will always be half of me, and I promise to live my life in a way that makes her proud. And her spirit will always be alive in me. Nancy, I love you, and I always will. Thank you."

Krista was then barraged with questions about her sister. She said she was older than Nancy by five minutes, "and I never let her forget it."

A reporter asked Krista if the twin sisters ever fought about anything.

"Clothes," Krista answered with a smile through her tears. "Nancy had such an eye for fashion."

She recounted how she'd always stolen Nancy's new clothes and then tried to return them to the back of her sister's closet. But Nancy always noticed, and the result was always the same—screaming matches.

Garry then shared one of his favorite memories of his daughter, whom he said had always considered herself a fashion plate. When she was about fourteen or fifteen, she started wearing her jacket off one shoulder because she thought it was stylish. One day the family was walking at the West Edmonton Mall, and Nancy was a little bit in front of the others, wearing her trademark off-the-shoulder jacket. The entire family decided to take their jackets off one shoulder, too. Suddenly, bystanders started pointing and laughing at the crazy-looking family all walking down the mall with their jackets hanging off one shoulder, and Nancy finally turned around to see her family imitating her. Everyone, including Nancy, burst into laughter.

"We're a family that spends a lot of time together hanging out and really enjoying each other. That's going to carry on," Garry said. "I'm certainly going to miss Nancy, but we're going to carry on and do the kinds of things she wanted us to do."

Despite her grief, Donna said she had so many funny stories about her daughter she wanted to share. She said they had come from Canada to North Carolina to see Nancy right after Bella was born. They had visited her in the hospital, and she was wearing a breast pump around her neck that someone had given her as a gift, pretending it was a necklace. She had a grin on her face from ear to ear.

"She just brought the room down, but that's our Nancy, that's our Nancy that we miss desperately and we love," Donna said with an unsteady voice.

"How did you all keep in touch; how did you keep that bond?" the reporter in the front row asked.

Garry said the family always spent a week together at Christmas, either in Canada or in North Carolina. He said they also took an annual vacation together and that, less than a week before Nancy went missing, several members of the family had vacationed with Nancy and her girls in Charlotte at High Rock Lake, and at the beach in Hilton Head, South Carolina.

"I'm always going to be really happy with that decision because I saw her within the last five days of her life, and we had a great time together, as I knew we would," Garry said with a peaceful look in his eyes.

He said he also talked on the telephone with his daughter at least once a week.

"I knew very much what was going on in her heart, what was going on in her life, what was going on with her kids," Garry said.

Krista said she had the most consistent and constant contact with Nancy. She spoke to her sister multiple times a day.

"Every morning on my way to work I called her and Bella," Krista said. "Bella in the back, 'Krista-Mum, Krista-Mum, are you coming for tea today?'"

Krista said then Bella would ask if Krista's dog, Teva, was coming for tea.

"Bella, Krista-Mum lives a little far away," Nancy would say.

Then Krista said they would talk again in the afternoon after Nancy and Bella returned from the pool, and Bella would tell her how well she had swam that day.

Another reporter followed up with a question wondering how the bond between the twins affected Krista's ability to cope with what must be an overwhelming amount of grief.

"I don't know if I can answer that. I'm on adrenaline. It's really hard to look in the mirror," Krista said allowing tears to tumble freely down her face without wiping them away. "When I see myself walking, and I'll do a double-take and go, 'Nancy.' So I'm not really coping yet, I don't think."

Garry then said he had something to add to Krista's thoughts about losing her twin sister.

"As I was holding Krista when we discovered that the body that had been discovered was in fact Nancy, Krista said to me, 'Dad I've lost half myself,'" Garry said looking up at the ceiling as if he had a visual image of the moment etched there for him to refer to. "And I think that probably expresses what she feels. There is a oneness about twins that is very special, very real."

A reporter asked when the last time was that the family had spoken to Nancy. Krista had called her on the Friday before she was murdered, when Nancy had been painting her house. Krista said the painting made her twin sister cranky.

"She was quite the princess. It wasn't her usual day at the pool," Krista said with a little laugh through her tears.

Her father recalled Nancy's passion for running, adding that other than being a mother, running was her greatest joy. Nancy's Crohn's disease, a gastrointestinal ailment, had sent her to the emergency room on more than one occasion, but regular exercise seemed to help keep the condition at bay to the point where she had gone months, or even years, without an attack.

She had discovered running as an adult. It was the one place where she always felt at peace with herself and the world. It was the thing that kept her centered and balanced. Garry said when he visited Cary, he and his daughter went running early in the day before it got too hot. She would cut him a break because he was not nearly as fast or in such good shape as she was. His favorite place to run with Nancy was around one of the beautiful lakes in Lochmere, Lake Lomond, which had a mile-long paved running path. When they finished their run, they would stop for a coffee at her favorite neighborhood haunt, Java Jive, which was just across the street.

Krista also ran with Nancy when she would visit North Carolina. Krista had stopped running for a while because of an injury, and Nancy was her coach and cheerleader, trying to get her back into the groove.

"She was teaching me to run again," Krista said with a renewed smile.

Nancy had bought her sister a stopwatch and was instructing her to run a little and then walk a little. Krista said she could tell Nancy would get bored with their slow pace when they trained together, but she never complained. She approached it with a sense of humor, as she did most things she wasn't fond of.

Nancy's mother, Donna, didn't run much anymore, but she especially enjoyed walking around Lake Lomond and watching Bella and Katie feed the ducks and the swans with stale bread.

"We have many happy memories of Nancy here and of her

wonderful friends who have taken us into their homes in happy situations, not just situations like this," Donna said with as much joy as she could muster.

"Nancy was a very outgoing person," Garry said. "Has a lot of friends, makes friends easily and supports people well," he said adding that she tried to help her friends out as much as she could. "I'm very proud of the way she handled herself as a friend. She was a lot of people's best friend."

"Most will remember her smile and her charisma, and her ability to make everyone in a room happy and smile and laugh," Krista said. "I was never sad. Nancy was an amazing lady."

One reporter asked if Nancy had missed Canada and if she had liked living in the United States.

"In [all] honesty, she loved it here," Garry said. "I think the problem that Nancy had, that she talked to us about, was that she missed family."

Krista said there were many things about Cary her sister adored. Nancy loved to see the symphony outdoors at the Koka Booth Amphitheatre. She said Nancy had season tickets, and it was one of her very favorite things to do. She especially liked bringing the girls and watching them dance to the music.

"If you had to sum it up in a few words, what would you want people to be left with in terms of her legacy?" the reporter in the front row asked.

"I have so many memories, so many," Donna said, her voice cracking with the weight of her grief. She stopped and put her hand to her mouth. "What people have been talking about is all true. She is all those things. She was such a wonderful mother. But I have to start reminiscing by saying this is the single most important, heart-wrenching tragedy that has ever befallen our family, and I'm having difficulty dealing with it."

The family said that their friends and relatives in Canada had also been very supportive. Their youngest daughter, Jill Dean, was holding down the fort there and dealing with everything on the home front, including running the family business and handling the

Canadian media. Donna said their phone had been ringing off the hook with old school friends of Nancy's, her teachers, and neighbors who all wanted to offer the family condolences.

"They are wondering themselves, 'What can I do, what can I say, how can I help?'" Donna said. "Such difficult questions to answer."

Then the conversation naturally turned to Bella and Katie and their well-being.

"I think if we can stabilize things for them, they'll be fine," Garry said.

"This decision [to seek custody] was not made with malice or any intent other than to support the children," Donna added.

A reporter then asked an elephant-in-the-room question about what the family would say to Nancy's killer, which came precariously close to violating the chief's guidelines. Garry answered before the chief could step in.

"I think it is an act of cowardice to take a life, to rob a family, to rob children of a mother. I guess what I would say is if you have a shred of decency, come forward and own up to your behavior because we're all responsible for our behavior," Garry said, more than a hint of anger in his usually even-tempered voice.

"I think it is selfish how someone could even fathom taking such a beautiful person off this planet. It's unbelievably selfish," Krista agreed, as tears once again welled up in her eyes.

Finally, a reporter asked if the family thought the case would be solved. Garry said emphatically that he thought the Cary Police Department was doing a great job and that he couldn't have asked for a better investigative team to be on the case.

"We have put our faith and trust in these people," Donna said, letting her words linger in the unusual momentary silence of the packed room.

PARTING WORDS

On Friday, July 18, 2008, the Cary Police Department held what would be its last press conference until an arrest was made.

Garry, Donna, and Jeff Rentz filed into the room to sit in their usual spots. Krista was absent, but her husband, Jim Lister, was present. Chief Pat Bazemore approached the podium. She was out of her uniform and back in her black suit, looking road-weary and somber.

"I am pleased with the progress that we are making at this time," Bazemore said, "and I remain confident that this case will be brought to a certain and appropriate conclusion."

Jim Lister told the reporters there would be a Friday night event at a Cary church just for family and close friends, but a public vigil would be held for Nancy the next day, Saturday, July 19, at the Koka Booth Amphitheatre in Regency Park, one of Nancy's favorite spots. He also announced there would be a service at the Grace Lutheran Church in Edmonton the following Wednesday, July 23, for Nancy's friends and family in Canada. Jim asked that in lieu of flowers, the family hoped people would make donations to a trust fund set up for the girls.

Garry Rentz then added that the family planned to return to Canada with Bella and Katie on Sunday, July 20, and then come back to North Carolina on Thursday, July 24, in order to prepare for the custody hearing on July 25.

The first question from a reporter in the crowd was whether the family had told the girls about their mother's murder.

"They, at the moment, don't know. I shouldn't say they don't know—we have not told them, and they have not mentioned to us that they know," Garry said. "So we're going to walk very gingerly into this area."

Garry said that after the press conference the family would be consulting with grief counselors about the best way to handle breaking the news to such young children. Donna added that they were also talking to a psychologist about how to help the girls deal with the long-term trauma of losing their mother.

"Our primary concern is care of these children, that what we do is not going to hinder or harm them in any way, and we're being very cautious," Donna said, her eyes puffy, but dry for the moment.

"I think the girls will come through it well if we handle it well," Garry said. "This is their first time through this kind of a tragedy, and I hope it never happens again."

Then a reporter asked an obvious but important follow-up question about whether or not the girls had been asking for their mother.

"No," Garry said simply without elaborating.

"We're fortunate that Krista has a striking resemblance to their mother, so that's comforting to them," Jim added.

Donna said Bella had always called Krista "Krista-Mum." She said her granddaughter had always been attached to her aunt but was especially connected to her right now in her mother's absence.

"It's a good thing," Donna said.

"Are the girls asking for their dad?" Another reporter chimed in.

"No," Garry said quickly.

WRAL photojournalist Chad Flowers asked Garry how the family was coping with Nancy's death. Garry responded by saying things were as good as they could be—that the media and the police had been very supportive and that they had been keeping busy with the girls and the planning of the memorial services.

"Ask me in two weeks, and there might be a different answer," Garry said honestly.

"It's been overwhelming to come down here and see what an impact that Nancy's made," Jeff said, "and the outstanding caliber of friends that she's made and, by that connection, as well, the outstanding caliber of people here in Cary. They've really gone above and beyond. Right from day one, from the search, to the posters, to the removal of the posters, to passersby on the street stopping to share a story about Nancy or to express their condolences and their grief, it's really been heartwarming."

Donna added that their friends in Edmonton were also reaching out to the family.

"Our phone rang many, many times last night. Our tree in front of our house is covered in white ribbons," Donna said as her voice trailed off and she finally broke down in tears. But she cheered up when she started to talk about Bella's relationship with her same-aged cousin Kennedy, the daughter of Nancy's youngest sister, Jill. "I have many memories that keep coming back to me, and they're keeping me going actually," Donna said with a tearful smile. "The fact that the kids are happy and away from the publicity, the rumors, and the talking. That's our goal. We want to have them in an environment where they're with people that love them and care for them and they're safe."

"The only legacy that any human being leaves behind are your children. And if you can't spend the time and the effort to rear children in a way that makes them people you're proud of, then you really have not done your job," Garry said. "And so we dedicate everything we can to our legacy."

Garry said he and his daughter talked at least once a week, while he was at work. "Nancy and I had a very open relationship and I knew every detail of what was going on, from her concerns to her worries," Garry said. "She shared everything."

"Were you worried about her?" a reporter asked, risking the chief's wrath.

"Honestly, no," Garry answered.

"I was worried," Donna countered, with a shake of her head.

Predictably, the chief jumped into the conversation at that point and said that the questions were supposed to be about the girls, not about issues relating to the criminal case.

One of the reporters then asked the family what they wanted to share of Nancy with her daughters as they grew up.

"Her love and pure joy for life. She had it from a young child until now," Donna said as she started to sob.

"You see a lot of Nancy in little Bella, too. She's very strong, very opinionated, and if she doesn't agree with something that you're doing, she lets you know. There's absolutely no doubt," Jeff said. "And Nancy was always like that. If Nancy was angry with you, you found out real quick. And if she was happy with you, you also found out quick."

The family said that Katie, Nancy's youngest daughter, also shared some special qualities with her mother. Katie was just about to turn two; her birthday would be celebrated by the family that week on the day before her mother's memorial service in Canada.

"She's a funny, happy little girl. She's just exactly like her mother. She loves everything she does every day," Donna said, smiling again at the mention of her granddaughters.

Talking about the girls obviously gave the family great joy, but beneath their smiles, the grief over Nancy's death was still very visible. It was as if they were on an endless emotional roller coaster. One minute they would be laughing and smiling about something funny or peculiar Nancy or the girls had done; the next minute their faces became drawn and they wept, remembering what they had lost.

"I would like to know why," Donna said as tears suddenly streamed down her face. "I'm sorry," she added waving away the question.

Garry picked up where his devastated wife had left off, returning to the themes he had mentioned during the previous press conference.

"I think this is an act of extreme cowardice by whoever did this, and I think if they had a shred of decency in their body that they would come forward and acknowledge their guilt," Garry said. "There can never be a rationale that would make sense for taking the life of another. And I think the pain that's been inflicted with this senseless act should be brought to an end, and one way to do it is to have the spine to come forward."

Clearly, the family was now touching on the off-limits investigation, but the chief was not going to stop them from sharing their feelings if they chose to do so.

"As a decent human being, to do something that causes this much grief to other people, to another family, to tear people's lives apart," Jeff Rentz added, "regardless of the consequences or the circumstances, I think you would want to come forward and acknowledge what's happened and your role in that."

As a police officer in Canada, Jeff had dealt with serious cases before. But for the first time in his life, he was on the other side, the victim's side. He had been the officer knocking on a family's door giving a death notification before; now he was the one who had been notified.

"Now when I go back and continue working, continuing to do my job," Jeff said, "it will be with a completely different perspective, and one that I never wanted to have."

One network reporter took a chance and boldly asked the family if they were frustrated that the case had still not been solved yet.

"The more time that goes by, it gets harder," Donna admitted.

"We have every confidence in what the police are doing and we trust them," Garry repeated. "Would I like it to be over tomorrow morning? Yes, I would. Am I uncomfortable that it's not? No. I'm going to allow them to take their time."

As the questions finally wound down, the chief resumed her spot at the podium.

"I'll see you again when we take a suspect or suspects into custody," the chief said, not mincing words.

PLAYING DEFENSE

"I speak to you today as a result of the wild speculation that has been internationally reported surrounding the death of Brad's wife, Nancy," said Seth Blum, one of Brad Cooper's attorneys later that same Friday afternoon at his own press conference. "The bizarre and unsupported theories that have been floating around television and the Internet have made it impossible for us to sit quietly and to say nothing."

Blum stood at a podium full of microphones in a park in front of the Raleigh Police Department, of all places, not far from his downtown office. To Blum's left stood his law partner,

Howard Kurtz.

"Brad Cooper is a very private man. He's not accustomed to the hot glare of the media spotlight. He never dreamed that he would see his face splashed across television news shows, or his name in headlines, especially not under these terrible circumstances. Brad Cooper is also a man in mourning. He's lost his wife. He is grieving," Blum said, pausing for effect. While Blum wasn't well known for handling high-profile murder cases, he *was* known for acting in local theatrical productions. His performance at the press conference revealed his well-honed dramatic skills. "Mr. Cooper wishes to mourn privately. He does not want to do it at press conferences. He does not wish to do it for reporters. He does not wish to mourn in the public eye."

Blum reiterated what Chief Pat Bazemore had been saying all week, that Brad had cooperated with police, that he had answered their questions and opened up his home and vehicles to their searches.

"He has asked, and continues to ask, that anybody who has information about the attack on Nancy, please come forward. Please do it now. Please share your information with the police immediately," Blum said.

Blum agreed to take questions but said he would not talk about privileged information his client had shared with him, or anything that might jeopardize the success of the investigation.

"He is not a suspect. He is not a person of interest, and he has been very, very clear with the police—he did not kill his wife," Blum said, burying the lead three and a half minutes into the press conference.

One reporter asked a question about the fight for custody of Bella and Katie.

"I'll say this. Mr. Cooper loves his daughters. They are two little girls who have done nothing to deserve what they are going through," said Blum putting the palms of his hands up toward the crowd of interrupting reporters to keep them at bay. "Like any good father, he wants to shield them."

Blum went on to say that Brad wanted the custody issue to be worked out between himself and Nancy's family in private without the intrusion of the media or the public.

The reporters continued to throw out questions about the allegations against Brad from the custody motion—his infidelity, his alleged emotional abuse of Nancy, the accusation that he cut her off financially. Blum's jaw visibly tightened.

"I can say this. Mr. Cooper is in mourning. I would ask that you respect his privacy and allow him the memory of his wife," Blum said as Kurtz took his arm and escorted him away from the podium with a quick "Thank you."

CHAPTER FOUR

REMEMBERED

JULY 19, 2008

Grief is the price we pay for love.
—Elizabeth II

"We didn't have a lot of time to grieve. We had a lot on our minds," Nancy's mother, Donna, said.

The family's focus had been on getting the children into a safe environment and then giving them the emotional help they would need to get through the tragedy. This meant that Nancy Cooper's parents and siblings had little time to consider their own feelings. The children's needs had to come first.

Grief counselors came to the hotel to help the girls cope with the situation. Luckily, Katie, at nearly two years old, was too young to really understand what was going on, but four-year-old Bella knew something was terribly wrong: Her mother was not there, and Bella and her sister were staying in a hotel with their grandparents.

The grief counselor told the family that they would need to tell Bella about her mother's death before she attended the public memorial service in Cary scheduled for Saturday, July 19. The idea was to have Brad Cooper come to the hotel and tell her in the presence of Nancy's family so that she would have a lot of support.

On the day of the service, Brad arrived at the hotel with his neighbor, Clea Morwick, and her two boys in tow. It didn't appear to Garry Rentz that Brad actually intended to have a heart-to-heart with his older daughter about her mother's death. Instead, all four children proceeded to play in the pool and get wild.

"Bella was wound up to the ceiling," Garry said. "[Brad was] wrestling with Bella, and she [didn't] have any interest in talking."

Garry, Donna, and Krista were panicking about how they were going to handle the situation. Surely, they could not take this child to a memorial service for her mother without first telling her the truth. She was young but smart, and it wasn't fair to keep her in the dark any longer.

"We're now fifteen minutes from the service," Garry said. "I said to Brad, 'I'll do it. This isn't working.'"

So, in the minivan on the way to the service, the family decided to handle it in the best way they knew how. Bella was in the van with Donna and Krista—her little sister, Katie, was following in a car with her uncle Jeff.

"Mommy was lost and they couldn't find her. When they found Mommy, the doctors couldn't help her. Mommy has died. Mommy is with the angels," Donna told her granddaughter.

"Mommy is not coming back," Bella said through tears streaming down her face.

"No, but we're all here. We all love you, and we're going to take care of you," Donna said, embracing the child.

It was the roughest part of the day for everyone, seeing Bella break down under the weight of the worst tragedy a child could ever imagine. But somehow, by the time they pulled into the amphitheater parking lot, she was calm and seemed ready to face what was ahead of her.

Bella hopped out of the minivan with her aunt Krista, carrying a pink backpack and wearing a matching pink baseball hat. Immediately, Nancy's friends surrounded the child, bending down to give her tender hugs. Nancy's brother, Jeff, walked up with Katie in his arms and gently placed her down next to her sister in the middle of the adoring circle.

Unlike a traditional funeral where everyone wore black, Nancy's family had chosen to dress in white and pastel colors to celebrate her life instead of dwelling on her death.

In the background, two musicians played the flute and the acoustic guitar. The beautiful, subtle melody drifted through the somber crowd. Nancy's friend, Hannah Prichard, held tight to Donna's arm and guided her toward the seats in the front row of the outdoor amphitheater, while Garry, who had donned a sun hat to keep his bald head from burning, walked behind them with Prichard's husband.

The family was also joined by Jessica Adam, the friend who had called 911. The group moved slowly together to the white plastic chairs in front of the stage. It was a typically beautiful North Carolina summer day with blue skies and plenty of sunshine. People in the crowd fanned their programs, trying to catch the on-again off-again breeze.

Despite the solemn mood everyone—including Krista, who bent down and gingerly guided Bella to her seat—managed weak smiles as they passed the hundreds of people already seated. The audience was made up of both people who had known Nancy and people who had not, but they shared one thing in common: They had been touched by the tragedy and wanted to pay their respects to her family.

White flowers adorned the stage, spilling over the edges of large flower pots. A blown-up black-and-white picture of Nancy and Bella sat on an easel in the center of the stage in front of the musicians. To the right of that picture sat another almost identical photograph of Nancy and Katie. Bella immediately noticed the photograph of her and her mother.

"Me and my Mommy," Bella said to her grandmother with a sad smile.

THE SERVICE

"We remember today, Nancy, mother and daughter, sister, friend. Thank you for giving her to us to know and love," said Pastor Mark Drengler from the Resurrection Lutheran Church. Drengler took to the podium after a soloist and harpist performed a haunting version of "Somewhere over the Rainbow."

Drengler explained that the soloist had been Bella and Katie's music teacher. She came to the stage again to sing Nancy's favorite song, "You are My Sunshine." She invited the crowd to sing along with her "for Nancy." A quiet wave of bashful singing spread across the amphitheater.

"I have to confess that I feel strange being here because I did not know Nancy. Our church is in the neighborhood where Nancy lived, and seeing people in need, we decided to see what we could do to help them, to care for them," Drengler said.

The pastor went on to say that when he discovered that Garry and Donna belonged to a Lutheran church in Canada, he decided it made even more sense for him to preside over Nancy's memorial service. Both Nancy and Krista had been baptized at a Lutheran church in Edmonton.

Drengler spoke of the vigil the previous evening where friends had gathered at the Triangle Academy Preschool to share anecdotes about Nancy with her family. He said he had learned a lot about Nancy through that experience.

"I guess I could sum it up by saying, Nancy Cooper loved to live life. A precious daughter, and all those memories of what it was like to grow up with such a wonderful family. A loving mom to her kids, Bella and Katie," the pastor said.

He said that there were so many stories about Nancy doing things with her kids, doing things for others, lending support to other parents. She got down on her hands and knees and caught frogs with the kids even though she hated amphibians. She loved to cook and entertain friends and family.

"What a blessing it was for Garry and Donna to hear those

stories," the pastor said.

But then it was time to address the tragedy, something he could not ignore. He had hundreds of pleading eyes staring at him, hoping he would provide the answers for which they were so desperately looking.

"This tragic, evil event—it's not fair. You know it, and I know it, but even more importantly, God knows it," Drengler said dramatically, raising his eyebrows and scanning the crowd with probing eyes. "God knows that it's not fair."

He went on to say that the evil was not caused by God and that Nancy's family and friends should not blame God for what had happened, but instead, use his strength to get through this difficult time.

"No one, not one person is exempt from tragedy. Not one of us is exempt from the unfairness of life," Drengler said.

He acknowledged that the crowd was angry and that it was like being in the middle of a raging storm, one that you weren't sure you would be able to survive. He assured everyone that when the storm passed they would be all right.

"Death is not final," Drengler said.

Nancy's friend, Hannah Prichard, then stood up in the front row and faced the crowd. She was wearing a wireless microphone and a nervous smile. Prichard was a strikingly attractive young woman with California girl looks. She had a long blond flowing mane pulled back in a tight ponytail, bright blue eyes, and porcelain skin dotted with small freckles. She wore a white halter dress with a large *N* on one side in honor of Nancy.

"I met Nancy, and my world changed. It's so rare to find someone you can spend every day with and never get tired of each other. She was a second mother to my children, and oftentimes they would rather be with her than with me. And she always gave more than she would take. And now my world has changed again, and I don't know what I'll do without talking to her first thing every morning to make our plans for the day. I do find comfort remembering all of our good times, and I know she will live on in my heart and in all of yours and especially through the sweet little girls, Bella and Katie," Prichard said as tears streamed freely down her face.

Prichard then shared a Native American prayer—I Am Not There—that she said had brought Nancy's friends comfort in the past week.

"I am the soft stars that shine at night. Do not think of me as gone, I am with you still at each new dawn," she read, the last line through tears.

"I loved Nancy," Prichard said, breaking down and walking into the comfort of her husband's arms a few steps away.

Then Nancy's friends Jessica Adam and Clea Morwick came up to the podium.

"Nancy was one of the best friends both of us ever had," Morwick began with a smile as she put her arm around Adam's waist and pulled her friend into her tightly. Morwick sported a short reddish pixie cut and a white sundress covered in black flowers. Adam wore a solid white sundress and had her jet black hair pulled back in a slick ponytail away from her olive skin. "She lit up our lives. She was the person who walked into the room and complimented everybody. She made everybody laugh. She got everybody a drink," Morwick said with nervous laughter. "She just made everything shine a little brighter, and we're going to miss her very much. She loves her family. She loves Bella and Katie so much, and she's watching us right now.

"Nancy was our shining star, and we'll miss her very much. We love you, Nancy," Morwick said drifting back from smiles into tears.

Then it was Adam's turn. She, too, wore a large *N* on one side of her dainty white sundress. She put her hand to her mouth for a moment and took a deep breath before beginning.

Adam recounted to the crowd how Nancy had brought her to that very spot, on the lawn in front of the theater at Regency Park, where she had continued her "never-ending introduction of new friends." She said Nancy was responsible for her making many friends when she moved to North Carolina.

"In case she hasn't heard me—Nancy, I have never, ever met

anyone like you. It's impossible to believe that I ever will. The gift of friendship that you gave to me, I aspire to pass it on," Adam said. "I love you and you will never, ever, ever be forgotten. And I look forward to the days when your girls are older, talking and sharing with them all the stories that we have. We love you."

The musicians performed Psalm 23, and then the pastor led the crowd in the Lord's Prayer. Garry took to the podium briefly to close the service.

"Once again from our family, thank you very much," Garry said with his usual graciousness. As he spoke, Krista led Bella by the hand out of the theater as television cameras zoomed in and followed their steps closely. The rest of the family stood to greet the hundreds of friends who had come to celebrate Nancy's life.

One person was conspicuously absent from Nancy's memorial service—Brad Cooper. His decision not to attend the service in Cary was hard to explain away. Still, his attorney tried.

"He feels his presence would be a distraction," his attorney Seth Blum had said.

CANADA MOURNS

On Wednesday, July 23, 2008, at Grace Lutheran Church in Edmonton, Alberta, where Donna and Garry were members, another memorial service was held for Nancy. The Rentzes wanted to be able to celebrate their daughter's life with their Canadian family and friends as they had done with Nancy's friends in North Carolina just five days earlier.

There was such a large turnout, the crowd spilled into the hallways and gymnasium of the church. The church staff piped in audio of the service to these areas so that everyone could at least hear what was going on, even if they couldn't actually see anything.

The event started off with a moving video tribute to Nancy. The first screen read, IN LOVING MEMORY OF NANCY COOPER. A touching country ballad by Garth Brooks played while photographs of the Rentz family scrolled past on the screen. At first, it showed Nancy and her siblings as young children, surrounding their parents, and then, as adults, in the same circle of love. The photographs portrayed a happy family—on vacation, celebrating holidays and birthdays, smiling with arms around one another. Nancy's smile always seemed to be the biggest one in the group as she tilted her head in toward her father's, or pulled her petite mother into her tall lanky frame with a wide loving embrace.

The words from the song flowing beneath the photographs tinged the video presentation with sadness.

"I'm glad I didn't know the way it all would end, the way it all would go," the country singer crooned with an aching twang.

There were many pictures of Krista and Nancy, identical twins with identical hairstyles, and identical smiles. They looked so much alike that one would imagine their parents must have had trouble telling them apart at times.

The music playing over the video presentation then changed to "You Are My Sunshine." Inspirational quotes from famous people flashed across the screen in between the pictures of Nancy and her family. The photographs in this segment were of Nancy with her children, Bella and Katie. In every photograph, Nancy had one or both of the girls in some kind of embrace that usually brought them cheek to cheek.

"Crazy Love" by Aaron Neville flowed out of the speakers next. And there were more pictures. A picture of Nancy in a cap and gown at graduation. Pictures of Nancy running races. Nancy on a boat. Nancy with her girlfriends. Nancy swimming. Nancy dressed up. Nancy joking around.

Conspicuously missing from all of the photos was Brad Cooper. A clear statement was apparently being made by the family: They had made up their minds about Brad, and he wasn't welcome there, in person or even in a photograph.

The last frame read, NANCY COOPER, 1973 TO 2008.

Nancy's brother, Jeff, then came to the podium to speak, followed by a parade of children—his daughter, MaKenna; Jill's daughter, Kennedy; and Nancy's daughters, Bella and Katie. It appeared as though the children's presence was unintended, but Jeff was undaunted by his little followers and started speaking as they played around him.

"As most of you know, Nancy made friends very easily," he began with a smile. He said many of her North Carolina friends could not be there but had sent notes to be read aloud. He started with words from Hannah Prichard.

"Nancy was the most generous, loyal, selfless person I have ever known. From the moment we met, we knew we would be friends forever, and it was such a privilege to be able to spend every day together with her and her children for the couple of years that I had her in my life," Jeff read from Prichard's note.

Jeff then read a letter from Jessica Adam. She talked about how the first time she and Nancy had met she remembered seeing a very tall, pregnant woman standing next to a very tan, pretty Bella. She assumed the mother and child must be from some exotic place. They had both shown up for their children's first day of preschool with their kids well groomed, carrying shiny new lunch boxes, but there was one problem—they both had the day wrong. Preschool started on Tuesday in the summertime, not Monday. The women insisted to the director that they couldn't have both possibly gotten the day wrong, so it must be her fault. They won the battle, and the school agreed to create an impromptu class for Bella and Adam's son, Max. Adam was thrilled, but Nancy began to cry.

"The thought of leaving her daughter even for the promised one hour was very difficult," Jeff read from Adam's note. She had consoled her new friend and encouraged her to leave Bella and walk out the front door. They slid along the side of the building and then peered into the window at their little angels to make sure everything was okay. Finally, Adam was able to convince Nancy to come to the nearby coffee shop with her for a latte.

By the end of their hour together, Adam had a new friend. Nancy took Adam under her wing, introducing her to her large group of friends. She invited Adam to join her book club, her girls' night out, and to attend a neighborhood July Fourth party.

The young cousins at Jeff's feet had by now gotten bored with the service, and instead of just fidgeting, they began running around the altar and up and down the aisles in their pretty fluffy dresses with untied bows in their hair flying behind them with wild abandon. But no one stepped in to corral the children, maybe because no one had the heart to deny Bella and Katie a brief moment of joy.

Nancy's longtime friend, Anna McRoberts, took Jeff's spot at the lectern. At first, she couldn't help but comment on how beautiful Nancy's little girls were as they raced around the sanctuary. Everyone seemed to be embracing the children's restlessness as a sign that Nancy's legacy would live on in these little blond spitfires.

McRoberts started by saying that, like everyone else, she believed she was Nancy's best friend, because that's how Nancy made her friends feel—like they were all her very best friends.

"She made us all feel so unbelievably special," McRoberts said, adding that the two had met in high school, and Nancy had been a grade ahead. "I thought she was so amazing and so cool. To me, she really was wonderment. She was everything I always wanted to be and still everything I hope I can be."

The close friends experienced many firsts together. They were evolving from being girls to being young women.

"I carry her with me every day. She taught me so many lessons and so many things that have stuck with me forever," said McRoberts. "She taught me how to have a family."

McRoberts spent a great deal of time with Nancy's family on their houseboat at the lake on vacation. Coming from a small family, McRoberts felt loved and enveloped by Nancy's larger one.

"Nancy also taught me how to be a friend, how to be a great friend. She was the centerpiece of our group of friends," McRoberts said with a chuckle. "Nancy just wanted us all to be happy and to be a part of everything."

Meanwhile, Bella, Katie, and their cousins continued to ignore the adults as they laughed and climbed over the pews and then alternately ran up to the altar and back into the audience again.

"She was everybody's rock, everybody's light, and she really was everybody's best friend. And I will live my life honoring the way Nancy taught me to live it, in joy and in kindness and in love. I love you, Nancy, with everything that I am," McRoberts concluded.

Glenn Sharples, Nancy's godfather, came up to the podium next and described Nancy as a joyous, delightful, happy child.

"She had a wonderful zest for life and for living which she displayed in everything that she did," said Sharples.

The history between the Rentz family and the Sharples family went back many years. They had spent numerous Christmas Eves together. It was always Nancy who was so excited about the holiday, he recalled. One year they had a Mexican Christmas Eve when he remembered Nancy attacking the piñata with more gusto than everyone else. On Hawaiian Christmas Eve, he said she performed a hearty hula dance for everyone.

"Nancy was very bubbly and full of energy," Sharples said. "Everybody loved Nancy. We watched Nancy grow into a very attractive, outgoing, and confident young woman. We felt very proud of Nancy and thoroughly enjoyed her. Nancy lit up the room and her laughter was contagious. She made you feel really good inside. You just wanted to be her friend."

After a poem, a prayer, and a song, Pastor Larry McKay stood at the podium in the front of the church.

"Today is a day that just should not be," he said. McKay went on to say that this was not something anyone in the family could have pictured while on the various joyous occasions they had shared together—Nancy's church confirmation with Krista, Jill's wedding, Bella's baptism in the very same church, Katie's second birthday on this day of all days. They had celebrated her birthday in advance so as not to draw attention to the fact that such a solemn occasion was taking place on what should have been a happy day.

"In a perfect world, no parent should ever have to grieve the death of their child, and never, ever, under such horrendous circumstances. The last ten days are days that should not have been, but their tragedy cannot be wished away. The pain and the horror that they have brought to each of you that love Nancy and still do are the sorts of things that we read about, we hear about. We maybe watch on TV, but we can never imagine them happening to us," he said.

He said he understood that the words of sympathy spoken to Nancy's family fell tragically short when it came to lessening their pain.

"God didn't take Nancy's life, but he knows your pain," McKay said. "One day you will soar like eagles above this grief."

"Nancy loved life. She celebrated it. She lived it. And she loved her little girls, Bella and Katie, even more. She was full of energy, always the organizer, never content to just sit still," he went on to say. "It would be so easy in all of the pain of missing Nancy to give in to a flood of despair. To nurse the bitterness and anger that can come so naturally to us, to replay regrets and give up hope, but to do so would be to give in to the evil of this world. To do that would be to depreciate God's gift of Nancy in your lives and to deprive Bella and Katie of the treasure of their mother's love, life, and legacy."

McKay said that the family would grieve together but each person would grieve differently. He urged Nancy's loved ones to be patient with one another, to lean on God, and to celebrate life in the way Nancy would have wanted them to.

The congregation sang "Joyful, Joyful We Adore Thee" as the family filed out solemnly. Krista, who was dressed in a black cocktail dress with her dark blond locks hanging down her back, looked strikingly like her sister as she carried one little girl in each arm. Like a woman who had been a mother forever, Krista held Bella and Katie effortlessly as they tilted their tired little heads into her shoulders.

CHAPTER FIVE

SHE SAID

JULY 2008

No one lies so boldly as the man who is indignant.
—Friedrich Nietzsche

"When we first met him, there was this quietness about Brad that was really nice. You got used to Nancy getting hurt by these people who had these big personalities and ended up treating her really poorly," said Jill, recalling her first impression of Brad. "He's smart. He's grounded. Maybe this is someone who will be really good for her."

Nancy had always been the life of the party, and as a result, she was usually attracted to life-of-the-party guys, but Brad was different. Brad was quiet and reserved. Unlike her previous boyfriends, he was perfectly willing to hang back and let Nancy shine in the spotlight.

Krista recalled not having been as immediately fond of Brad as her little sister Jill was. For Krista, something didn't sit right with her from the very beginning about the introverted man.

"He was such a departure from Nancy's usual boyfriends, such a departure," Krista said. "He was just so closed. Trying to have a conversation with the guy, it was like pulling teeth."

At the time, Nancy worked for a company in Calgary and Brad was an information technology specialist employed by IBM who was contracted to work with the same company.

Nancy had been trying to fix Brad up with a friend of hers from work. He shared with her that he had just gotten out of a messy relationship with a woman named Jennifer to whom he had been engaged prior to their breakup.

"Brad was complaining to Nancy about just having left this relationship where he had been mistreated, and he was kind of battered and bruised," Garry said.

At the bar where Nancy was trying to introduce Brad to one of her friends, she and Brad got to talking and decided they were interested in one another. Krista and her then boyfriend and future husband, Jim Lister, went on a double date with Nancy and Brad. After dinner, the two couples went back to the apartment Nancy and Krista shared in Calgary to watch a movie. Krista recalled that Nancy fell asleep on Brad's lap on the couch, and he was such a gentleman he didn't want to wake her. He was forced to watch *Steel Magnolias* by himself after Krista and Jim went to bed. From there, the relationship blossomed into a romance.

"We watched him pursue her. There was no question about who was doing the pursuing," Donna said.

Like Jill, Donna had immediately liked Brad. Garry, on the other hand, thought Brad was somewhat antisocial compared to their gregarious daughter, though very bright. He even asked Brad to build the first computer system at his office in Edmonton.

Like all of the people the Rentz children dated, Brad fell in love with Nancy's family. His own family, comprising his parents, Carol and Terry Cooper, and his younger brother, Grant, was not close and overly loving like the Rentzes. His father was an organic chemist who had high expectations for his son, expectations that Brad sometimes found hard to meet. Overt expressions of love were rare in his home life growing up. So being welcomed into the warmth of Nancy's family was something Brad had seemed to quietly embrace. Krista said Brad's reserved demeanor always made him secondary to Nancy's wide open persona, but Jill said he fit right in when the whole family stayed up into the wee hours of the morning drinking wine, talking, and playing games. Jill had a particularly close relationship with Brad. She played practical jokes on him and brought him out of his shell around the lively group. He referred to Jill as his "little sister," a moniker she gladly accepted.

When Nancy first moved to Calgary from Edmonton, the family didn't see her as much as they wanted to. But once she started dating Brad, he brought her home more often. His interest in her family actually helped reconnect them to Nancy. He also spent a great deal of time with the Rentzes in their vacation home in Canmore, Alberta, a serene place Brad grew to love as much as Nancy's family did.

Still, Krista thought Brad was just about the most antisocial person she had ever met and always felt uncomfortable trying to have a conversation with him. But Jill said they all overlooked his oddness because he had become part of their loving family.

"When it's your family, you excuse the behavior because it's just who that person is. It doesn't mean you like him any less. So we accepted him as part of us," Jill said frankly.

During the winter holidays in 1999, Brad proposed to Nancy at her family's home in Edmonton, and she gladly accepted. A large wedding was planned for the spring of 2001. Nancy booked a hall and even found the perfect wedding dress. But even in the midst of her excited planning, she was still having second thoughts.

Nancy had always been sought after by men, but she had a penchant for older men. The man she had been serious about when she'd met Brad, Brett Wilson, was a successful divorced businessman with grown children. Despite her love for him, however, and the fact that he had always been very supportive of her, Nancy was convinced he was not interested in having more children. For Nancy, this was a deal breaker. It had always been her dream to have a family. She shared her internal conflict with her mother.

"Which one do you love?" Donna asked her daughter.

"I have feelings for both. I think Brad is less flamboyant, probably more reliable," Nancy told her mother. So Nancy wrestled with her decision and finally chose Brad over Brett, children over passionate love.

"I think the reason she ended up with Brad was because she wanted to have a family. She wanted to have kids. The guys she was dating before were much older and had done that," Jill said.

Ultimately, Brad and Nancy decided to cancel the big traditional wedding and get married in a hurry after Brad was offered a job with Cisco Systems in North Carolina, where he was recruited by his old boss from IBM. Legally, the only way Nancy could move to the United States was to be married to Brad. They ended up getting married a week before Brad left for the United States in a rushed ceremony in front of a justice of the peace. Brad's parents didn't even attend. It was just Nancy's family and close friends at the ceremony, none of Brad's family or friends, followed by a small reception at a local restaurant that Krista managed.

"They got married in a week, and it was devastating. I was devastated," Jill said. She'd already felt like she had lost her sister when Nancy had moved three hours away to Calgary. To Jill, North Carolina was a world away from Edmonton.

As much as Jill liked Brad, she was skeptical about the move. Nancy was on a fast career track. She had even owned her own clothing store for a period of time, honing her business and management skills. Plus, Nancy's entire family was in Canada.

"She was so successful here, and she gave up everything to go there and try something new, and she just wanted a family," Jill said of her sister, who was in her midtwenties at the time. "She wanted to buy the house. She wanted to have the two-point-five kids and the two cars. So she was willing to give up so much of herself and what was important to her to make it happen."

THE AFFIDAVITS

Prior to the custody hearing on July 25, 2008, both sides filed a slew of affidavits from Nancy's and Brad's friends and family. The detailed documents gave the public a peek at what had been going on inside Brad and Nancy's troubled marriage.

Because the case was a custody case, the affidavits spoke primarily to the Coopers' marriage and Brad Cooper's parenting abilities. But unlike other custody cases, there was an elephant in the middle of the room about which everyone was reluctant to speak—Nancy's murder. Most of the affidavits didn't address the issue, maybe out of an extreme sense of caution, but her two closest friends took the plunge.

"From my personal knowledge about the history of the parties' marriage and the circumstances of Nancy's disappearance and death, I believe that Brad murdered Nancy," Jessica Adam said boldly in her affidavit.

"There is no doubt in my mind about what happened to my best friend, Nancy Cooper on July 12, 2008. She went home at midnight, got into a fight with Brad, and he killed her," Hannah Prichard said in her affidavit.

Nancy's friends had strong negative opinions about Brad Cooper. Most of their first impressions of Brad included descriptions of him as "a loner" who was "quiet" and "socially awkward." And those opinions hadn't seemed to change over the years, even with the close neighbors who saw the Coopers on a regular basis. They said in their affidavits that Brad's standoffish behavior kept them from ever really getting to know him.

On the rare occasion when he did attend neighborhood functions or his children's play dates, Nancy's friends said he mostly kept to himself.

Diana Duncan was Nancy's first friend in Cary. The women lived across the street from each other. Duncan's son, Caelan, was about Bella's age, and the two played together frequently. Duncan and Nancy had shared many confidences over the years, and developed a deep bond of friendship. Duncan said in her affidavit that Brad made her very uncomfortable when Caelan played with Bella and Katie.

"He stood apart and shunned us. He seemed to resent having to watch the girls, and also seemed to resent our child," Duncan said in the court filing.

Nancy's friend Dr. Theresa Hackeling said in her affidavit that her husband made a sincere effort to befriend Brad after she became friends with Nancy, but to no avail. He told her Brad made it too difficult, because he was so self-absorbed. Hackeling said Brad "demonstrated very narcissistic behavior."

Nancy's friends said Brad was rarely around. They said not only did he eschew neighborhood gatherings, he did not participate much in the household or parenting duties.

"Nancy, I saw as a single mom because Brad was constantly unwilling or unavailable to help with the house or the children," Nancy's friend and neighbor, Clea Morwick, said in her affidavit. Morwick had taken charge of Nancy's children on the day she disappeared while her husband, Michael, headed up the massive volunteer search for Nancy.

Brad worked many hours as a network engineer at Cisco Systems. He specialized in Voice Over Internet Protocol, known as VOIP, which involved a phone system that was routed through the computer. When he was home, Nancy's friends said Brad was usually sleeping, studying for his MBA at North Carolina State University or training on his exercise bike for Ironman triathlons. Jessica Adam's husband, Brett Adam, said in his affidavit that sometimes Brad would ride his stationary exercise bike for eight hours straight in an extra bedroom with the door closed so that he would not be bothered by Nancy and the girls.

"Those outside activities consumed [him] and left very little time if any time for family," Michael Morwick stated in his affidavit. Morwick was known among his friends as having a crush on Nancy, and he wasn't the only one. Diana Duncan's husband, Craig, was also said to be smitten with the Canadian beauty. Their affection was unrequited, but nonetheless they were part of the large group of people who adored Nancy and tolerated Brad. After Nancy's death, they no longer had any reason to pretend.

"I would describe Brad as socially inept, selfish, moody and unpredictable. Nancy walked on eggshells around Brad and did her best to appease him so that she could avoid confrontation with him. If she made him angry, he punished her in calculated, manipulative ways," Jessica Adam said in her affidavit, not mincing words.

BRAD THE PARENT

While, legally, a custody case is supposed to be just about what is in the best interests of the children, the Cooper case was about so much more. It was not only about how Brad Cooper parented his children, but how he treated his wife when she was alive, and whether or not he had anything to do with her death. Still, Brad's parenting skills were the cornerstones of the court affidavits.

Nancy Cooper's friends said from what they had witnessed, Nancy had done most of the daily caretaking of the children, and Brad did very little.

"She adored her girls and had an amazing capacity to make every day special for her daughters," Clea Morwick said in her affidavit. "She was the homemaker who did all the cleaning, laundry, cooking and shopping for the family. She got minimal help from Brad."

Nancy's friends said Brad's lack of involvement with his daughters made it impossible for the girls to even really know their father. They said he rarely, if ever, attended the girls' birthday parties, dance recitals, school functions or doctors' appointments.

"Brad spent so little time with the girls that he was in essence a stranger to them," Jessica Adam said in her affidavit. "I have often witnessed hesitation by the girls to go to their father."

Brad's parents also seemed to dislike Nancy, according to Nancy's friends. They said his mother, Carol Cooper, gave Nancy the cold shoulder and refused to include her in family outings when they all got together. Nancy's friends said Brad did nothing to stand up for his wife in these situations.

"Brad's mother, in particular, was terribly mean to Nancy," Jessica Adam said in her affidavit. "I have witnessed Brad's mother attempt to forcibly remove Katie from Nancy's arms despite

Nancy's objections."

Clea Morwick recalled a story in her affidavit that Nancy had told her about a visit Brad's parents made from Canada to Nashville, Tennessee, where they were joined by the Cooper family. Nancy told Morwick that Brad's parents wanted to take the girls and Brad to the zoo but didn't want Nancy to come. Nancy agreed to stay behind but only with the understanding that they would all have dinner together after the zoo trip. Nancy told Morwick that Brad, his parents, and the girls returned late that evening after dinner, never even having called once to check in with her.

"Brad's mother did everything possible to undermine Nancy's parenting," Morwick said in her affidavit.

Nancy's friends said she was in total charge of the girls' lives, from school, to activities, to play dates, to their health care. Nancy's friend Michelle Simmons recalled in her affidavit that Bella had broken her nose in early 2008. She said Nancy stayed with Bella in the doctor's office with Katie in her arms while they did a procedure to fix Bella's nose, because Brad would not leave work to help.

One morning Brad decided he would drive Bella to the Triangle preschool. Nancy told her friends that Bella was crying hysterically and did not want to go with her father. Nancy put Bella into her car, and Brad followed behind them to the preschool.

"At the school, he physically took Bella into the school crying and calling for her mommy," Theresa Hackeling said in her affidavit.

Nancy's friends said Brad not only didn't know how to handle his girls, he didn't know what they did or didn't like. In short, he didn't know the basic things every parent knows about their children. This became painfully obvious when Nancy found a note in the months just prior to her murder that Brad had written about his daughters. She showed the note to Hannah Prichard and Diana Duncan. It listed the girls' favorite colors and foods.

"It had each girl's name listed on it with different facts underneath like 'Bella's favorite color is yellow,' and 'loves chicken nuggets.' We found it quite strange since these were not things that you would forget," Prichard said.

On the back of the note the women said there was a to-do list that included things like closing bank accounts, checking on the value of their cars, checking life insurance policies and their wills.

"She asked me what I thought it meant. I said I found it extremely creepy and offered that she come stay with me. She declined," said Duncan.

BRAD THE ABUSER

Hannah Prichard said that Nancy had multiple miscarriages before Bella was born, as well as in between the births of Bella and Katie. In her affidavit, Prichard said that Brad had so little regard for his wife that she was forced to take taxis to the emergency room after her miscarriages because "Brad was too busy to come home, and she did not have a car [of her own at the time] to drive herself."

Nancy's friends said Brad's selfishness was just the tip of the iceberg when it came to his mistreatment of his wife. They said he punished Nancy in many subtle ways, but his main weapons were his sharp tongue and the emotional jabs that undermined her natural confidence.

"Brad would scream at Nancy, calling her names in front of the children, and he would tell the kids, 'It's all Mommy's fault,'" Prichard recalled.

Nancy's friend Desiree Jackson said in her affidavit that "Brad told Nancy he hated her at Christmastime 2007, in the presence of Bella. Not surprisingly, Bella was very upset and cried uncontrollably."

Another friend, Michelle Simmons, remembered the same incident. Simmons said at the time, Bella turned to her mother and said, "Why does Daddy hate you?"

Nancy's friends said that what Brad was really good at was the most subtle form of domestic abuse—control. While Nancy didn't display any obvious signs of domestic violence, such as black eyes and broken bones, they said she had emotional wounds just as deep as any bruises or cuts. They just weren't visible. Brad chipped away at Nancy's self-esteem, one little blow at a time, and her confidence diminished slowly before her loved ones' eyes as her marriage disintegrated. The formerly strong-willed, opinionated woman with a biting sense of humor who ran road races and collected new friends daily was suddenly a shell of her former self. Her life was spinning out of control while her friends and family watched helplessly from the sidelines.

"Nancy said that she actually feared for herself and the kids and did not trust Brad. She would sleep with the girls in her room with the car keys in her pants pocket and the bedroom door locked from Brad," Hackeling said in her affidavit.

Nancy's friends said Brad's primary form of control involved money. Clea Morwick said in her affidavit that Brad had made it very clear that he was the breadwinner and that gave him control of the family. She said Nancy referred to her husband as "the Budget Nazi" because she said he only allowed her a small weekly allowance that he sometimes denied her depending upon his mood.

"He said Nancy had no right to the family money, and he would decide what amount of money she needed per week," Morwick recalled.

Universally, all of Nancy's friends said in their affidavits that Brad had cut Nancy off from money.

In January 2008, many of Nancy's friends remembered the water being turned off at the Cooper home after he failed to pay the bill. Because Brad had closed the bank accounts that Nancy had access to, and had opened new ones in his name only—and did the same thing with the credit cards—she had no ability to get the water turned back on. Nancy called Brad at work to ask him for help but Diana Duncan said Brad didn't seem to care.

"Brad did not seem concerned about how the lack of water would affect the children," Duncan said.

And it wasn't just financial control that Brad exerted over Nancy, according to her friends; it was also control over where Nancy went, what she did, even who she talked to.

Because Brad was one of a handful of experts in the world who dealt with telephone service through the Internet, Jessica Adam believed Brad was using this technology to monitor Nancy's phone calls. She said on many occasions she would be talking to Nancy and the call would be mysteriously disconnected for no apparent reason. Eventually, the women started talking only on Nancy's cell phone. Brett Adam witnessed the calls between his wife and her friend being disconnected on more than one occasion and came to believe the same thing they did.

The week before Nancy disappeared, Nancy and the girls were having dinner at the Adams' home in Apex. Jessica and Brett Adam recalled in their affidavits that Brad called Nancy on her cell phone during the meal, and she excused herself from the table and took the call on the porch. They said minutes later, Nancy returned saying that Brad was angry because, in Jessica's words, "Nancy had no right to decide where the girls ate dinner that night," and Brett said Brad instructed Nancy that she was to take the children and leave immediately.

A few months before Nancy disappeared, her friend Michelle Simmons said she and Nancy had a plan to meet up after a playdate. She said Nancy called from the playdate and told her that "Brad was angry and yelling at her to come home." She told Simmons later that Brad was waiting for her in the driveway when she returned home and took away her cell phone for several days as a punishment for not obeying him.

"This was the first time I told Nancy how afraid I was for her. My husband and I begged her and the girls to move into our home," Simmons said in her affidavit.

BRAD THE ADULTERER

It was no surprise to anyone that Brad Cooper, given his history of control and emotional abuse of his wife, was also an adulterer.

Brad traveled out of the country for work, often for weeks at a time, during which times Nancy Cooper told friends he rarely called or even e-mailed her to see how she and the girls were doing. When Nancy would try to contact him, she got no response. She told her friends this happened in the summer of 2006 when he spent two weeks in Europe, leaving Nancy at home with Katie, who was a newborn at the time, and Bella who was still a toddler. She said it also happened in the spring of 2007, when he went on a trip with his MBA class to France, and then again in June of 2008 when Brad traveled to Ireland on business and said he'd be gone for a weekend but extended his stay by a week. Later, Nancy put the pieces together and told friends that she thought her husband had had multiple affairs on business trips, and she suspected he may have had others even closer to home.

"She could not believe this was the man she had married," Damia Tabachow said in her affidavit.

"Mr. Cooper is deceitful. He found lying quite easy," said Dr. Theresa Hackeling in her affidavit.

Both Jessica Adam and Hannah Prichard said Brad was prone to disappearing at times. One weekend in the fall of 2007, Nancy told Prichard and Adam that Brad had left early one Sunday morning, saying he was going to a boat show for a project with his MBA class, and didn't return until 5:00 A.M. Monday morning. After some research, Nancy found no evidence of a boat show and believed he had been with another woman.

But the worst was Brad's affair with a married woman from Nancy's close circle of neighborhood friends. Nancy and Heather Metour had become fast friends, bonding over afternoon glasses of wine and trips to the local swim club with their children. Everyone was used to seeing the young, pretty women together.

Metour, along with Diana Duncan, had even thrown Nancy a baby shower at Duncan's house when Katie was born. But Metour had a secret, one which abruptly ended their friendship.

In their affidavits, eight of Nancy's friends referenced Brad's affair with Metour as the real turning point in the Coopers' marriage. It was a betrayal that Nancy could not overcome; it was simply too close for her to ignore.

The story was that Brad and Metour had had sex in the closet of Nancy and Brad's bedroom. To make matters worse, Brad was supposed to have been watching Bella at the time. Both Michelle Simmons and Damia Tabachow said in their affidavits that Nancy told them Bella was asleep in the master bedroom nearby when the alleged sexual encounter took place.

"This total lack of care that Bella could wake up and see them is so upsetting," Tabachow said in her affidavit.

"When Nancy found out about the affair, she confronted Brad immediately," said Nancy's friend Jennifer Fetterolf in her affidavit. "Brad turned angry, defensive, and emotionally abusive towards Nancy and denied it. Brad had her convinced that it didn't happen, and Nancy turned apologetic and felt guilty that she had possibly blamed him for something that he didn't do."

This denial, according to friends, lasted for a full year as Nancy continued to question Brad about the affair. "After a year of lies and aggressive heated arguments over the affair, Brad admitted it had occurred and that he had been in love with Heather at the time," Nancy's friend Clea Morwick said in her affidavit. "This was the final slap in the face for Nancy. She had been ridiculed, verbally badgered, and humiliated again and again by Brad."

THE DIVORCE

By March of 2008, Nancy Cooper had had enough of her troubled marriage. The couple were sleeping in separate bedrooms and barely speaking to each other except about issues that involved the children. Nancy and Brad Cooper had even halfheartedly gone to counseling to see if there was anything worth saving, but the confirmed affair with Heather Metour was the last straw.

"Nancy told me that she simply could not forgive him," Damia Tabachow said in her affidavit. Nancy consulted with attorney Alice Stubbs about creating a legal separation agreement—the first step toward divorce. Tabachow said at the time Brad seemed willing to let Nancy and the children go back to Canada to live with her twin sister, Krista Lister, and her husband, Jim. But according to all of Nancy's friends, Brad made some bizarre demands in return for agreeing to let her go.

"When Nancy told Brad the marriage was over, he told her he wanted to spend the summer with the girls and then for her to take them and for him to never see them again. At a later date he told Nancy they could go their separate ways and each take one child," Michelle Simmons said.

"Brad told Nancy they should just take one girl [each] and be done," Hannah Prichard said in her affidavit.

Nancy's friends said Brad became anxious, as if he wanted to get rid of his family immediately. Clea Morwick said in her affidavit that Nancy wanted Bella to finish her spring semester at preschool, but Brad insisted they be out by April 26 so that he could list the house for sale. Nancy began packing up the house, and friends started planning a going-away party for Nancy. Nancy also painted the house herself and got it ready to sell.

"He then told her, one day, he wanted her and the girls out as soon as possible," said Simmons. "He would fight with her on a regular basis about when she was leaving, and around three weeks before she was scheduled to go in April, he tried telling her to be out in a few days. I would talk to her about how unbelievable it was that he was so eager to get her and the girls out."

But then something changed. Nancy's friends said Brad discovered he would have to pay Nancy alimony and child support.

"Brad would not let her leave once he found out that he would have to pay her money for supporting the girls," Tabachow said.

"We couldn't believe it since this was the man who kept trying to kick her out sooner and moving up the dates," Simmons said.

Nancy's friends said Brad exercised one last measure of control over his wife that ensured she would not be able to leave the country with her children. Nancy had been keeping the girls' passports and other important papers in her car because she didn't trust Brad. Duncan said in her affidavit that Brad made an excuse to go back to

Nancy's car while they were at a local arts festival with the kids. He then took all of the paperwork Nancy had hidden for safekeeping, including the passports.

"Brad changed his mind and stole the kids' passports from her and told her that she could go, but the kids were staying here," Prichard said.

"Since April 2008, his attitude changed. According to Nancy, he had decided to move for full custody," Duncan said in her affidavit. Nancy's friends felt like Brad wanted custody solely so as not to pay Nancy any money. "He suddenly became friendly and started to actively take care of the girls. Nancy told me that she believed the only reason for this was because he had been advised to do so."

Michael Morwick, Clea's husband, also said in his affidavit that after the move to Canada was canceled, Brad started to "play the good dad." But Morwick said Nancy was sure Brad's intentions had everything to do with money and very little to do with actually wanting to be with his daughters.

"Nancy told me she felt that all his decisions and behavior since then seemed driven by money," Duncan said.

Fast forward to July 2008. With Nancy now out of the picture, her friends feared that Brad might be able to retain full custody of the girls, because in North Carolina it had to be proven that the parent was negligent in a major way in order to circumvent his or her rights.

"Brad seems like he is in a dark place, and I am very concerned for Bella and Katie if he obtains custody. He is unstable, and I would hate for those beautiful girls to get caught up in an incident that would put their safety in jeopardy," Keith Prichard, Hannah's husband, said in his affidavit.

HILTON HEAD

The week before Nancy Cooper's disappearance she had been on a family vacation with her girls, her parents and Krista and Jim first at High Rock Lake in Charlotte, and then at Hilton Head in South Carolina. Brad Cooper had not attended the gathering.

Whenever the Rentzes and their children got together, they had a wonderful time, and this vacation was no exception. But when Nancy got home, friends said she paid for her joyful week by returning to find her house in total disarray.

In five affidavits filed by her friends in the civil custody case on behalf of Nancy's family, the disgusting mess Nancy returned to was graphically described.

"Brad had not cleaned up a thing after himself, allowing the house to become infested with bugs," Hannah Prichard said in her affidavit. "There were even worms everywhere in the kids' playroom."

According to Nancy's friends, Brad had left dirty dishes and decaying food in the kitchen that had attracted ants. Even the dishes Nancy had used to feed the girls on the day they'd left for her weeklong vacation were still in the sink, unwashed.

Clea Morwick was also privy to the story about the status of the house when Nancy returned from her vacation. In her affidavit she said the bathrooms were filthy, and Brad had not replenished any of the food, so there was nothing for the girls to eat.

"Nancy was very angry over this situation and spoke of how disrespectful Brad had been and how unwilling he was to change," Morwick said.

On Friday afternoon, July 11, the day before she disappeared, Nancy spoke on the telephone with her friend, Dr. Theresa Hackeling. In her affidavit, Hackeling recalled that Nancy told her about the disturbing scene at the house the week before, when she'd returned from her trip with the girls late at night.

"I remember Nancy's being extremely upset with Brad," Hackeling said. "She returned to a home in shambles. There were ants on the table, bugs on the floor, and no food for her kids."

Just a few hours after this conversation with Hackeling, Nancy, Brad, and the girls attended a neighborhood party. It would be the last time any of her friends ever saw Nancy alive again.

THE PARTY

Diana and Craig Duncan, Nancy Cooper's friends and longtime neighbors, hosted a party on the night of Friday, July 11, 2008. They invited their friends, along with their children, to come over for a cookout and a few drinks.

As usual, guests at the party said that Brad kept to himself while Nancy chatted with everyone. The party guests said Brad left with the children around 8:00 P.M., and Nancy stayed. Everyone said there was obvious tension between the couple.

In Diana Duncan's affidavit she said that Brad got very annoyed with almost-two-year-old Katie at the party when she got fussy, because he didn't understand what she wanted. Duncan said she remembered Nancy telling Brad he needed to pay closer attention to his daughter and try to understand Katie's signals because she still wasn't able to verbalize her needs.

Duncan also said that earlier that day when Brad had found out that Jessica and Brett Adam were paying Nancy to paint their home, he told her he would not be giving her any allowance that week because she obviously didn't need it.

"She told me it was hard just feeding herself and the children on what he was giving her," Duncan recalled.

Damia Tabachow was also at the party that night. According to her affidavit, Tabachow spent about an hour and a half talking with Nancy one on one, and recalled that Nancy said the couple was "back in hate mode" and that Brad was now "playing nice" in front of the girls and their friends because he had been advised to do so by an attorney. No one at the party that night would ever forget what Nancy said to them, because it would be the last time any of them ever spoke to her.

DISAPPEARING ACT

On Saturday, July 12, 2008, Jessica Adam said Nancy was supposed to be at her house around 8:00 A.M. to start painting. She had agreed to pay her friend to paint in order to help her earn some extra money. Adam said in her affidavit that when Nancy didn't show up by 9:25 A.M., she called her cell phone.

"I became anxious," Adam said.

When Nancy didn't answer her phone, Adam called the Cooper house and was surprised when Brad picked up the phone because, she said, he rarely did so.

"Nancy went for a run with Carey, and she should be back soon," Adam recalled Brad telling her.

"I immediately felt strange because I knew that Nancy would have informed me if she was meeting Carey for a run," Adam said in the court filing.

Adam didn't know Carey's last name or have her number. She was a relatively new friend of Nancy's. The three women were supposed to run the road race together in August. Adam said it didn't make sense that Nancy would not only go for a run without her but also that she would do it at 7:00 A.M. when she knew the two had plans to meet at 8:00 A.M. to paint that same day.

Adam called Nancy's cell phone again. Still no answer.

"I immediately knew something was wrong," Adam said in the affidavit. "I was immediately concerned that Brad had done something to her."

At around 12:30 P.M. Saturday afternoon, Adam said she received a call from Brad.

"I felt sick as soon as I heard his voice," Adam recalled.

"Do you have Carey's phone number? Nancy is still not back, and I'm trying to get a hold of her," Brad asked.

Adam told Brad she did not have Carey's number and was worried about Nancy. She offered to watch the girls while he went to look for her. She said he declined her offer and said he would put the girls in the car and handle it himself.

Adam, still sensing something wasn't right, hung up and immediately called 911 to report Nancy missing. By that time several friends had gathered at Adam's house to share their concerns about Nancy being unaccounted for, including Hannah Prichard and neighbor Mary Anderson. After the 911 call, Adam and Anderson then drove to the Cooper house and met with the Cary police.

"I was in a total panic by this point," Adam said.

THE EXPERT

The Rentzes' attorney asked a local psychologist, Ginger Calloway, to weigh in on the case. She read the affidavits and the case file and made judgments as to whether or not Brad should have custody of the children.

She looked at everything from the fact that Brad did not report his wife missing, to the fact that Brad had talked about suicide and seemed to have a history of emotional instability according to Nancy's family. She indicated over and over again in her affidavit that Bella and Katie Cooper needed to feel secure after experiencing such a traumatic loss.

"They also need a safe, trusting and emotional environment where they are safe to disclose their fears and knowledge about the death of their mother," Dr. Calloway said. "It is not known at the present time what the children may have witnessed or heard regarding the death of their mother."

It was the first time anyone raised the issue of where the children had been when Nancy was killed.

Dr. Calloway went on to say that the children needed to be cared for by people who were not distracted by their own emotional needs.

"If the father of the children is under intense scrutiny because of the criminal investigation and attendant media scrutiny, I am concerned that he will of necessity be overly attentive to his own defense and not able to adequately attend to his children's needs and feelings as they require," Dr. Calloway said.

She said that if the children did have knowledge or information about their father's involvement in their mother's death, they would be less likely to disclose it around him or his family for fear they might hurt him.

She concluded that based on all of the information she had been given that there was a strong potential the "stability for the children would be at risk" if they were to remain in Brad's custody. She recommended that Brad undergo a mental health evaluation to see if he was capable of caring for the children.

To that end, on July 24, 2008, the Rentzes' attorney, Alice Stubbs, filed a motion to have a psychological evaluation done of Brad. The motion called Brad "mentally unstable" and said he had engaged in a "bizarre pattern of behavior" that led Nancy's family to believe he was "not fit to care" for the children and that there was a "substantial risk of bodily harm" to the kids if they remained with him. The motion also pointed out that there was a strong possibility Brad would attempt to leave North Carolina with the girls if he were left with them unsupervised.

It was the first step toward getting inside Brad's mind—a mind many people thought was the mind of a killer.

CHAPTER SIX

FAMILY SECRETS

OCTOBER 2000

You don't choose your family.
They are God's gift to you, as you are to them.
—Desmond Tutu

Nancy Cooper's family read the affidavits from her friends in the custody case with great interest. In their opinion, the people closest to Nancy had watched her marriage unravel; they had only seen it from afar in Canada. But when they really began to soul-search as a family, they realized that the red flags had been there all along. From twin Krista's initial distrust of Brad Cooper's reserved demeanor, to younger sister Jill's devastation when he abruptly took Nancy to the United States, separating her from her family, the signs of a bad relationship were all there.

The affidavits dredged up old memories for Nancy's family, reinforced what they already knew and filled in the gaps with some pieces they hadn't previously been aware of. Together, as a family, they sat down and pieced together their version of Nancy and Brad's story—a story that all agreed by this point had a chilling ending.

NEW FRONTIER

"When she moved to North Carolina, things just started to slowly unravel," Jill said with bitterness in her voice. "She always dated someone that held his ground with her, and Brad couldn't. She overpowered him. And I feel like when they moved it was a deliberate move on his part. It was an immediate power shift."

In Canada, Nancy had actually made comparable money to Brad, but all of a sudden in Cary, North Carolina, Brad was the sole breadwinner. Without a green card, Nancy was unable to work at all.

"I think for him, in a sick way, looking back, it felt good for him. It was like he had a thumb on her," Jill said tearfully. "I think he got some kind of sick joy from making my sister feel small. It made him feel big."

Krista said it was after the move, when Nancy was far away from her family, that Brad's true colors started to show.

"He was so tight with *his* money, *his* house, *his* car," Krista said. "Nancy was his last concern, last thought. Nancy got really lonely, very sad, very depressed. She was miserable."

"Brad's approach to life is that if it doesn't shine on him, make him look good, he won't spend the money," Garry said.

To the outside world, Nancy and Brad's life looked idyllic. Nancy sported a large diamond engagement ring. They lived in a nice home in an up-and-coming neighborhood. Brad drove a BMW. But these were all things the world could see. Jill said that's how Brad was—eager to show everyone he was the big successful man with a beautiful wife, who took care of his family.

"I'm smarter than you because I can cheat on you and get away with it. I'm smarter than you because you don't have a bank account, and I can control your finances. I'm better than you, that makes me better than you. Yes, you can have a humongous diamond ring on your finger because that makes me look like a big man," Jill said, imagining Brad's thought process.

Nancy's reaction to her discontentment was to get out of town as often as possible. She traveled to Florida with a Calgary friend and went home to Canada to visit her family frequently. In her first year of marriage, Nancy came home to Edmonton for Krista's wedding to Jim, as well as for an extended visit.

"She wanted to leave. She thought, 'This isn't what I bargained for,'" said Jill. "But most of us tried to convince her to make it work."

According to Jill, Nancy had met a man in Florida with whom she was taken. He was just a symptom of the problems in her marriage. But the lure of him only increased her unhappiness. "It was not a good situation. She was feeling vulnerable. She was out of her comfort zone. She was not herself, and she got into this situation. I think when you're looking to get out of a marriage, you're doing self-destructive behaviors," Jill said.

Jill made it clear that she didn't approve of Nancy's interest in other men while she remained a married woman. She and her two best friends sat down and counseled Nancy.

"I just regret that entire thing," Jill recalled of the intervention, "because I got really upset with her. Everyone has that moment with a sibling or a parent where they're not your hero anymore. They have faults, too. That was my moment with her. [Until then, Nancy] could do no wrong in my eyes, and when she did that, she really disappointed me. I thought she was better than that."

Brad came to the Rentzes' vacation home in Canmore, Alberta, to try and win Nancy back.

"Brad had convinced her that he would change and he would make more of an effort to make a life down there for both of them," Krista said.

Jill advised Nancy to stick it out, to give the marriage another shot.

"I told her how upset I was with her and, ironically, that I thought Brad deserved more and that it was unfair the way she was acting," Jill said.

So, heeding her family's advice, Nancy Cooper returned to her husband like a dutiful wife.

MOTHERHOOD

When Bella arrived in early 2004, everything changed for Nancy. She seemed to settle down and be more content with her situation.

"I don't know if it changed or Nancy stopped caring. She got what she wanted. She got a baby," Jill said. "I'm pretty sure Brad could have been the biggest ass in the world, and she would not have noticed. She was on cloud nine."

Krista agreed that motherhood seemed to allow Nancy to make peace with Brad, albeit temporarily.

"They had finally kind of found their way, and Nan was happy. She had a kid. She had a great friend network, wasn't necessarily happy in her marriage, but happy in her life," Krista recalled.

But the happiness didn't last for long. While the Coopers outwardly looked like they were living the American dream, on the inside of the marriage, things were very different. "When I look back, I see all of the controlling behavior from the very beginning—moving there in the first place, not [initially] allowing her to have a car. At the time there were all of these excuses. But peel away what he's telling everyone, and he's really trying to control her," Jill said.

Nancy never had an ATM card or access to cash. Jill said she was forced to charge everything on the joint credit card, from groceries to gas for her car.

"He had her completely trapped," Jill said, in hindsight.

In order to have a little money of her own, Nancy took work under the table. When Nancy wanted a small television for the kitchen, Brad told her to get a job. She watched other people's children in her home for minimum wage to earn the money for the TV. According to Jill, Brad thought it would be "character building" for Nancy to earn the television set herself. In Jill's mind, this was a long way to fall for a well-educated woman who'd been a business owner and had had a successful career before getting married.

Krista said the biggest shift in Brad's behavior came when Nancy was pregnant with Katie, when he became even more arrogant, as well as verbally and psychologically abusive. After Katie was born in

July of 2006, Nancy shared with her family that the couple was no longer intimate.

"She noticed he was going back to [the way he'd acted] when they first moved to North Carolina—very mean, very degrading, very Brad, Brad, Brad, Brad, Brad, Brad," Krista said.

"The old Brad is back," Nancy told Krista over the phone after Brad returned from a business trip to Europe. "He was a different man. Something happened in Europe. I think it's a woman."

Nancy had always suspected Brad of cheating, but most of her suspicions had never been confirmed. Yet every time Brad had a new experience away from home, he seemed to come back changed. After that particular trip he'd told her he wanted to learn to play guitar, speak French and move the family to France.

"He had a growing ego. I think it was, 'I'm doing so well in my philandering that I must be a wonderful person,'" Nancy's father Garry said. "There was a real change in the man."

THE OTHER WOMAN

Because Brad was often away, working, at school, or exercising, Nancy counted on other young mothers in the neighborhood for their friendship and support. Unfortunately, both of Nancy's sisters said she had a habit of attracting hangers-on who would use her instead of being true friends. In the Rentz family's opinion, Heather Metour was one of those people.

"She was a home wrecker. She was an awful person. I don't know why on earth my sister would ever connect herself with this person," Jill said.

Jill had met Metour when visiting Nancy, and was put off by the brash woman who seemed to need to be the center of attention with everyone. Jill asked Nancy why she would be friends with such a person. Nancy said Jill just didn't know Metour the way she did.

"Watch out for her, Nancy," Jill told her big sister.

Jill recalled going on a beach trip with Nancy and her neighbors one summer, before Katie was born, when Brad and Metour appeared to be too close. They took a two-hour walk alone on the beach together one day. At the time, the word among the group was that Metour was sleeping with the husband of another woman in the group. Still, it looked to Jill like the woman was moving in on her brother-in-law.

"Heather was always obsessed with Brad, and it was obvious," Jill said. "For some reason I didn't think Brad could do something like that."

On that same trip, Brad was training for an Ironman triathlon with his friends. All of the wives, the kids, and Jill spent four hours at the beach one afternoon watching Brad and the other men train. It was Jill's birthday, and she was hot and annoyed and wanted to go back to the hotel room. Nancy refused to leave. As a result, the sisters got into a fight.

"She would put everything aside to support him in what he wanted to do," Jill said. "At the end of the day, no matter what had happened, she still wanted to support him."

"When Brad was in a situation when Nancy was all about him, he was fine," Jill said, remembering how they had all stayed up drinking wine and playing cards that night. "But if there was ever a situation where she wasn't paying attention to him, or he wasn't the center of her universe, that's when things started to go awry."

That same night, Jill remembered Brad making fun of Metour, saying how pathetic it was that she was having such an obvious affair with another man in their group of friends. Jill said she bought his act.

"Sometimes I think he's two people. It's very hard for me to understand how the person I know and the person I spent time with is the person that I'm hearing all of these things about and that I know has done horrible things," Jill said. "You started to think, did I ever know that person? Or is that just someone I made up in my head because I wanted him to be that person?"

Krista had similar feelings about Metour when she first met her—that she was trouble, someone she didn't want her twin sister hanging out with.

"Heather made me feel very uncomfortable. She was very possessive over Nancy," Krista said.

In late 2007, Brad sided with Nancy's sisters, suddenly deciding that Metour was not an appropriate friend for his wife, and he told her so, according to Krista.

"Brad didn't want Heather around anymore, said she was a bad influence, and he didn't want Heather in his house, *period.* He just hated her, just all of a sudden," Krista said.

As a result, Nancy had to keep their friendship under wraps. One evening Metour and Nancy met for dinner. Both of the women had a lot to drink. By the end of the night, Krista said, Metour dropped a bombshell. She told Nancy she had slept with Brad. The next day, after they had both sobered up, Nancy called Metour to confirm what she had told her. At the same time, Metour had been named in a lawsuit after allegedly sleeping with another married man, John Pearson, and breaking up his marriage. It was clear that through the process of the lawsuit all of her extramarital affairs could become part of the public court record. Krista said Metour had wanted Nancy to hear it from her and not from someone else. Nancy ended the friendship immediately and confronted Brad, who promptly denied the allegation.

"'How dare you not trust me. How dare you go with Heather—she's just trying to split us up because she doesn't like me,'" Brad said to Nancy, according to Krista.

"Nancy bought into it," Krista said.

CHRISTMAS 2007

Being the oldest child in the family, not to mention the big brother to three little sisters, Nancy's brother Jeff had a lot of protecting to do. Like his mother and sister Jill, Jeff had liked Brad Cooper from the beginning. In Jeff's opinion, Brad had seemed like a solid guy.

Once Nancy moved to North Carolina, he only saw the couple

when they returned on visits to Canada, but Jeff and Nancy had always made it a point to stay in close contact by phone.

Then, around Christmas 2007, Jeff had a very awkward phone conversation with his brother-in-law. They talked about nothing in particular, but Jeff said even speaking about mundane, everyday things like work and the holidays seemed to be more difficult for Brad on this occasion than ever before. Sure, Brad had never been a great conversationalist, but Jeff had always had a way of making him feel comfortable, more like a brother than a brother-in-law. Yet, during this call, the two men seemed more like strangers.

"It was the strangest conversation I've ever had with him. It was like pulling teeth," Jeff said, remembering the painful twenty minutes he spent with Brad on the phone. "I asked him a question. He would answer and then pause. I had known a totally different Brad."

Just prior to Christmas, Garry and Donna had traveled to North Carolina to celebrate Brad's graduation from his MBA program. They remembered Brad talking about the Heather Metour situation, saying he was so upset by what she had told Nancy that he was considering suing her.

"That lying bitch. I'm going to take her to court, going to nail her for defamation of character. What a terrible person," Brad said, according to Garry.

"Well, go for it, Brad, you should do that. It is a terrible thing to do," Donna said to her son-in-law.

But finally, on New Year's Eve 2007, Krista said Brad told Nancy the truth—that he had in fact slept with Metour.

"Brad admitted finally that it was only once, and Heather had always said it was only once and that it didn't mean anything. It was a drunken night," Krista said.

EARLY 2008

Nancy's mother told her daughter to consider forgiving Brad for his indiscretion.

"Can you find it in your heart to forgive a person for a one-night stand? I mean they happen sometimes," Donna said to Nancy.

"No," Nancy replied. "I can't."

Brad was desperately trying to win Nancy back again. He knew she had always been unhappy with the size and layout of their house. In addition, there was now the added bad memory of Brad and Metour having had sex in their home. Brad told Nancy they could build a new house. They had started looking for a new home in the fall and then decided to look at empty lots in the area finally settling on a neighborhood in Apex, the town next to Cary. They spent several weeks working with the builder and his wife to nail down the final plans. Nancy was excited about the prospect of finally having her dream home.

The couple had also decided to go to therapy in an effort to rebuild the marriage, in light of Brad's admission about Metour. It was in therapy that Nancy told her family she learned the whole truth about the affair.

"We're sitting there, and he acknowledges in front of the counselor that this has been a longstanding relationship," Nancy said to her father.

"In therapy, that's when Nancy found out the affair went on for years," Krista recalled Nancy telling her. "And that he loved Heather."

Around the same time, Nancy told her family that she had been approached in a grocery store by a woman from Brad's MBA program. The woman recognized Nancy from a picture of the Coopers that had run in the school newspaper, taken on Brad's graduation day the previous December. She gave Nancy a cryptic message.

"If you're divorcing your husband, I'm glad to give you evidence," the woman told Nancy.

As if this was not enough, the final straw was when Nancy heard that Brad had also had an affair with one of his co-workers' wives. Several men from the neighborhood who Brad had gone out for a bachelor party with at a local bar to play pool told her about it. They said Brad had detailed his exploits to them during the game after a couple of beers. "He was bragging about the affair,"

Garry said.

"We're done. I can't rebuild the trust. The trust is completely gone," Nancy told Krista.

On the day of the closing for the new house, Brad called the builder and told him the deal was off, that they would not be building the home after all. Naturally, the builder asked Brad why he would pull out after more than one hundred hours of work had already gone into the project.

Brad told him Nancy was terminally ill and that as a result they would not be moving forward. It was true that Nancy had had pneumonia and during a test a spot had been found on her lung, but nothing had come of it. When Nancy's family learned this chilling detail of what the builder had been told after her death, they were shocked that Brad would have told such an ugly lie, but in retrospect they strongly believed it foreshadowed his future intentions.

SPRING 2008

In the spring of 2008, when Nancy finally opened up to her brother Jeff about her problems with Brad, his uncomfortable conversation with Brad at Christmas started to make more sense. But even as she expressed her frustration and discontentment to Jeff, he never felt like she was seriously at risk.

"I didn't get the impression from that conversation that she was in danger," Jeff said, remembering how they talked on the phone for several hours. "The Nancy that I knew was very confident and very secure, very strong, and very self-reliant. If she was scared, had she indicated a fear, that would have been my cue. She didn't indicate she was scared at all. She indicated that she was very frustrated and that things weren't going well for her, but there was no element of fear at all."

Jeff felt like Nancy simply needed to tie up the loose ends in North Carolina and move on with the divorce. The upshot of their conversation was that she was making plans for her future and the future of her children and wanted his advice on what he thought would be her best options.

Jeff wished now that the signs had been more obvious, that something would have triggered him to realize his little sister might be in real danger. It's a thought that has stayed with him since her death.

"Ask more questions. If I had done that, if I had asked more questions I may not have gotten the answers that would have made me nervous for her, but at least then, if something is to happen, you can go on knowing that you did everything you could. At the end of the day, the person that is in the peril is really the only person that knows she's in peril," Jeff said with regret.

"She was always the person who was there when you needed her. That's what I miss most about her," Jeff said. "What really hits me the hardest is that I couldn't do that for her. I couldn't be there for her. I couldn't help her when she needed it the most. That's the part that crushes me and stays with me."

Jill was also having conversations with Nancy in the spring of 2008 about her sister leaving Brad for good.

"We thought, 'He *owes* you.' You are owed your fair share. You left everything. You left your life for this person. You had his children," Jill said, recalling the family's advice to Nancy. "Stick up for yourself, and that's always what my dad has taught us. Stick up for yourself and fight for your rights, and that's what she was doing."

"We were all saying, 'We can make it work, just get home and we'll figure it out from there,'" Krista said of Nancy's desire to move back to Canada.

Nancy was torn between moving to Edmonton, where she would have support from her parents, as well as from Jill, Jeff, and their spouses, or moving to Toronto where she could be close to Krista and Jim. Ultimately, Nancy settled on the Toronto area, to be near Krista and Jim. Krista looked at nine houses for Nancy in the hopes that Nancy could get some equity out of her house in Cary and maybe, with a little help from her parents, afford a modest home outside Toronto. Krista and Jim also looked into buying a bigger home where Nancy and the girls could come live with them so that they could help her get back on her feet. Nancy knew that after eight years of being out of the job market it would take time for her to get reestablished professionally.

A moving truck was booked, and Krista headed to North Carolina to help Nancy get the house packed and painted and ready to sell. It was on that trip that Krista realized it was not going to be easy for her sister to get out of her marriage.

"It was odd, surreal," Krista recalled of her visit. "[Brad] would follow us everywhere, put gas in her car, follow us to the grocery store, come in, pay for the groceries."

In February 2008, Krista was in town helping Nancy prepare for Bella's fourth birthday party. They were shopping for items for the party with Brad in tow everywhere they went. At one point, Nancy wanted a balloon to hang up at the party. Krista said Brad refused to buy the $1.50 balloon. She offered to buy it for her sister.

"Don't, because it's going to make my life a living hell when you leave because I'll get shit for telling you stuff," Nancy said to Krista.

Krista also remembered how anxious Nancy had become. The situation was taking a serious toll on her sister and her ability to parent. She was snapping at everyone.

"You're losing yourself in your bitterness and anger, and you need help," Krista told her.

One evening when they were walking back to Nancy and Brad's house from a dinner at Clea and Mike Morwick's, Krista said Nancy pulled Brad aside and apologized for her negative demeanor.

"I want to apologize. I'm under a lot of stress, and I'm going to try to be nicer. I'm going to try not to be so angry, and I'm going to be there for our kids and make sure this is okay," Nancy said to Brad. "I need you to be part of the plan to make it work so we cannot harm our kids, not be angry, and just do this like adults."

Krista said Brad agreed to a truce from their ongoing daily battles and said he, too, would try to make the transition smoother. But as soon as Krista returned to Ontario, the truce apparently ended. Shortly after she got home, Krista got a call at work from

Nancy who was hysterically crying, telling her that Brad had taken the children's passports and was not going to let her leave. Krista hung up and promptly called her parents, who were vacationing in China at the time.

"Nancy's in trouble. Cancel your trip, come home," Krista pleaded on her father's voice mail. "Dad, get down there and shake Brad and say, 'What the hell are you doing to my daughter?' And make him stop because you're the only one he's going to listen to."

Krista then called her little sister, Jill, to fill her in on the situation. Krista was beyond emotional at this point, but she knew her logical little sister would help walk her through this chaotic situation and figure out a plan.

"We need to get her out of there now," Krista said on Jill's voice mail.

Jill received the voice mail at work and couldn't believe how hysterical Krista was.

"Krista was hyperventilating on the phone, crying. She swore a couple of times, couldn't believe how bad it was. She was afraid for her," Jill recalled. "It's like someone blindfolding you. It's like losing your arm. It's so odd not to be able to know what's going on with your loved one and you can't do anything about it."

Jill immediately called Krista back and tried to get a better sense of what was happening to Nancy. She wanted to cut through Krista's emotions and figure out what steps they needed to take to get Nancy out of the desperate situation she was in.

"I just remember this sense of panic. I had this impending sense of something bad [was] going to happen," Jill said.

The sisters had always relied on their father to make the big decisions in the family, but with Garry and Donna on holiday in China, the girls felt lost. They wished he was there so they could tell him in person how scared they were for Nancy.

"In my head, I'm like, 'why are we not doing something? Why don't we handcuff her onto an airplane and take her and the kids?' I don't know why we didn't do anything," said Jill. "They're in the middle of a divorce. They hate each other. They're living in the same house. You've gotten to the point that the marriage is not going to be safe."

The next day Jill decided to call Nancy directly and get the whole story. Jill was on a business trip and had a long drive from Edmonton to a town several hours away when she called Nancy on her cell phone. She asked Nancy directly if she felt like she was in any danger. Nancy said no, but Jill couldn't help that nagging feeling that something more was going on, something Nancy wasn't telling her.

"Nancy, I love you. I'm your sister. I want to be there for you. You need to tell me everything that's going on even if it's embarrassing," Jill said to Nancy on the phone as tears streamed down her face and she gripped the wheel tightly with one hand and tried to concentrate on the road in front of her.

After she hung up with Nancy, Jill also called her parents in China to tell them what was going on.

"This is not good. She is not herself. She is just a shell," she told her father. If her sister had a broken nose or bruises, the abuse would have been obvious enough for them to yank Nancy out of her home, but instead, it was like a subtle poison slowly eating away at Nancy's confidence. Jill stepped back and tried to look at the situation rationally. She decided Nancy just needed to bide her time until she could get out of the marriage and out of North Carolina.

"Of course she's feeling poorly about herself. She doesn't know what she's going to do with her life," Jill said. "We all tried to be there. We all tried to help her and get her out, but the thing is she never in her mind thought this would happen, and to be honest none of us did either."

Nancy had always been the tough one, the one who could take care of herself. In a fight between Nancy and Brad, odds were always on Nancy. She had a way of putting people in their place. Jill kept reminding herself of this fact as she thought about Nancy's situation.

"She thought she could do it. She thought she could handle it," Jill said. "She's so tough. That's why we left her. If she was someone in any way that we were concerned about emotionally not making it through, physically not being able to put up with it, we would have gone down there."

Through Nancy's friend, Hannah Prichard, the family located attorney Alice Stubbs. She agreed to take Nancy's case and started working on a separation agreement so that Nancy could leave North Carolina and get on with her life in Canada as soon as possible. Her parents agreed to pay for Stubbs' services.

"I can do this. I can make this work out until I get there," Nancy said to Krista after she connected with Stubbs. "I'm not worried. I'm angry, and I want to move on."

SEPARATION ON HOLD

Brad knew Nancy had contacted an attorney and asked her to draw up a separation agreement. What he didn't know was that divorce would mean he'd have to pay child support and alimony. Once Brad got wind of the details of the separation agreement and realized he would owe Nancy money, Nancy told her family that his agreeable tune regarding the move changed. He changed the plan, and they were back to square one again.

Garry said Brad even went to a class given by a law firm about how to mitigate your damages during a divorce. He learned that there was no way he was going to get out of paying.

"He had gotten nasty. He had gotten degrading again—mean," Krista said.

Brad also took away from the class that he needed to participate more fully in parenting if he hoped to get joint custody. Again, Nancy told her family that she felt Brad only wanted the custody so that he would have to pay less in child support. Nancy jokingly referred to him as "Superdad," Garry said, but she meant it in a sarcastic way, because his motivations were so transparent.

Nancy told her father about the fight in the preschool parking lot where Brad had insisted on prying a crying Bella out of Nancy's arms and taking her inside.

"He's going to take the kid to school whether she wants to or not, so he grabs her," Garry said. "He takes her to school kicking and screaming."

"[Nancy] was at that point worried that the kids were seeing too much, witnessing too much. Bella had gone to wetting her pants, crying a lot, not wanting to leave Nancy's side, had gotten mad at Brad for making Mommy cry all the time. She needed it to end, but Brad wasn't moving fast enough. She was worried that he wouldn't let her go," Krista said.

Nancy felt strongly that Brad was stalling, trying to make her stay so he wouldn't have to pay her any money.

"I'm not paying you. Why would I pay you? Get your family to pay you. Your family is going to take care of you," Brad said, according to Krista.

Krista also claimed that Brad came up with various crazy scenarios: offering to pay Nancy to be his nanny and watch the children during the day, then go home to an apartment at night. He also again made the bizarre suggestion that they each take one child, and they would be even.

"He was trying to work every angle on not having to pay her a red cent," Krista said.

Krista said Brad even pretended that he wanted to try to work things out again, something that seemed preposterous to Nancy after everything they had been through.

"I don't know why you don't want to work on things, Nancy. I do and I want to fix the marriage and you don't and all you want to do is separate," Brad said, according to Krista.

Nancy told Krista she thought Brad must have received advice from an attorney to act this way. This would allow him to say in court that the divorce was all Nancy's idea and that he had been willing to try to repair the marriage.

But by the time the family gathered in Hilton Head for what would be their last vacation together, there was no "fixing" anything. Nancy made it clear that she was desperate to leave Brad and get back to Canada with the girls. She was ready to be surrounded by her loving family again.

FINAL FAREWELL

Garry and Donna said they knew their son-in-law was trying to keep Nancy from leaving. They had stopped talking about the situation on the home phone or through e-mail because they were certain Brad was monitoring Nancy's calls and her computer. By this point, he had cut her off from all money, with the exception of a small allowance that she said was not enough for her and the girls to live on.

"With that kind of water torture going on, it was pretty clear he was trying to demoralize her, and she was trying to fight it out based on her lawyer's advice," Garry said.

Nancy came to Hilton Head with just a few dollars in her pocket, so Garry and Donna basically picked up her tab for everything. They were also paying for Nancy's attorney, and were happy to do so, but Nancy had become embarrassed by what she viewed as her pitiful financial situation.

When they left each other at the end of the trip, Nancy and Krista sobbed and held each other.

"Nan and I were a mess. Bella bawled and ran after me and begged me not to go," Krista said. "I think Bella saw her mother was happy that week for the first time in a long time."

The next day, it was Garry and Donna's turn to leave Nancy at the airport in Charlotte. It was the last time they would ever see their daughter alive, a good-bye they would never forget. Nancy clung to her mother and cried. She wanted more than anything to get on the plane with her parents, but she didn't have passports for the girls.

"She wanted to come home. She was sobbing. She was in my arms," Donna said tearing up as she recalled the good-bye.

"Mom, I just want to come home," Nancy said to her mother in between sobs.

"We watched her walk away," Donna said of the last time she ever saw her daughter.

"That was a tough thing to do," Garry said, but he managed to take some comfort: "I was really thinking that we would very quickly be bringing her home."

As bad as things were between her and Brad, the entire family assumed Nancy would come out of this terrible situation on top, as she always had. Nancy always seemed to be able to get out of bad situations and pick herself up again.

"I never thought, 'Brad's a killer, he's going to kill her,'" Jill said.

"None of us saw the violent potential," Garry said.

CHAPTER SEVEN

HE SAID

JULY 23, 2008

A lie which is a half truth is ever the blackest of lies.
—Alfred, Lord Tennyson

Brad Cooper submitted his own affidavit in the child custody case on July 23, 2008. In it, he gave a detailed account of what he said had happened in the hours before Nancy Cooper's disappearance. Never before in Wake County had a potential murder suspect come out and talked about specifics related to a crime like this.

Brad started by saying the family had attended the neighborhood party at Diana and Craig Duncan's on the evening of Friday, July 11. He said that while he socialized a little, he mostly kept Bella and Katie occupied while Nancy visited with her friends, and then that around 8:00 P.M. he took the girls home and put them to bed while Nancy stayed at the party. His account up until this point differed very little from what Nancy's friends had said in their affidavits.

The next morning, Saturday, July 12, Brad said he went to the local grocery store, Harris Teeter, at about 6:15 A.M. to buy milk. He said when he returned home from the store, about two and a half miles from the house, Nancy asked him to go back and pick up some laundry detergent. So, at 6:30 A.M. he said he headed back to the store. He said Nancy then called him on his cell phone around

6:40 A.M. while he was in his car on the way to the store and asked him to also pick up some juice. He said at 6:45 A.M. he purchased Tide detergent (not bleach as had been widely rumored) and Naked Green Juice, a favorite of Bella's.

Soon after he returned home from the store, around 7:00 A.M., Brad said Nancy went for a run. He indicated that Nancy usually went running with a friend who lived nearby, a woman he simply knew as Carey. At this point in the investigation the mysterious Carey still had not been heard from publicly. Despite her friends' statements to the contrary, Brad said Nancy never carried her keys or a cell phone when she ran.

Brad said he had plans to play tennis with a friend, Mike Hiller, at 9:30 A.M. that Saturday morning. When Nancy had not returned by 9:15 A.M., Brad said he called his friend to postpone the tennis game. Eventually, Brad said he called his friend and canceled the game when Nancy was still not back by midmorning.

Brad said that he wasn't worried about Nancy because it was not uncommon for her to stop and get coffee and visit with friends after a workout.

Brad said Nancy's friend, Hannah Prichard, called the house between 10:00 A.M. and 10:30 A.M. He told her that Nancy had not returned from her run and was probably just having coffee with someone. He said that between 10:45 A.M. and 11:00 A.M. another one of Nancy's friends, Jessica Adam, also called the house asking for her. Again, Brad told Adam that Nancy was running late and might be getting coffee.

"At noon, I began to get worried," Brad said in the court filing.

He said he started calling Nancy's friends asking around for Carey's number. He said neither Prichard nor Adam had Carey's number or knew her last name because she was a fairly recent friend of Nancy's.

"By 1:00 P.M., I was very concerned about Nancy's not coming home. I fed Bella and Katie lunch, dressed them, and put them in the car. We drove around looking for Nancy at the places she usually goes," Brad said in the affidavit.

He said he searched the Lochmere neighborhood and the adjoining Regency Park neighborhood, as well as the area around nearby Lake Johnson. Brad said he also checked in at the gym the family belonged to, Lifetime Fitness, to see if Nancy was there. He said he drove by the area where he knew Carey had a condo but did not know for sure in which one she lived and did not see her car.

Brad said that around 3:00 P.M. he received a call from the Cary police, who had been called by Jessica Adam about Nancy's disappearance. He said he returned home immediately to speak with them. In the affidavit, he addressed the question of why he hadn't called the police.

"Once I knew the police had been called, there was no longer any point in my calling them again," Brad said.

He went on to say that he thought someone needed to be missing for twenty-four hours before the police would take a report. He defended his initial lack of involvement in the search by saying the police had asked him to stay at home, close to the phone, in case Nancy or someone else with information, called. He called no one, not even Nancy's family, to tell them she was missing.

"I did not call Nancy's family because I was focused on helping police find Nancy by answering their questions," Brad said in defense of his silence.

BRAD THE LONER

One of the things Brad clearly anticipated Nancy's friends would say about him was that he was too wrapped up in his own career and hobbies to be a good husband or parent. As one of the few experts in the world in VOIP phones that ran through the Internet, Brad worked long hours.

Now that Nancy was gone, Brad said he would change his ways, and was confident that he would be able to handle the parenting duties on his own. Still, he needed to address his absence from parenting duties when Nancy was alive. Brad said Nancy had encouraged him to get his MBA so that he could earn more money and be able to provide more opportunities for their children.

But work and school weren't the only distractions that kept Brad away from his family. He was also training for Ironman triathlons, something that required hours of intense exercise. He said that in June 2007, he stopped training when he realized his marriage was in trouble and decided to refocus his attention on his family.

"I dropped my extra activities and evening workouts so that I could come home directly from work and spend more time with Nancy, give her a break from the girls, and help her more around the house," Brad said. "I loved Nancy very much, and I wanted to stay married to her."

BRAD THE PARENT

Nancy's friends had all been very consistent in their affidavits stating that Nancy was Bella and Katie's primary caregiver. They said that they rarely saw Brad doing anything with his family, let alone taking care of his girls. But in his own affidavit, Brad painted a very different picture of himself as a father.

He said he watched the girls in the mornings when Nancy went jogging, and in the evenings when he returned from work. He said he often changed diapers, prepared bottles, gave the girls baths, helped them brush their teeth, read to them, and put them to bed. Brad said sometimes he let Bella come in and snuggle with him when Katie got fussy and kept her awake at night.

"Nancy and I shared the daily care of our children," Brad said in the affidavit.

Brad said that on the weekends Nancy often took a "mommy's day off" where she would shop or spend time with friends, and he would care for the girls by himself all day long.

Brad also challenged the accusations from Nancy's friends that he was not a part of the girls' medical care. Brad said that although Nancy usually took the girls to the doctor while he was at work, they discussed the girls' medical care and made decisions about it together.

Brad said he played games with the girls and often took them on outings to museums and parks. He said he read to them every day. He said he even helped Nancy plan the girls' birthday parties. For Bella's most recent birthday, Brad said that he took her and her friends horseback riding at Dead Broke Farm.

"She loved it," Brad said.

Brad painted himself as a patient and affectionate father.

"I tell my daughters 'I love you' many times a day. We hug and kiss and Bella says 'I love you' to me," Brad said.

In addition to child care, Brad claimed to be a full partner in the domestic duties around the house, something Nancy's friends had vehemently denied. He said he often went grocery shopping and even bought clothing and shoes for the girls.

"I helped with the laundry, cleaning and household chores," Brad said. "Nancy sometimes referred to me as 'Superdad.'" Nancy's family claimed this moniker was a joke, a nickname Nancy began using sarcastically when Brad started taking on minor childrearing responsibilities.

Brad said that since his wife's death, he had done everything possible to shelter the girls from the media spotlight. He said that he and the girls had been staying with friends so that they could avoid the investigators and the daily media circus surrounding their house. On the occasions since Nancy's death that he did have to leave the girls briefly, Brad said he made sure that they were with family members, close friends, or neighbors with whom they felt comfortable.

"I love my children very much and have tried to protect them from being publicly shown in the media. They are too young to understand the tragedy of their mother's death and all the cameras and people are confusing to them," Brad said.

BRAD THE ABUSER

"I am neither mentally nor emotionally unstable," Brad said. "I have never attempted or threatened to commit suicide."

Brad said that other than marriage counseling with Nancy, he had never had any type of mental health counseling or been on any kind of medication for psychological issues.

He admitted that he and Nancy had had arguments on occasion but said they were rarely in front of the children and usually did not involve yelling.

"I have never raised my voice or been abusive or neglectful in any way to my children," Brad stated. "I have never emotionally or physically abused my wife. I have never belittled her in private or in the presence of others."

Again, this was in direct opposition to what Nancy Cooper's friends had said in their affidavits about Brad. He listed all of the reasons that his statement should be considered credible. He said the police had never been called to a disturbance at his home. He said there had never been any actions against him involving "domestic violence of any kind." Brad said again that he had opened up his home and cars to searches and that he had cooperated with everything the police had asked of him, including answering all of their questions.

Brad then ripped a page right out of Chief Pat Bazemore's playbook, using her exact words from the press conferences: "I am not a suspect or even a person of interest regarding the death of my wife."

BRAD THE CONTROLLER

Brad had a very different take on the financial control Nancy's friends said he wielded over his wife. He said Nancy had expensive tastes, tastes that had ultimately put the family into debt, claiming that their credit card debt had reached forty-five thousand dollars at one point.

"Nancy liked to buy eight thousand dollar paintings, designer clothing, Tiffany jewelry," Brad said in his affidavit. "Status was important to Nancy, and I indulged her too much."

Brad said the previous Christmas, Nancy had bought him a twelve-hundred-dollar Louis Vuitton laptop case, which he asked her to return. He said in October 2007, he bought Nancy a nearly three-thousand-dollar diamond pendant necklace that she wanted. He said Nancy wanted a BMW X5 fully loaded, which he had purchased for her.

Brad denied withholding money for Nancy's and the children's basic daily needs. He said he paid all of the household bills and then gave Nancy 80 percent of what was left over. Brad claimed in the affidavit that this amounted to about three hundred dollars per week. He said that Nancy complained that the amount he was giving her was not enough and that he would often try to give her more.

"I have never refused to give my wife money to buy groceries, clothing, and anything else she needed or wanted as long as we could afford it," Brad said.

He said if anyone had loaned her money, as was repeatedly alleged by Nancy's friends and family, it was for "items that we could not afford to buy."

Brad also said he never tried to control his wife's movements. He said that she often went out without him in the evenings and stayed away from the house for five or six hours "without letting me know where she was."

BRAD THE ADULTERER

Brad admitted to one affair in the affidavit, the one with Nancy's former friend, Heather Metour. Despite what Nancy told her family, that Brad had revealed during therapy it was a long-term affair, Brad denied this. Instead, he claimed it was merely a one-night stand.

"Three years ago I made a mistake while married to Nancy. I had a single indiscretion and slept with another woman one time. I tried to hide it from Nancy because I worried what it would do to our marriage, and I deeply regretted, and still regret, that it happened. Nancy suspected, and our marriage began to deteriorate nevertheless," Brad said.

Heather Metour had been instructed by her attorney, John McNeil, not to talk about the Cooper case. But McNeil did make a statement to WRAL regarding his client's potential involvement in this case.

"She's upset any of this that occurred four years ago is being brought up at all. It's got nothing to do with the custody case," McNeil said.

Brad said he and Nancy had not had sex for two and half years, not since Katie was conceived. He ultimately admitted his infidelity with Metour to Nancy, and they decided to go to counseling. Brad said during the counseling Nancy also admitted that she had had an indiscretion.

"Nancy admitted she had an extramarital relationship while married to me four years ago before Bella was born. Nancy insisted that she did nothing wrong, that her relationship with the other man only happened once," Brad said.

THE DIVORCE

Clearly, it was Brad's admitted infidelity with Heather Metour that had sent the marriage into an irreversible downward spiral. Although Nancy had always suspected her husband of other affairs, this one he had confessed to. Even more hurtful was the fact that it had occurred with her close friend. Not even counseling could get the couple beyond the transgression.

Nancy's attorney, Alice Stubbs, drafted a separation agreement for the couple. On Tuesday, April 15, 2008, Stubbs e-mailed the agreement to Nancy. At the time, Brad's attorneys said Nancy had forwarded the e-mail to him. Just how Brad intercepted that e-mail would later become part of the criminal trial.

The separation agreement itself, a thirty-five-point document, was never signed by Nancy or Brad. Under the draft, Brad would have to pay Nancy an undetermined amount of alimony on the first of the month every month until April 30, 2016. Only four things could make this requirement disappear: an agreement between the parties, Nancy's marriage to someone else, Brad's death, or Nancy's death.

Beginning on May 1, 2008, according to the agreement, Brad would have to pay twenty-one hundred dollars in child support every month until Katie turned eighteen. They would share custody of the children, with Nancy having primary physical custody and Brad having regular visitation.

In his affidavit, Brad eschewed allegations from Nancy's family and friends that the pending separation agreement was a strong motive for murder. Brad instead said that it proved that Nancy thought he was a good father, and therefore, in light of his wife's death, he now deserved full custody of his girls.

"Nancy and her attorney agreed that I was a fit and proper parent to have the [joint] care, custody, and control of the children," Brad said in his affidavit.

The separation agreement did in fact refer to Brad as a "fit and proper" parent who was entitled to joint custody. It indicated that while the children would live with Nancy in Canada, Brad would have the children on alternating weekends and for two weeks in the summer. The agreement also indicated that the couple would share in all major childrearing decisions.

Brad indicated that this proved Nancy would have wanted him to have the children in the event of her death. He said he only took the girls' passports from Nancy because he was afraid she would take them to Canada without his permission before the details of the separation were finalized.

THE CUSTODY BATTLE

"I regret that the Plaintiffs are using Bella and Katie as a tool to try to hurt me," Brad said. "Nancy also would not have approved of the Plaintiffs' actions. Unlike the Plaintiffs, I sheltered Bella and Katie from the horrors of this ordeal."

Brad said that he also didn't appreciate Nancy's family talking about intimate details of the girls' lives at the press conferences, especially the fact that they were in psychological counseling. He was also upset that he had not been consulted about the girls' attendance at Nancy's memorial services in Cary and in Canada. Brad also did not approve of Garry and Donna allowing the media to photograph the girls at the services.

He said he felt like his hand had been forced when it came time to finally tell the girls that Nancy was dead.

"I had to tell Bella about her mother following the advice from a child psychologist because they were going to Nancy's memorial service. Bella became upset and did not want to listen," Brad said.

Brad's version contrasted sharply with Nancy's family's account of how Bella learned of her mother's death. They had said that Donna and Krista told Bella in the car on the way to the service after Brad had failed to do so.

Brad said he planned to have his own private memorial service for Nancy with his close friends because he did not feel comfortable attending the services in Cary or Canada. Yet, no one was ever invited to such a memorial and there was no evidence one took place.

"I regret that I couldn't even attend my wife's memorial service for fear that it would detract from the focus on Nancy and cause tension with her parents," Brad said.

But in truth, tension between Brad and the Rentzes had grown exponentially every day since Nancy's body was found, and now the custody battle had touched off an all-out war between Brad and Nancy's family. In his affidavit, Brad readily hurled insults at them.

He said that the girls only saw Nancy's family for a few weeks every year, and, as a result, did not have a close bond with them. He said Donna had had multiple car accidents and would therefore not be a proper caregiver for Bella and Katie. He said Krista, like Nancy, had Crohn's disease, a gastrointestinal ailment that sometimes required hospitalization. Given this fact, he said that Krista was not a fit caretaker for his daughters.

He implied that Nancy's family was trying to "replace" Nancy with Krista, Nancy's identical twin. He said they had asked for Nancy's sunglasses, jewelry, and hat, which he surmised would be used to make Krista appear even more like Nancy.

"This would confuse Bella and Katie and dishonor Nancy's memory," Brad said.

Brad argued in the affidavit that taking Bella and Katie away from their home, their friends, their school, and out of their comfort zone would be severely detrimental to them during this very traumatic time in their lives.

"Plaintiffs have wrenched Bella and Katie from the only stable, familiar caregiver and environment they know. They lost their mother, and [the] Plaintiffs have taken them from their father and from their home," Brad said. "Bella and Katie need the love and stability only their father and their home can provide."

CHAPTER EIGHT

REBUTTAL

JULY 24, 2008

Betrayal is the only truth that sticks.
—Arthur Miller

On the morning of Thursday, July 24, 2008, the front page of the local newspaper, the *News and Observer*, had a story about all the filings in the custody case along with details about Nancy's memorial service in Canada. The headline read, Filings lay bare a bitter union.

The story then jumped to page 10A. There was a box with the caption in all capital letters that read, she made many "feel so special." Beneath the caption was a photograph that summed up Nancy's loss without words. It was a picture of one of Nancy's black-and-white photographs on an easel from the service in Edmonton the previous day. In it she was holding Katie. A blond, tanned Bella wearing a pink flower in her hair in a white sundress covered in black flowers was pressed up against the photograph, her left cheek flush with the picture, her arms crossed in front of her.

The photograph in the newspaper captured the child from behind, with only a slight hint of her right cheek visible. It was so subtle yet so powerful. It looked as though Bella were hoping that if she closed her eyes and wished hard enough, her mother might reach out from the photograph and put her arms around her again.

FIGHTING BACK

On Thursday, July 24, Brad Cooper's attorneys filed a slew of new affidavits aimed at rebutting what Nancy's friends had said about him.

"I am normally a private person and to date have not disrespected Nancy by correcting any half-truths or exaggerations that she told me during our marriage," Brad said in his rebuttal affidavit. "While I wish Nancy to be remembered for her good friends and the many good times she shared with friends, I feel that I need to set the record straight on a few issues."

Brad went point by point through all of the allegations waged against him by Nancy's friends. He said they exaggerated his workout training schedule. He said that the MBA program that took up so much of his time was at Nancy's request and that she had wanted him to finish it as soon as possible, even if it meant putting in more hours.

Brad said Nancy's friends also exaggerated the amount of travel he did for work. He also maintained that he was always in touch with Nancy by cell phone and through e-mail when he traveled, despite what her friends said. Brad also said he never left Nancy without money when he went on his trips.

As for "disappearing" one weekend, Brad said he did go to a boat show in Greenville, North Carolina, with his MBA team on Sunday, September 30, 2007, "to perform a market analysis on boat customers and dealers." He said he was at the boat show for a few hours, returned to a classmate's house to compile the data, and then returned home a little after 10:00 P.M. that evening, not at 5:00 A.M. the next day.

Brad denied allegations that he was controlling of his wife in any way. He said he did not disconnect or monitor Nancy's phone calls. He said, in fact, he had done away with the Cisco VOIP system in his home that would have allowed him to do this and had instead changed to a standard cordless handset in May. He said that when the water was turned off in the spring of 2008 because he had "overlooked" the bill, he called the town of Cary and immediately had the service restored.

Brad denied the implication that he did not want Nancy to have a car. He said Nancy only wanted a BMW X5, and they had to wait until they could find one with just the right features. As a result, for a few months, they shared a car.

Brad said he did try to help Nancy get the house ready for sale by doing small repairs but that, for the most part, she made it clear that she didn't want his help. As far as spending time with his daughters, Brad said that despite allegations that he'd missed his children's birthday parties, he was at every one, including Bella's party at the horse farm in 2008.

He said he also spent time with his girls—swimming at the neighborhood pool, attending Bella's soccer camps and dance recitals, and going on vacations with them. He said he had been to their school on numerous occasions to drop them off, pick them up, or attend class functions.

"I have a wonderfully loving relationship with my children," Brad said.

As far as the sexual encounter with Heather Metour, Brad said that, despite what others said, it was not a serious love affair, just a one-night stand.

"I was never in love with Heather during this time. The day after the indiscretion, I called Heather to indicate that it was a mistake and should never have happened and would never happen again," Brad said.

After Nancy's death, Brad took the children and stayed with Metour's ex-husband, Scott Heider, and his kids. Nancy's friends indicated that they thought this was a strange choice—to take your children and stay with your ex-lover's ex-husband. But Brad defended his choice in the affidavit, saying that the children knew each other and were comfortable together and that he felt as though he needed to get away from the media frenzy. He also added that Heider and Metour had been divorced for some time, and the affair was clearly water under the bridge at this point.

At the end of his rebuttal affidavit, Brad's attorneys attached a series of pictures: Brad and the girls at the beach, in the pool, riding ponies, dressed up as Eeyore on Halloween. The pictures showed Brad as a doting father: with a sleeping baby on his chest tucked beneath his chin, smiling as he held an infant gingerly over his shoulder, balancing a baby on his lap on a raft in the pool as she held her arms outstretched. The pictures were so normal, so mundane, it seemed that either this man was being set up or he was a master of deception.

FAMILY AFFAIR

Brad's family—his mother, Carol Cooper; his father, Terry Cooper; and his younger brother, Grant Cooper, all native Canadians—filed brief affidavits on Brad's behalf. All three categorically denied that Brad had ever attempted suicide. They also said they had never noticed any discord between Brad and Nancy.

Brad's father said that he was aware that his son and daughter-in-law had money problems. He said Brad and Nancy took out an eighty-thousand-dollar home equity loan to pay off their credit card debt.

"Brad was concerned about their spending," Terry said.

As far as his relationship with the kids, Brad's family maintained that he was a good father and that it was obvious his children loved him. His brother, Grant, said Brad constantly spoke to him about his children. Brad's mother said when she visited the couple's house in Cary, she noticed that Bella was especially close to her father.

"Bella was very attached to her daddy. When she was tired and cranky, all she wanted was her daddy," Carol Cooper said. "Brad loves his kids. He spends time with them and cares for them. Brad looks after them very well."

"Bella would hug and kiss Brad," Terry said.

But it was the characterization of Brad's demeanor that was

the most interesting element of the three affidavits. Brad's family said he was a person who kept to himself, someone who was very calm and nonviolent, someone who could never have killed his wife.

"Brad was usually a very quiet, docile person," Terry Cooper said. "Brad would never do anything violent—it's just not in him."

A LITTLE HELP FROM FRIENDS

Five of Brad's friends and two teachers from the preschool also submitted affidavits on his behalf.

It was clear from their comments that the teachers barely knew Brad and had little to say about him one way or the other. Both teachers at the Triangle Academy Preschool, Kathy Dorr and Tracey Vancott, said that Bella and Katie were well dressed, seemed happy, and never showed any signs there were problems at home.

They had seen Brad drop the girls off or pick them up on several occasions but said that he rarely came to school functions.

"Bradley Cooper seemed to be a very typical father and I never noticed anything that would set him apart from other fathers," Dorr said. "Both children seemed happy and well-adjusted."

"I also never noticed him behave in an inappropriate manner," Vancott said.

Brad's friends had varying degrees of detail in their affidavits. They all painted Brad as a quiet person who kept to himself, just like his family had said. He was clearly not the buddy type of guy, but they said he could be helpful and friendly at times. At gatherings, they said he often kept to himself or concentrated on the children while Nancy mingled.

"Nancy was a social butterfly who liked to socialize," said Mike Hiller, Brad's neighbor and friend of seven years.

Hiller was the friend whom Brad was supposed to meet for tennis the morning Nancy disappeared, though he made no mention of that in his affidavit. Instead, he talked about how Brad had been making a real effort recently to spend more time at home with his family. He said he never witnessed the couple fight.

"His parenting skills are very good, and Brad is a good father. I never saw Brad yell at his children. I never saw Brad act violently toward the children," said Chris Wall, the husband of a woman Brad worked with at Cisco Systems. "I never saw Brad yell at Nancy. I never saw Brad put Nancy down."

Before Nancy's death, Wall had run into the family at Frankie's, an amusement area for kids. He talked about how attentive Brad seemed toward Bella specifically, following her around, keeping an eye on her as she made her way around the play area.

Another person who seemed more like an acquaintance than a friend, Paul Dittner, who used to live near the Coopers, also talked in his affidavit about how he had never witnessed Brad doing anything untoward to his wife or children. He said he had run into Nancy a few weeks prior to her death at the Hillers' home, and she had told him that she and Brad were getting a divorce.

"Nancy told me that Brad was a good father and that she knows Brad loves Bella and Katie," Dittner said.

Michael Morwick, Clea Morwick's husband, and a neighbor of the Coopers, was the only person to put in affidavits for both sides. While he had said some pretty negative things about Brad in the affidavit he filed on behalf of Nancy's family, he painted a completely different picture when it came to his affidavit for Brad's side.

He said that since learning Nancy and Brad were getting divorced, Brad had been making a much bigger effort with his children and had even made more of an effort to socialize with Nancy's friends. Morwick said Brad felt as though he had fallen out of favor with everyone because of his affair with Heather Metour, but Morwick said they were all trying to welcome him back into the fold for the sake of the kids.

Morwick had seen Brad and Nancy together at his home the Wednesday before Nancy disappeared. He said that Nancy's Crohn's disease had acted up that night, so she had gone home, but Brad stayed there with the kids. He said Brad had been friendly toward him that evening. Later it would be discovered that it had nothing to do with the Crohn's disease, but that Brad and Nancy had had a fight over what she deemed his controlling nature, and she had left to go to her friend Jessica Adam's house.

Morwick gave the first account of how Brad acted right after Nancy's disappearance. He and his wife, Clea, took the girls to their house that day so that Brad could concentrate on the search for Nancy. Morwick said he remembered talking to Brad in front of the house as police did a preliminary search inside.

"He was sitting on the curb with his hands holding his face. He was worried. He kept asking why the police dogs were not there to search for Nancy, and why the police didn't get something for the dogs to smell so they could find Nancy," Morwick said.

Mike Hiller also talked about Brad's demeanor after Nancy's disappearance. He recalled that after the police press conference announcing Nancy's body had been discovered, Brad told him that he never knew Nancy to run in the area where her body was found. Hiller said his friend was clearly distraught over his wife's death.

Right after Nancy's body was discovered, Brad went to stay with his friend Scott Heider. On Wednesday, July 16, at 3:00 A.M., Heider recalled that the Cary police came to his house to get a DNA sample from Brad. Bella and Katie spent most of that week, Heider said, playing with his children as Brad tried to keep things as normal as possible for his daughters.

The oddest part of the situation was that Scott Heider was Heather Metour's ex-husband, so the natural question was why would he take in the man who had an affair with his ex-wife? In his affidavit, Heider explained their friendship despite this adversity in one simple sentence: "I was angry at Brad, but we have still remained friends."

Heider said that in his opinion Brad gave Nancy and the girls everything they could possibly have needed or wanted. He also talked about Nancy, saying they had run together on several occasions. But even as he spoke about the seemingly benign facts of the Coopers' lives, he was the only person whose deposition mentioned anything negative about Nancy.

"Nancy often exaggerated details of stories for dramatic effect," Heider said. "She liked to tell people stories to get attention."

The big question anyone who read the affidavits was left with was, who was telling stories now that Nancy was dead?

CHAPTER NINE

RECKONING

JULY 25, 2008

We are all born for love. It is the principle of existence,
and its only end.
—Benjamin Disraeli

While the majority of Nancy's family made their way to the courthouse for the custody hearing that Friday, Donna stayed behind with her daughter-in-law, Shannon Rentz, Jeff's wife, in order to keep an eye on the children. Nancy's friend, Jessica Adam, had arranged for the family to stay at a house in Cary while the court proceedings were going on.

Donna was in the kitchen cooking when she heard some commotion coming from the bedroom upstairs where Bella was staying. Bella had been having tantrums in the days since she'd learned about Nancy's death, and while she was still working with the grief counselor, the child seemed to be on an emotional roller coaster that made it hard to predict her mood from one minute to the next. Donna ran upstairs to check on her granddaughter.

"She was just screaming and crying for her mommy," Donna said, her voice heavy with emotion as she remembered the day.

"Mommy, where are you? Where are you? Where are you? Where are you? Where are you? I need you! I need you!" Bella screamed at the top of her lungs. Donna saw that the child had ripped the blinds away from the windows.

"She was looking for her mom, and she was looking for her mom in the sky. She knew her mom was with the angels, I guess. I don't know," Donna said shaking her head. "She was beyond control."

Bella slammed the door and refused to let Donna into the room three times. Finally, Donna sat down on the floor outside the bedroom and told her granddaughter that she would be there, waiting until she was ready to talk. Donna had lost her child, probably the biggest tragedy anyone could ever face. But in this moment she knew that Bella's grief over losing her mother took precedence. In this moment she was not a grieving mother, but a grandmother who needed to support her granddaughter. Donna had gone through some old photographs and had found some of Nancy that Bella had never seen. Through the closed door, she offered to show them to her. Bella finally opened the door.

"She came over, sat beside me, took the pictures. She cried, but she settled down," Donna remembered with a sigh of relief.

Finally, she left the child alone with the photographs and her memories and went back down to finish cooking, telling Bella that she hoped she would join her in the kitchen soon. Eventually, the child came downstairs and took her grandmother's hand and led her back to the bedroom.

"I made something for you," Bella said. She showed Donna three little hearts made out of Play-Doh.

And that wasn't the only thing Bella had made. In the stepstool next to the bed there was a little compartment with a lid. Inside, Bella had begun to collect memories of her mother—photographs, mementos, anything that reminded her of Nancy. It was the beginning of what would later become a very large, very private memorial from Bella to her mother.

In addition, everywhere she went, the child carried a photograph of Nancy with her, a lasting reminder of the mother she would never get to see again.

RESOLUTION

Photographers chased Nancy's family as they walked the few blocks from their attorneys' office to the Wake County Courthouse on the morning of the custody hearing. Garry Rentz, Krista and Jim Lister, and Jill and Chad Dean followed. They seemed calm and unflustered by the gaggle of cameras in their faces.

Another swarm of media surrounded Brad, Carol and Terry Cooper, and Brad's attorneys as they made the walk from their office to the courthouse. Brad looked pale and serious in a dark suit. He towered over his diminutive lawyers, Seth Blum and Howard Kurtz, who flanked him on either side, the tops of their heads coming just slightly above his shoulders.

But for all of the drama leading up to the main event, the day ended quietly. There would be no custody battle. Instead, the lawyers met behind closed doors and hashed out an agreement. Anxious reporters paced in the hallway as Judge Debra Sasser worked out the details.

This was not a big surprise. Lawyers around town had speculated that Brad would never take the stand to fight for his children, because once he did he would open himself up to questions about his wife's murder. Being the obvious prime suspect, he couldn't risk that.

After about an hour of legal wrangling in the judge's chambers, everyone surfaced and told the journalists waiting in the hallway that an agreement had been reached. Nancy's family would continue to have temporary custody of Bella and Katie and could return with them to Canada. The custody hearing would be continued on October 13.

"We are very pleased with the decision the court has made," Garry said. "We respect the judgment of the court and the quality of the work that has been done. So we are just very satisfied with where we are."

Brad's attorneys also played up the agreement as if it were exactly the thing Brad had been wanting all along. They said that Brad wanted the girls to be away from "the spotlight of media scrutiny" and that this goal would be best achieved in Canada with Nancy's family.

"While he will miss the daily joys of fatherhood, he fully intends to remain a vital force in his children's lives," the attorneys said in a written statement released after the ruling. "Though it is painful to contemplate any additional day without his girls, Mr. Cooper accepts this as a heartrending, but necessary step toward achieving justice."

The agreement allowed Brad to speak to the girls via phone or webcam four times a week for at least fifteen minutes at a time. It also allowed Brad to have two weekend supervised visits with the girls at a family center called Time Together in Raleigh where he could see his daughters for four hours a day on each weekend day. Both parties would split the cost of the girls' transportation between Canada and Raleigh.

The order further stated the children needed to be kept away from the media and any information about the case.

"None of the parties shall disparage the others and none of the parties shall discuss the circumstances surrounding the death of their mother or the pending custody," stated Judge Sasser.

Nancy's family had just won their latest battle, but they knew the war would continue. If Brad wasn't charged with Nancy's murder by the next court date, it would be hard to argue that he should not have custody of his own children.

NEW PARENTS

"It's been one of the real difficult things that Donna and I have dealt with," Garry said of deciding where the girls would live now that they had extended temporary custody.

In the whirlwind of the custody battle, Garry and Donna had had little time to really consider where the kids would live permanently. They felt that they were too old to care for both of the girls on a full-time basis, and they didn't want to split the sisters up because they had such a close bond; but at the same time it was not obvious which of their family members could take on the burden of two little children. They were also trying to be mindful of Nancy's wishes. Jeff and Shannon already had one daughter and another one on the way. Jill and Chad also had a daughter but were in between houses and living in Donna and Garry's basement. Krista and Jim had no children, but both had demanding careers; Krista as an interior decorator, Jim as a sales representative for a major beer distributor. Still, Krista had the closest and most consistent relationship with her nieces, and her undeniable likeness to their mother couldn't hurt.

"Kris and Jim had no background as parents. Of all of our kids, if I'm going to dump two young needy people on somebody, do you pick someone who's never thrown a fast ball, or do you pick someone who has parented?" Garry said. "The big question was, can I leave both of these kids with two rookies, and can they make it?"

After many discussions, Krista and Jim were decided to be the most logical choice. With Bella being so fragile at this point, Krista seemed to be the only person who could truly comfort her. Katie could have been happy anywhere, but it was decided that Bella's bond with Katie was so strong that separating them was no good.

"The connection between [Katie] and Bella is so significant," Garry said. "Bella takes care of her."

"Bella wouldn't let me out of her sight," Krista said. "We had a really good relationship and a really close relationship. She just needed that familiar face and that familiar relationship that she had with Nancy and me."

So despite not wanting to separate the girls, Bella went back with Krista and Jim while little Katie temporarily traveled to Edmonton to stay with her grandparents. Meanwhile, Krista and Jim readied their house as they were suddenly parents to two young girls. It wasn't the way Krista would have wanted to have children, but she and Jim lovingly took on the responsibility.

"I always wanted kids—to get them this way, no, but the cool thing is they've got my DNA. Nan and I shared that. It's the closest thing to having kids for me," Krista said.

But for Krista and Jim, loving these children also involved risks. They knew there was a chance that, in the end, they could lose them.

"I was always worried that [Brad] would get them back," Krista said. "I knew that if something major didn't happen in three months he would get them back, and that would destroy me."

SETTLING IN

Nancy's family found Dr. Huzar Altay through a connection at the University of Toronto. She ended up being a great fit for the girls, especially for Bella. Initially, Dr. Altay met with the entire family in her offices but would leave the door open so that the girls could wander in and out and not feel pressured to sit down and talk. One day Katie wandered in looking for Krista, and Bella came in after her sister in a very protective manner.

After the very first visit, the doctor told the girls they could take a toy home and bring it back the next time. Bella chose a police car.

"All of Bella's early interactions with Altay were all around trauma, crime, and emergency," Garry recalled.

Slowly, Bella started to spend more and more time wandering into the doctor's office. Little by little she started to open up to Altay and, eventually, grew to like and trust her.

While Katie seemed to remember nothing, her speech was delayed and her sleeping patterns were disrupted. Nancy's family knew that no amount of therapy or love could ever erase the tragedy that had befallen these little girls' lives.

"What are they aware of? What do they know?" Garry said of Bella and Katie as he wondered if they had witnessed anything the day their mother died.

CHAPTER TEN

DOG DAYS

AUGUST 2008

We must never be afraid to go too far,
for the truth lies beyond.
—Marcel Proust

Nancy's brother, Jeff Rentz, felt as though the best thing he could offer his family as a police officer was insight into how a criminal investigation worked. He tried to explain to them that it took time to put together a strong case, that the police only had one shot at it, and if they didn't have enough evidence to convict, a guilty man might go free.

"It's really important in policing to do things the right way," Jeff said. "If you don't take your time and you don't do things the right way, ultimately you're going to screw yourself."

It was frustrating and difficult for the entire family to play this waiting game, but Jeff assured them that in the end justice would prevail. They clung to this belief in the midst of their grief when they had little else to hold on to.

"Something had to be done. We wanted something to happen," Donna said. "We shared our frustration."

"This is a guy who's pretty angry at us," Garry said. "We felt the kids were at risk and we were at risk."

On one of their trips to North Carolina to allow Brad to have his court-ordered visitation with the girls, Garry and Donna met with the district attorney, Colon Willoughby, and the first assistant DA, Howard Cummings.

"I do not want to give these children back to the man who probably murdered their mother," Donna said to the prosecutors that day.

"We have one chance. If I'm not ready, or I go too soon and we lose, I don't get another chance," Cummings said, echoing what Jeff had already told them.

WEB DEFENSE

Brad Cooper's attorneys, Seth Blum and Howard Kurtz, had paid attention to the proactive legal defense techniques that had become part of the playbook for modern-day high-profile cases. They knew their client was not looking good in the public arena. The case had caught the attention of the national media. The slant was obvious: "Man in upper-class neighborhood murders his wife and then tries to cover it up." The story itself was actually more common than most murder cases, but because of all of the titillating details coming out of the custody case, the public had a rare, intrusive glimpse into the Coopers' lives. They were "every couple" in a way. And people could relate to them.

To combat the steady stream of negative publicity surrounding their client, Kurtz and Blum created a special section on their law firm's website to defend Brad's reputation, which they saw as the fastest and most efficient way for them to connect with the highest number of people.

"We are reaching out in this way in an attempt to bring twenty-first century communication techniques to bear and to help motivate any possible witnesses to speak up now," the attorneys said in a statement released Friday, August 1, 2008.

The web page provided a description of what Brad had said

Nancy Cooper was wearing when she disappeared on July 12, 2008. It also asked the public to come forward with any information they might have about the case and either bring it to their attention or to the attention of the Cary Police Department.

"We know that coming forward can be intimidating. However, the help of the community is our best tool to ensure that justice is served. We appeal to your sense of civic responsibility," the page read.

The site went on to say that Brad had been in touch with police and was helping with the investigation. "He has cooperated extensively with law enforcement in an attempt to find the killer or killers," the site said.

This assertion would later be strongly challenged by investigators, who said Brad was *not* cooperative.

THE NAIL

On Wednesday, August 6, 2008, an affidavit taken on July 24 was filed by Alice Stubbs, Nancy's family's attorney. It was simple and straightforward—just one line—but its impact would turn out to be great.

It was not detailed or emotional like the other affidavits filed by Nancy's friends, but in its simplicity it helped in part to answer the burning question that many people close to the case had been grappling with: Did Nancy Cooper go jogging on Saturday morning, July 12?

The affidavit was from Carey Clark, the woman with whom Brad Cooper said he believed Nancy was jogging the morning she disappeared. While her name had been bantered around shortly after Nancy's death, the police had refused to comment on Carey Clark or whether or not she had seen Nancy the day she died. "I had no plans to run with Nancy Cooper on Saturday July 12, 2008, and I never ran with Nancy Cooper on July 12, 2008," Clark said in her affidavit.

Brad's attorney, Seth Blum, immediately downplayed the latest filing by saying that his client had simply "thought" his wife was jogging with Carey Clark that morning but didn't know for sure.

Clark's affidavit added more fuel to growing speculation that Nancy had never gone out jogging, an issue her family and friends had already raised in the custody filings. And if she didn't go jogging, there was only one conclusion anyone could reach—Brad Cooper was lying.

CHAPTER ELEVEN

UNDONE

SEPTEMBER 2, 2008

Someone who lies about the little things
will lie about the big things too.
—Terry McAuliffe

On Tuesday morning, September 2, 2008, reporters lined up at the Wake County Clerk of Criminal Courts Office to get a copy of the search warrants that had been under seal since the Cooper home was searched in July.

The main thing everyone wanted to see, besides the list of what had been taken out of the house, was the probable cause affidavit detailing what Cary police believed had happened to Nancy Cooper.

The search warrant for the Cooper home in Cary was issued on July 16 at 2:00 A.M. The affidavit covered everything from the 911 call from Jessica Adam on July 12, to how police had responded to the Coopers' home, to how Brad Cooper had eventually shown up and told them his version of his wife's disappearance.

According to the warrants, Officer Daniel Hayes and Detective Adam Dismukes were the first police officers on the scene that day. They said Brad had allowed them into the home to look around, where they saw a key ring, which included a car key and a house key, lying on a piece of furniture near the door. The car key belonged to Nancy's 2004 BMW, which was parked in the driveway. They also found a cell phone in the house that Brad said belonged to Nancy.

According to the affidavit written by Jim Young, a senior police officer, Brad told the police that on the day of Nancy's disappearance he had gotten up with Bella around 4:00 A.M. Sometime later, he said he made two separate trips to the grocery store to get milk and laundry detergent and then took Bella into his home office. He said at that time Nancy was downstairs, and he heard her call up and say she was looking for her running shirt.

"Brad Cooper stated that he heard a door of the residence open and close and assumed Nancy Cooper had left the residence for her run," the affidavit stated. He had "guessed" it was a white T-shirt because he saw her that morning doing laundry in the same shirt.

Detective Dismukes said he saw cleaning supplies on the countertop in the bathroom attached to the room where Nancy slept. He also noted a "dried stain" on the fitted white sheet covering the bed in her room.

The affidavit went on to say that Detective George Daniels had arrived at the house, and together all of the officers fanned out and started interviewing friends of the Coopers. They learned from those interviews that Nancy was seeking a divorce from Brad because of an affair he'd had and that she wanted to return to Canada with the girls to live with her family. They also learned that Brad had removed Nancy from the couple's financial accounts. Nancy's friends told police that she'd kept important papers like her passport and divorce documents in her car. But most important, police were told that Nancy always kept her keys and cell phone with her.

"Nancy Cooper did not trust Brad Cooper and would always keep her cell phone and key to her 2004 BMW X5 on her person regardless of where [she was] or what activity she was performing," the affidavit stated.

The officers learned about two arguments Nancy and Brad had had—one on July 7, when Nancy returned from her vacation with her family in Hilton Head to find her home a mess, and one on

Friday, July 11, regarding money she had been paid by Jessica Adam for helping her paint her house.

Detective Daniels interviewed Brad on Saturday July 12 about his wife's disappearance. At that time, the detective noticed "small red marks or scratches on the left side of Brad Cooper's neck." According to the affidavit, Daniels also interviewed Brad on Sunday, July 13, 2008. Brad told him he had been cleaning the house the day his wife disappeared—scrubbing floors, vacuuming, and doing laundry—because Nancy had been so mad at him about the state of the house when she'd returned from vacation. Officers saw Brad's behavior as a big red flag because Brad was not known by Nancy's friends or family as someone who took part in domestic chores.

"The information provided by Brad Cooper regarding the extensive cleaning of the residence on Saturday, July 12, 2008, is not consistent with information gathered from multiple interviews with individuals who knew Brad and Nancy Cooper extensively during their marriage," it said.

Brad also told the detectives he had cleaned the trunk of his car, a 2001 BMW 325i, while his wife was on vacation. He told them he had "spilled gas." Police looked in the trunk and noted that it had been recently vacuumed, but they smelled no odor of gas. They also noticed that the passenger area in Brad's car had not been cleaned. It was full of mail and receipts and had clearly not been vacuumed. It seemed odd to them that someone would clean the trunk of a car, but not go ahead and clean the interior of the car at the same time.

Brad confirmed for detectives that Nancy wanted to move to Canada, even though he had offered her multiple alternatives. According to the warrant, he also admitted to taking the children's passports.

"He had taken the passports of both children into his possession, but offered to provide Nancy with the passport of one child so that both Nancy and Brad would be assured that neither would attempt to leave the country with both children," the warrant stated.

The affidavit concluded with the fact that Nancy's body was found lying facedown in a "drainage pond" in the 4700 block of Fielding Drive in an undeveloped phase within The Oaks at Meadowridge subdivision on July 14 less than three miles from the Cooper home. It went on to say that she had died under "suspicious circumstances."

The affidavit stated that the chief medical examiner for the State of North Carolina, Dr. John Butts, had positively identified Nancy on July 15 and classified the death as a homicide.

Based on this affidavit, the officers requested to search the Cooper home, the couple's cars, and Brad Cooper's person, which included getting a DNA sample from him. They said they were looking for items that "illustrate and/or provide evidence of the marital discord of Bradley and Nancy Cooper and/or provide evidence regarding the homicide of Nancy Lynn Cooper."

SEIZED

As part of the search, police took Brad Cooper's fingerprints and a DNA swab from inside his mouth. They also took photographs of him.

In total, thirty-three separate items or categories of items were taken from the Cooper home by investigators. There was clothing: a green dress, a black sports bra, a red shirt, gray tennis shoes, high heel shoes, and flip-flops. There were household items like a pillow and bed linens. There were documents from the couple's home office, two cameras, and three computers. There were curious items: "brownish green vegetable material collected from 2001 BMW" as well as grass, a piece of "green colored plastic," and what appeared to be a broken pink fingernail.

Investigators spent a great deal of time searching Brad's car. They took a fiber from the trunk lid that they suspected was a piece of hair, a hair from the front right bumper, and a hair from the left front tire well. Investigators took swabs from the interior door handle on the driver's side of Brad's car. They even confiscated the trunk floor and the seat covers in the car. It didn't take a cop to see that police seemed to be focusing in on Brad's car. It raised the obvious question—did they suspect that Nancy's body had been in the trunk?

WORKPLACE SEARCH

Another one of the search warrants unsealed on September 2 was for Brad Cooper's workplace at Cisco Systems, which was searched on July 21, 2008.

Brad was an engineer with the prestigious international technology company located in an area just outside of Cary known as Research Triangle Park. To date, the company had been very quiet about the investigation. They would only say he was still employed.

Investigators seized seven categories of items from Brad's office, including several computers and external hard drives, a thumb drive, multiple discs and documents.

On the face of these warrants, there was no new information connecting Brad to Nancy's death. But it was clear that investigators intended to do a thorough computer forensics search, something that might just blow the case wide open.

BRAD'S WAY

Brad Cooper answered the complaint filed against him in a formal court document by denying the majority of the allegations against him. He spent most of the time rehashing denials he had stated in previous filings—that the reason he hadn't called the police was because he'd been out looking for his wife, that he hadn't denied his wife money, that he hadn't had multiple affairs but a "single one night indiscretion."

One curious change involved his knowledge of Nancy's run that morning. Brad had stated previously that he never actually saw her leave, that he simply heard the door close. In this filing, he said more explicitly that he didn't know if she ever really went jogging.

"Brad has no way of knowing whether she actually went jogging on that morning. Brad denies that he was the last person to see Nancy alive," the document stated.

Brad admitted to removing the children's passports from Nancy's car, but his explanation was that "important legal documents, such as passports, should not be kept in cars."

In the document Brad also undermined Nancy's family, saying he doubted they could provide a good home for the girls, that they had never spent much time with the children because they lived so far away, and that all of the times they'd been with the children, Nancy had always been there as well.

"The minor children love their grandparents, but they did not know them very well before the Plaintiffs took them using this action," it stated.

Brad's attorneys also filed a motion to strike all of the allegations made against Brad in the custody case by Nancy's family. In this document they refuted each allegation on the basis that they were made to imply Brad killed his wife.

"At best, Plaintiffs show a careless disregard for the truth in making these conclusions," the motion read. "The statements have been designed to create the perception that Brad was responsible for Nancy Cooper's death without any factual basis."

He again challenged the assertion that he had "disappeared" without Nancy's knowledge on a September weekend in 2007. He said on Sunday, September 30, 2007, he and his business class had gone to a boat show in Greensboro. This time, to prove his whereabouts, he produced cell phone records showing he and Nancy spoke six times between 11:57 A.M. that day and 8:25 P.M.

Brad also refuted allegations that he'd taken away Nancy's cell phone at one point. He produced Nancy's cell phone records showing that Nancy had made 3,456 cell phone calls between January and June of 2008.

He also challenged the accusation that he'd been out of touch with Nancy when she went to Hilton Head with her family the week prior to her disappearance. He produced cell phone records showing twenty calls between the two from June 28, 2008, to July 6, 2008.

Brad denied there was trouble between Nancy and his mother, Carol Cooper, saying the only reason Nancy didn't go to the zoo with him and his parents during their November trip to Nashville was because she was sick. He said despite what Nancy's friends stated, Nancy had eaten dinner with everyone else that night.

As far as Jessica Adam saying she did not know Nancy was running with Carey Clark on July 12, Brad chalked it up to the fact that Clark and Nancy were faster runners than Adam and that Nancy didn't want to tell Adam they were running without her. Despite the fact that Clark had filed her own affidavit denying she was running with Nancy that day, Brad implied that Nancy may not have told Adam for that reason.

Finally, Brad's attorneys filed a motion to dismiss the custody case. They said all of the allegations against their client were based upon "gossip, unwarranted deductions, assumptions and hearsay."

"We're trying to help him get his life back," Brad's attorney, Seth Blum, told WRAL. "We don't know of any other way to protect Brad's reputation."

WEB CAMPAIGN

Howard Kurtz and Seth Blum continued their campaign to clear their client's name via the Internet.

The Cooper section on their law firm's website addressed the accusations against Brad: "We hope that Brad will be afforded the same dignity and presumption of innocence that each of us would demand for ourselves. We pray that the distorted focus on Brad Cooper will not allow the guilty to escape detection."

Another page referred to Nancy's friends as the "Cary Clique." In this segment, Kurtz and Blum said that the negative anecdotes about the Cooper marriage came from friends who heard only one side of the story—Nancy's side. They said that everything the "Cary Clique" expressed about the Cooper's marital problems was tainted and exaggerated.

"How can anyone in the midst of marital problems whose wife or husband is murdered ever even hope for fairness from such people?" the site read.

The next page turned its attention to the Cary police chief's statement that the crime was not random.

"One hopes her statement is based on more than the wish to maintain Cary's reputation as a safe place to live," the site said. "The statement does nothing but create an unsupported presumption that Brad is somehow involved."

The site went on to stress that Brad was continuing to speak with police, again, something the police would later assert was not true. It also pointed out that he had not attempted to flee.

"It is of paramount importance for people to keep in mind that lack of proof with respect to guilt of another does not equate guilt on Brad's part," the site stated. "Somehow, this focus on Brad has led a few people to assume the worst."

The defense attorneys were aware those assumptions in part came from rumors surrounding Brad's early morning trips to the grocery store on the day Nancy disappeared. In the early days of the investigation, there was a widely circulated rumor that Brad had gone to a grocery store very early Saturday morning to buy bleach. The speculation was that he was cleaning up a murder scene at the house and possibly washing the dress Nancy had worn to the party, which might have been stained with blood.

The public scrutiny of this issue began when a Canadian journalist asked Chief Pat Bazemore about the alleged bleach purchase at one of the early press conferences. She answered by saying she could not comment on the issue, which only fueled more speculation.

"Volumes of suspicion have grown out of this question," the site said. "We cannot allow slanderous assertions against Brad Cooper to continue without redress."

The attorneys posted surveillance video from the grocery story from Brad's trips that morning to show when he was there and exactly what he purchased. Each video showed him entering the store, checking out at the register, and exiting the store.

Brad first entered the Harris Teeter at 6:22 A.M. on Saturday, July 12, according to the video time stamp. He purchased milk, according to the receipt, which was also included on the site, and then departed the store three minutes later at 6:25 A.M. Brad said he went home and then turned around at Nancy's request and returned to the store for detergent. The site said just before his client entered the store a second time, he got a call from Nancy asking him to also get "Naked Green Juice," a supposed favorite of Bella's. The video showed that Brad reentered the store at 6:41 A.M. He purchased laundry detergent and juice and again checked out three minutes later, at 6:44 A.M.

While the videos were meant to eliminate rumors and exonerate their client, they raised only more questions in the community. For example, why was Brad wearing what appeared to be a sweatshirt and long pants on a day where the high was eighty-nine degrees? Surely, even in the early-morning hours it could not have been that cold on a North Carolina summer day. Was he hiding something, such as scratches, maybe? Interestingly, he also wore a long-sleeved button-down shirt the night that he spoke at the press conference at the Cary Police Department on July 14, and he was photographed in another long-sleeved button-down shirt the day he left his home as a result of the police search on July 16. On both days the temperature hovered between eighty-eight and ninety-one degrees.

Another question raised was, why would Brad go to a store two miles away when the Lowe's grocery store was just a little more than a half mile from his home and was also open at that hour? After all, he had purchased beer there on his way to the neighborhood party the previous evening; he surely knew where it was and had shopped there before.

The site did address the scratches the police said they saw on Brad's neck when they came to the house on July 12. It showed pictures of his neck supposedly taken on July 17, five days later, with no visible scratches.

"He did not have scratches on his neck, and no one asked him about the scratches on his neck," the site stated, adding that officers should have photographed those scratches if police were truly concerned.

There was one strange inconsistency in the videos of the two grocery store visits that Brad's attorneys did not address. In the first video, Brad was seen wearing sneakers, but in the second video, he was wearing sandals. How did he even have time to change his shoes and why would he do so? Only sixteen minutes had elapsed between the time he purchased the milk and the time he reentered the grocery store on his second trip. With the two stop lights he would have had to go through on his way home, his travel time would have easily been four or five minutes each way. This left him with just six or so minutes at the house before he would have had to turn around and leave again.

Another question the videos raised: Did he have time in between the two grocery store runs to dump a body on Fielding Drive, roughly four and a quarter miles from the store with an estimated drive time of about eight minutes each way? It was possible if he had gone straight there, dumped the body quickly, and returned immediately to the store. Because the area where Nancy's body was found was so muddy, it would have been likely that he would have had to change shoes—possibly from sneakers to sandals.

In their effort to divorce their client from the rumor mill, Brad's attorneys ended up raising even more questions than they answered.

CHAPTER TWELVE

REVELATIONS

SEPTEMBER 29, 2008

Truth exists; only lies are invented.
—Georges Braque

On Monday, September 29, 2008, the custody case between Brad Cooper and Nancy Cooper's family came to court for the very first time. At issue were several motions filed in the case. Brad Cooper did not show up for court, but his attorney Deborah Sandlin was there representing her client.

The first motion heard was filed by Nancy Cooper's family and asked that Brad Cooper undergo psychological testing. Alice Stubbs, the attorney for Donna and Garry Rentz and Krista Lister, told Judge Debra Sasser that Brad Cooper's mental health was "in controversy." Stubbs said she wanted to make sure Brad was not a danger to the children. She asked the district court judge to pick from a list of three psychologists to perform the evaluation.

Sandlin pointed out that Brad had already hired a psychologist, Jonathan Gould of Charlotte, to perform his own evaluation. Brad had paid twelve thousand dollars out of his own pocket for Gould's services. But Stubbs said she believed it was necessary for a neutral third party, not someone paid by the defendant, to do the evaluation.

Sandlin said that while Gould's final report was not back yet, he had given Brad a very "comprehensive evaluation" that involved a "battery of tests" over an eight-hour period on August 8, 2008.

"Every test known to man was conducted," Sandlin said. "Mr. Cooper is very anxious to have his children back."

She said she worried that more psychological testing would further delay reunion with his children, but Stubbs disagreed.

"We're not trying to delay the hearing," Stubbs said. "We think it's in the best interest of the children."

Sasser ruled that another psychologist could evaluate Brad, but the assessment would have to be paid for by Nancy Cooper's family.

The court then considered a motion filed by Brad's attorneys for a protective order that would limit the questions Nancy Cooper's family attorneys could ask Brad during his deposition. His attorneys also objected to a request for Brad to turn over documents and records dating back to January 1, 2008, saying that this was an undue burden and clearly had to do with the murder case, not the custody case, and therefore was not relevant.

"It is my understanding that the murder of Mr. Cooper's wife, that he is very upset about, is no closer to being solved since the day she was killed," Sandlin said.

Brad was asked to turn over phone records, e-mails, bank records, tax returns, and copies of his computer hard drives—ironically, a lot of the same information his attorneys had asked Nancy's friends to turn over. While Sandlin said her client would turn over "whatever he has," she added that some of the requests were not reasonable. For example, according to one of Brad's other attorneys, Howard Kurtz, the police had confiscated all of Brad's computers; therefore, he had no access to the information on his hard drives.

"There's not a single request they haven't rejected," said Stubbs, adding that Brad had turned over nothing to date. "We are eagerly waiting."

Judge Sasser denied the bulk of the motion but agreed with the defense attorneys on a few specific points. She agreed that not all of Brad's work e-mails—fourteen thousand in total since January

1—should be scrutinized and that turning over every receipt since July 1 was a burdensome request. But the judge also ruled that bank accounts and retirement accounts were relevant, especially if they showed that Brad had taken out money just prior to his wife's death.

"The elephant that sits in the room is that if there is evidence that Mr. Cooper is in any way responsible for his wife's death, that's certainly relevant in the custody case," Sasser said.

Sandlin said that the emotions surrounding this case and the murder investigation were so high that she was afraid it would keep her client from getting a fair shake in the custody case.

"I *will* have to determine—did Brad Cooper kill his wife?" countered Sasser.

"Whether or not Brad Cooper killed his wife is a factor," Sandlin admitted. But at the same time she said, "There must be corroborating evidence."

Stubbs agreed with the judge that it was impossible to separate the custody issue from the murder investigation.

"If you were to find by clear and convincing evidence that Brad Cooper murdered Nancy Cooper, it would not be in the children's best interest to grant him custody," Stubbs argued.

In many ways the motions were just a sideshow to the main event. Everyone in the courtroom knew that if there was not an arrest before the hearing took place in mid-October, Judge Sasser would be forced indirectly to rule on whether or not Brad Cooper had killed his wife.

AUTOPSY RELEASED

After nearly three months, the autopsy results were finally released, on Monday, September 29, 2008.

Because Nancy's body had been in the woods and partially submerged in water for several days, major decomposition had begun to take place. Her body, which had been found facedown in a watery ditch, was bloated and discolored. Not only had birds gotten to her, but insects had also started to infest her body. As a result, the medical examiners had to use dental records to positively identify her remains. But even with the damage, the medical examiners were able to determine how she died.

"There is a faint linear mark across the central neck in the area of the thyroid approximately 1.3 inches in length," the report said. They also found "fine petechial hemorrhages" in Nancy's eyes and discovered that the hyoid bone in her neck was fractured.

"Based on the history and the autopsy findings, it is my opinion that she died as a result of external causes, homicidal violence, most likely asphyxia by strangulation," Dr. Michael Papez wrote.

Nancy Cooper's autopsy revealed that she was found wearing only a jogging bra.

"She is clothed only in an elastic halter athletic style bra of black, gray and red coloration that is pulled up above the breasts," the report read. "There is a clear stone stud earring in the left earlobe."

The report indicated that the doctors had performed a rape kit on Nancy Cooper to see if she had been sexually assaulted, but it also noted that there were no obvious signs of trauma in her genital area.

The day the autopsy was released, Cary police also released a statement regarding the investigation.

"Outside her family, no group is more committed to resolving Nancy's murder than the Cary Police Department, and it's been since the day she disappeared," Chief Pat Bazemore said.

Nancy's father also released his own statement in reaction to the autopsy.

"The journey to the truth and justice can be long and arduous," Garry Rentz said. "Today's news marks a point that is particularly poignant and painful, but necessary to further the evidentiary process leading to a conviction of the person or persons responsible for Nancy's murder."

MUDSLINGING

It seemed as though the entire community was caught up in the Cooper saga, and there was no middle ground. You were either on Nancy Cooper's team or Brad Cooper's team. Diplomacy was not an option.

Another affidavit filed by the defense that drew yet another definitive line in the sand came from Brad's friend, Mike Hiller, the man with whom Brad was supposed to play tennis the morning Nancy disappeared.

In a new deposition taken on September 29, 2008, Hiller stated that he and Brad had made a date to play tennis at 9:30 A.M. on Saturday, July 12. Hiller noted that he had asked Nancy the prior evening at the neighborhood party whether Brad could play, and she had agreed. But Hiller said that on Saturday morning, Brad had called him at 9:15 A.M. to say that Nancy had not returned from her run.

"Brad was very easy going about it. He said he thought maybe Nancy had stopped for coffee," Hiller said in the affidavit.

They spoke three times and finally, a little after 10:00 A.M., Hiller told Brad he would have to postpone their game because he had another one scheduled for 11:00 A.M. Hiller and his wife also had plans to go to the Coopers' house that evening to socialize.

Hiller said Cary police first interviewed him over the phone right after Nancy disappeared. They interviewed him again two weeks later in person at the police station, and then again in person at the end of August. He claimed that during the last interview police tried to force him into saying something that wasn't true.

"The police officers used good-cop bad-cop tactics and tried to coerce me to admit that I made calls on Nancy's cell phone to help Brad establish an 'alibi,'" Hiller stated.

Hiller said police told him they were investigating Brad simply because he was the husband and that it was standard to rule out the husband first. Hiller asked them why they had said the murder was not random.

"The officer told me 'That is the town speaking so people like you would be more comfortable,'" Hiller said.

Hiller said Jessica Adam told him the day Nancy disappeared that she "just knew" Brad had something to do with it. He also accused Adam of pressuring Nancy's other friends into writing their affidavits by saying, "They were either on the side of 'Brad did it' or they were not in her 'circle' of friends."

Just like Brad's other friend Scott Heider, Hiller said Nancy exaggerated and that on one occasion, when Hiller and his wife were eyeing a house for sale that Nancy and Brad had also looked at, she had called him, and they had gotten into an argument over whether or not the Coopers could afford the property.

"She called me up and said that I didn't know how much her husband made and that she could afford both the house on the lake and the BMW the dealer was trying to find for her," Hiller stated.

It was clear Mike Hiller didn't care for Nancy Cooper.

CIRCLING THE WAGONS

In early October, both sides began the tedious process of taking depositions from all of the players involved in the custody case.

For the first time publicly, Nancy Cooper's family gave detailed accounts of how they watched Nancy and Brad Cooper's marriage unravel one small strand at a time, even though they weren't always fully aware that they were witnessing an impending crisis. In his October 2, 2008, deposition, Jim Lister, Krista's husband and Nancy's brother-in-law, recalled Nancy and Bella visiting them in Vancouver, Canada, in July 2005. He said Brad had inexplicably had them fly into Seattle, a full three hours from Vancouver, simply to save money. Bella, who was just a baby at the time, was cranky and exhausted from the long trip.

Jim also remembered on that same trip that Nancy had paid her mother-in-law a visit with Bella. Jim said he knew that Nancy did not care for Carol Cooper, largely because she did not pay much attention to Nancy or Bella. On the Vancouver trip, Jim and Krista accompanied Nancy to a party with Brad's parents where Jim said he witnessed firsthand Carol Cooper's lack of interest in her daughter-in-law and granddaughter.

"Nancy explained they had a very strained relationship, that she not only disliked Brad's mother, but felt she was a horrible person, selfish, unloving and rude," Jim said.

Not only did Carol Cooper and her husband rarely, if ever, visit their son once he moved to Cary, but Jim said they had not even made an effort to attend Brad and Nancy's whirlwind wedding or the send-off dinner when the couple moved to the United States.

Jim surmised that Brad's family, and specifically his mother, had made Brad into the unemotional person Jim knew him to be.

"To me, Brad seemed almost orphaned; devoid of any meaningful family contact and clearly uncomfortable and unfamiliar around the large and loving family setting of the Rentz family," Jim said.

In her October 2, 2008, deposition, Jill recalled a car trip she had taken in 1999 with Nancy and Brad. At the time, the couple were just dating. Jill said in her affidavit that Nancy had told her how Brad had become depressed after a car accident and tried to commit suicide. Since Brad was listening to the conversation about this in the car and never disputed what Nancy was saying, Jill assumed it to be true.

Jill said that once they married, Nancy took on most of the responsibilities for the children, yet Brad still treated her with a lack of respect. Jill said in her deposition that she and her family "started to grow increasingly concerned" about Nancy, Katie, and Bella around March 2008 when the water at the Cooper house was shut off and Nancy discovered that the credit card had been canceled. In addition, Nancy told Jill that Brad had taken the girls' passports. "Brad was trying to control her and show her how powerless she was," Jill said.

Jill recalled that when she visited Nancy when Bella was just one and a half and her own daughter was almost one, Nancy and

Brad shared a car. Occasionally, he would let them drive him to work so that they could use the car during the day, but most of the time Jill said that they had to walk anywhere they wanted to go with the babies in the strollers in the sweltering North Carolina summer heat.

But ultimately, Jill said it was Brad's unfaithfulness, not his controlling nature, that had made Nancy want out of the marriage.

"Things started to go downhill in Nancy's marriage when she realized that Brad had been unfaithful to her and that he had lied to her," Jill said. "Nancy decided that the marriage was over. She then tried to decide when to leave."

Krista also sat for a deposition. She talked about how she had tried to help her twin prepare for her move. Krista said Nancy had planned to relocate to Oakville, Ontario, to be close to her and her husband, Jim.

Krista described the March 2008 trip she made to Cary from Canada to help Nancy pack up her house and paint it in order to get it ready to put on the market. She recalled Nancy asking Brad to pick up some paint and he had refused. She also recalled preparations for Bella's fourth birthday party during which Brad followed them everywhere they went. Krista said they first stopped at the gas station where Brad put gas in Nancy's car. Then at their next stop, a party store, the couple argued over the prices of the snacks for the celebration because Brad thought they were too expensive.

The party was held at a horse farm that Brad had picked out for the event. Krista said it was cold and rainy, and there was no shelter, so the kids spent most of the time in the car watching movies. Krista said Brad stood in the slow drizzle and cooked food on the grill for the guests.

"Brad was visibly angry, unfriendly towards all the children and parents attending," recalled Krista.

On Sunday, Krista and Nancy left the girls with Brad and went to visit Hannah Prichard, who was then pregnant and on bed rest. Before they got there, though, Nancy decided to turn around and go back to the house to check on the kids. Krista said she could not reach Brad by phone and was worried about whether or not he was keeping a close eye on Katie.

"Nancy communicated to me that she had told Brad that he needed to be more responsive and responsible with the children as they prepared to separate and was livid about his attitude and selfishness," Krista said.

Krista and Nancy eventually went to visit Prichard, and when they returned, Krista said Brad had taken spackle and touched up areas where they had just spent hours painting. As a result, their work had to be completely redone.

"I left the next day feeling absolutely horrified with Nancy's situation. I felt very sorry for her and expressed to my husband Jim that we needed to get her out of North Carolina fast. Brad was trying to control everything Nancy did," Krista said. "I was also horrified with the obvious change in Nancy's personality. She appeared to be tired of all the fighting and the drama and was near the end of her rope so to speak. She seemed to be ready to give up."

Another one of the October affidavits was from a woman named Shirley Hull, who had witnessed what had now become the legendary fight between Brad and Nancy on May 24, 2008, in the parking lot of the Triangle Academy Preschool. It was a key affidavit since, unlike the others, it came from someone who was not friends with either Brad or Nancy.

"I observed a man that I now know to be Brad Cooper screaming in the parking lot at his wife Nancy," Hull said. "Nancy was crying, and she and Brad were screaming at each other."

"Give me the girls!" Nancy yelled at him, adding that he could keep the house.

"I also heard him scream obscenities in front of Katie and Bella, who were screaming and crying hysterically," Hull said.

JIM THE FATHER

Becoming instant parents was a bit overwhelming for Krista and Jim Lister, a couple who had previously spent their days working on their careers and their nights out at restaurants or socializing with friends. It was understandable that Krista would embrace her young nieces, but Jim also rose to the challenge, taking seamlessly to his new role as a father. When Krista first started dating Jim, she had told him she was unable to have children. She didn't want to get serious with anyone who had hoped to have biological children. At the time, Jim had said that he was on the fence about having kids and that it didn't matter to him that Krista wasn't able to have children. Fast-forward ten years, and Jim was the overnight father of two little girls.

"He's so amazing. The girls so adore [him]," Krista said. "He just took it on."

As part of the custody agreement, Brad Cooper was entitled to four fifteen-minute webcam visits with his daughters on a weekly basis. He was also entitled to four four-hour supervised visits in Raleigh. Jim had facilitated all of these visits. To be able to do what the court had asked of them, Jim and Krista had to put aside their anger toward Brad for the sake of the girls. Jim had stepped up to the plate in the midst of this tragedy and had the best interests of the children in mind. He said there were few issues with the face-to-face visits at Time Together, a facility in Raleigh especially designed for supervised parental visits in contentious custody battles, and they had allowed the children to visit with Brad per the court order during the weekend of September 6 and 7, and during the weekend of September 27 and 28 without any issues. But the webcam calls were another story.

In Jim's affidavit he stated that the Tuesday, Thursday, Friday night, and Sunday morning calls with Brad had become chaotic. The children were agitated before and after the calls. Their limited attention span did not permit them to stay engaged with Brad for more than a few seconds unless Jim or Krista was playing with them in front of the camera. Jim said he felt like he was coercing the girls into participating in what was a very unnatural interaction and suggested to the court that the calls be limited to a shorter duration or maybe scrapped altogether in favor of basic phone calls.

PROFESSIONALLY SPEAKING

The girls' psychologist in Ontario, Dr. Huzar Altay, also weighed in on the custody issue. Altay had been hired by Nancy's family to counsel Bella and Katie. She said it was clear from the very beginning that Nancy's family was committed to doing whatever was necessary to create a safe and comfortable environment for the girls.

When they initially sought Altay's help, there were issues with separation anxiety. Bella would not let Krista out of her sight and would have frequent tantrums. Katie had a hard time going to bed at night and would also cling to Krista and Jim. Both girls often refused to sit at the table and eat.

In the office visits, Altay said that the girls played together in a frenetic manner and were initially unfriendly toward her, but eventually they warmed up as they began to trust her.

Altay reported that after just a few weeks of "parenting coaching" with the previously childless couple, the girls' behavior had improved remarkably. Altay attributed the majority of the improvements to Krista and Jim's willingness to do whatever it took to make the transition smoother for the children.

For example, Krista drove Bella by her new preschool every day and pointed it out until the day school started. They also paid an early visit to the school so that Bella would feel more comfortable on her first day.

Krista had quit her job as an interior designer to be home with the kids. She used her skills to decorate the children's room and even sought their input. Altay said Krista created a "family wall" in their room complete with photographs of Nancy and Brad. Krista also created a scrapbook about Nancy for the girls with Bella's help.

Krista enrolled the girls in ballet and gymnastics, and Bella quickly made friends with a next-door neighbor. When Altay visited the Listers' house, Bella excitedly gave her a tour and referred to the house as "my home."

Altay said Donna and Garry were very supportive and stayed involved in the girls' care even though they didn't live in the same city. Altay described Garry as "the rock of the family." She said he was "extremely rational, even-tempered" and that his skills as a "facilitator" and an "organizer" kept the family on course throughout the crisis.

Altay said while Jim was initially "overwhelmed and worried" about his ability to adapt to being a new father, he immediately took to his role.

"He demonstrates a deep and natural affection, respect and love for the children," Altay said, adding that Bella in particular had warmed up to Jim and become attached to him as a father figure.

Altay also interviewed Bella's preschool teacher in Canada, Karen Taylor, who was impressed by Bella's adaption to the class. Taylor told Altay that Bella was very "matter-of-fact" and "age appropriate" regarding how she looked at the world and the tragedy that had befallen her family.

"My mommy was lost, then found, but was so sick the doctors couldn't fix her, so she is with the angels," Bella told her teacher repeating the words her grandmother had told her on the way to her mother's memorial service.

Altay said it was clear the family was not afraid to talk with the girls about the fact that Nancy was gone, but at the same time they had said nothing to disparage Brad. He was included on the "family wall." They made him part of the girls' prayers at night, and they facilitated the webcam calls even though the situation was less than ideal.

"I believe the family had not done anything to malign the children's father," Altay said.

Overall, Altay felt as though the girls were in a stable environment and appeared to be emotionally healthy despite what they had gone through. Altay attributed this to the sacrifices Krista and Jim had made to make the girls feel constantly loved and safe, along with the support of the extended family.

"This is a remarkable family who indeed thinks and behaves in whatever way is required to serve the best interests of these children. I have not had any reason to question their collective integrity and commitment to do whatever is necessary to provide Bella and Katie with a happy, healthy life which will be devoid of their mother, but they certainly endeavor to keep Nancy Cooper very much alive for her children to access and to relate to and to continue to be influenced by her inherent character and her many strengths," Altay said.

CHAPTER THIRTEEN

CHARADE

OCTOBER 2, 2008

The only abnormality is the incapacity to love.
—Anaïs Nin

On October 2, 2008, Brad Cooper did the unexpected. He arrived at the offices of Tharrington Smith on Fayetteville Street in downtown Raleigh to give a deposition in the custody case. For a man now widely considered the prime suspect in his wife's murder, he was taking a big risk by opening himself up to questioning under oath. While the civil case and the criminal case were separate, there was no denying that anything he said in the civil deposition that might implicate him in Nancy's murder would also be used by investigators as part of their criminal case.

Brad wore a pale blue button-down shirt beneath a dark-colored blazer. He sat directly in front of the camera and appeared calm, even occasionally bored as he stared off into the distance while the lawyers argued off camera over minor legal points. He would casually sip his coffee or water and glance back at the camera, his face blank, absent of any obvious emotion. The only telling motion he made throughout the six plus hours that he sat for the deposition was that he frequently played with his wedding ring, twisting it around and around again with his right hand.

Alice Stubbs, the attorney for the Rentz family and Nancy's former divorce attorney, asked Brad the questions. The thin, blond, athletic lawyer with sharp features looked more like a pretty college girl than a formidable attorney. But Stubbs, a former district court judge, was more experienced than her youthful appearance implied. She had the rare gift of being able to glide slowly into a pattern of questioning as innocent as a lamb, and then, without warning, pummel the defendant with a lion's force.

With Stubbs on the other side of the table, it was entirely possible that Brad Cooper had finally met his match.

BRAD COOPER

Brad Cooper was born in Canada on October 9, 1973. He grew up in a small town called Medicine Hat, where his parents, Carol and Terry Cooper, still resided. His father and his younger brother, Grant, both worked at Medicine Hat College. Grant lived with his girlfriend, Joy, and they had a little boy together. Brad said he had never met his nephew and couldn't recall his name.

Brad appeared to remember very little of his upbringing. He recalled that he attended St. Vincent's Elementary School and Crescent Heights High School, but he couldn't remember the names of any of his friends. He said he did not stay in touch with anyone with whom he had grown up.

"Have you ever considered taking your own life?" Stubbs asked.

"No," Brad said.

"Have you ever told anybody you considered taking your own life?" Stubbs followed up quickly.

"No," Brad replied.

Stubbs asked him about the handwritten note that had been found in the house with lists of the girls' favorite things and financial information regarding his family, including life insurance and wills. Stubbs asked him if that list was not, in fact, a preparation for suicide. He denied this.

Brad attended Medicine Hat College from 1991 to 1992 and then went on to study computer science and graduate from the University of Calgary.

While Brad seemed to remember few male friends, he did remember some of his girlfriends. He said that he lived with and was engaged to a woman named Taylene Lyon from 1992 to 1994. His psychologist had requested Brad locate Lyon to help back up his claims that he was not abusive in his relationships with women, but Brad said he had had no luck in finding his old flame.

Brad said he also lived with a woman named Jennifer Wilson for a year in Calgary to whom he was also engaged after he broke up with Lyon.

Brad started his job as an engineer with the technology giant Cisco Systems in January of 2001, and soon after he and Nancy had moved to Cary from Canada. In December 2007, Brad received his MBA, something he said he did to help him work his way up the career ladder at Cisco.

Stubbs asked Brad if he had used Cisco's VOIP technology, in which Brad was a trained expert, in his own home, to which Brad replied that he had. She wanted to know if he could monitor calls from a remote location. Clearly, this question was related to the allegations from Nancy's family and friends that her phone calls were, on occasion, mysteriously disconnected.

Brad replied that he could see if someone was on the line, but not actually listen in on the call.

Stubbs also wanted to know if Brad could initiate a call from a remote location. Reading between the lines, she was clearly getting at the possibility that Brad had programmed his home phone to call his cell phone in between the early morning grocery store visits on July 12, 2008, in order to prove that Nancy was alive and calling him from the house. Brad said he could do this, but it was not something that was "normally done."

THE MARRIAGE

Brad Cooper met Nancy Rentz in 1998 at TransCanada Pipelines where he was a network engineer and she was a desktop support person. He claimed in the deposition that she asked him out twice, and he turned her down because he had just gotten out of a relationship and wasn't yet ready to date. Eventually, however, Brad said the two ended up at the same party and soon began dating. One year later, on Christmas Day 1999, they were engaged.

Nancy and Brad married in front of a justice of the peace in Calgary on October 13, 2000, with only her family in attendance. They needed to be married in order for Nancy to go with Brad to North Carolina where Brad had a job with Cisco Systems.

Prior to the birth of Bella, Brad said Nancy had had five miscarriages. He claimed that when these occurred, despite what her friends had said about her taking a cab to the hospital, he had, in fact, come home from work to care for her. He also said Nancy's frequent bouts with Crohn's disease landed her in the emergency room on multiple occasions, with him by her side.

Isabella Nancy Cooper, nicknamed Bella, was born on February 23, 2004. Almost two and a half years later, Gabriella Kathryn Cooper, nicknamed Katie, was born on July 23, 2006.

"Was Nancy a good wife?" Stubbs asked Brad.

"I would say so, yes," Brad responded.

"Why?" Stubbs asked as casually as if she were asking him what his favorite color was.

"She was supportive of myself and the children and very loving and generous," Brad replied.

"Was she a good mother?" Stubbs asked.

"I would say she was a great mother," Brad said.

According to Brad, the marriage started to unravel after Katie's birth. The couple no longer had sex, and Nancy ultimately learned about Brad's affair with her close friend Heather Metour. As a result, the couple went to counseling in February of 2008 with therapist Maria Arthur, but Nancy simply couldn't get beyond the affair.

"She was upset and shocked," Brad said. "You want your marriage to get over the affair, you've got to come clean and tell the truth and be able to rebuild the trust."

But Brad said Nancy would have none of it. She couldn't get past it. They were done.

"Did you have a good marriage?" Stubbs asked.

"I'd say we had our ups and downs," Brad responded, and then added that since January 2008 their marriage "was more in the down side of things."

In the deposition, Brad admitted that he'd had sex with Heather Metour in late 2004 in the closet of the master bedroom while Metour's two young sons and Bella, who was not yet one at the time, were nearby in the house. He said the entire incident lasted less than fifteen minutes. Brad said that this was the only time he had intercourse with Metour or any other woman since he had been married to Nancy.

However, he did admit during the videotaped deposition that he had kissed Metour on several other occasions, had oral sex with her one time in his house, and had fooled around with her once in the car.

Brad said Nancy eventually learned about the affair from Metour herself.

"I initially denied it for approximately one year," Brad said. "I thought if I told her about it, it would ruin our family and our kids would be affected. I thought that by denying it, it would go away, and we could remain as a whole family."

But eventually, the pressure from Nancy became too much for Brad. He decided to come clean.

"I told Nancy that it happened, that it only happened once, and, as soon as it did happen, I immediately contacted Heather telling her it was a mistake and that it would never happen again," Brad said.

But the tension between the couple after he admitted to the affair didn't lessen as Brad had hoped it would. He said the issue constantly came up and was the focus of frequent fights.

"Why did you have to sleep with her?" Nancy reportedly asked

Brad on more than one occasion.

Ironically, after Nancy's murder, Brad turned to the one friend who was willing to stick by his side, Scott Heider, a co-worker from Cisco and Heather Metour's ex-husband.

After Nancy's death, when Brad and the girls went to stay with Heider, Brad said he felt as though it was necessary to have a discussion with him about the affair. At the time, Metour and Heider had long since been divorced. Still, Brad said he felt that he had to clear the air, given Heider's generosity.

"The essence of the conversation was that it was bad that it happened, and I apologized for it happening," Brad said of his conversation with Heider.

But Nancy had not been so accepting of Brad's apologies. For her, the affair was the final straw in her already troubled marriage.

"She basically said she did not want to continue with marriage counseling, and she couldn't get over the incident with Heather," Brad said.

THE MONEY

Another thing the couple simply couldn't get past was their differences over money.

"I'd say she spent more than we had which was unfortunate, and she drank a little bit more than I would have wanted her to," Brad said when Stubbs asked him about Nancy's weaknesses.

Brad said that even though he was doing well at Cisco, the couple had gotten into serious credit card debt, mostly because of Nancy's overspending.

"When possible, I tried to indulge her requests, and when impossible, I had to say that we could not afford something," Brad said.

He gave several examples, like the time Nancy wanted a pricey painting from Canada. Brad said he told her it was not something they could afford, but he said she purchased it anyway on a credit card without consulting him first.

In the fall of 2007, Brad said Nancy wanted a diamond pendant necklace. She had admired one at a local jeweler that cost seven thousand dollars. Again, Brad said he put the brakes on and said it was not something they could afford. But he agreed to get her a similar necklace for about twenty-eight hundred dollars.

This was a diamond necklace friends said Nancy never took off, yet it was found in the couple's home during one of the searches. Brad said Nancy wore the necklace "fairly frequently" but insisted she did take it off on occasion for cleaning and stored it in a desk drawer. The implication was that if she was wearing it when she was killed, Brad must have taken it off and kept it.

As a result of their issues with money, Brad said he put Nancy on a three-hundred-dollar per week budget and cancelled the couple's credit cards and joint bank accounts, opening new ones in his name only. He said that while Nancy wasn't responsible for all of their debt, she was responsible for the bulk of it. For example, in 2007, he said Nancy spent twenty-seven thousand dollars on their American Express card, while he spent seventeen thousand dollars. Her family later explained that because Brad never gave her cash, Nancy used her credit card for all purchases including groceries and gas.

These actions prompted weekly arguments about money. Brad said she referred to him as "the Budget Nazi." Brad said their arguments got heated and often resulted in Nancy's calling him an "asshole" or a "bastard." But, he said, he rarely got as angry as she did. He admitted to calling her a "bitch," once, but said it was not in front of the children.

"I'm not one to raise my voice," Brad said. "Nancy's more inclined to raise her voice."

"Did Nancy mistreat you?" Stubbs asked, sounding almost sympathetic, clearly a strategic tactic to try to get him to open up.

"I'd say there were some actions and some conversations that were probably uncalled for. I'm not too sure I'd classify it as mistreatment," Brad said coolly.

One of their most volatile fights Brad said occurred when he forgot to pay the utility bill and the water to their home was shut off. While he eventually got it turned back on, he said Nancy was livid because she could not wash dishes or clothes or bathe herself or the children.

"She blamed me," Brad said.

THE SEPARATION

By the spring of 2008, Brad said it was clear the two were headed toward separation.

Initially, he agreed to let Nancy and the girls move to Canada to be with her family. He said he even applied for a job with Cisco in Toronto, looked at real estate and schools there, and priced moving costs. Brad said he thought that being near the girls would be the best possible situation despite the dissolution of the marriage. But he didn't get the job in Toronto, so they were back to square one.

Brad said he had intercepted through Nancy's e-mail account a copy of the proposed separation agreement that Stubbs had written. He made it sound like Nancy had given him access to her e-mail account, which would later be a major point of contention. While at first he was in favor of the separation, he admitted he soon grew resistant to the idea.

"I was worried about the effects on the kids with Nancy and I separating," Brad said.

Things had gotten so bad, Brad said the couple was simply coexisting in the home and only talking when it had something to do with their children. Still, Brad vehemently denied the allegations that he and Nancy were screaming at each other in the parking lot of Triangle Academy Preschool in May 2008.

"Did you and Nancy ever have an incident at the school in May of 2008?" Stubbs asked.

"No," Brad replied.

"Do you recall having an argument with her in the parking lot of the school?" Stubbs countered, undeterred.

"No," Brad responded calmly.

But one thing Brad was not denying was the fact that he did not like the draft of the separation agreement Stubbs had written for Nancy.

"I thought it was somewhat unreasonable, and I told Nancy I thought I should see an attorney to see what was reasonable and what my rights were," Brad said.

Specifically, Brad said the visitation was not equitable and not something to which he could agree.

"I realized that seeing the girls every other weekend would not be sufficient," Brad said.

He also said the money requested on a monthly basis for child support, twenty-one hundred dollars, along with the girls' school tuition, health care costs, and money for their activities was more than he made in a month after taxes at Cisco. He estimated the actual cost to be somewhere between five and six thousand dollars per month.

Given his concerns about how the whole situation was shaping up, he said he was afraid that Nancy might try to take the girls to Canada before a legal separation agreement was signed. This, he said, prompted him to remove the girls' passports from Nancy's car without telling her.

"Nancy indicated that you told her she could travel to Canada with the girls and file for custody there," Brad said directly to Stubbs, who sat across the deposition table from him. "I was concerned about that, so I took the passports out of the car, took one to work, and left one at home."

Brad said Nancy didn't discover the missing passports for about two months, but when she did she got very upset with him. He denied the rumors that he had ever suggested they each take one child and then cut ties permanently with one another. He said he instead suggested they each take one passport, not one child.

"To make us both feel comfortable, why don't we each have control of one passport and that way we would both be guaranteed that neither parent would remove the children from the country?"

Brad said to Nancy.

But no matter how gently Brad Cooper presented these marital woes, it sounded as though he was giving himself the perfect motive for murder.

THE INVESTIGATION

Since Nancy's murder, Brad had been working from home. He said this was at the suggestion of Cisco managers, who said they wanted to give him time to deal with his grief.

"The last few months have been a blur," Brad said.

But he had had several sessions with a psychologist and said he was now doing better and was eager to get back to the office by the end of October. He seemed unflappably optimistic despite his obvious status as a murder suspect.

In addition to regular sessions with a therapist, Brad had also undergone a battery of tests and had been evaluated by a psychologist named Jonathan Gould for the purpose of the custody case.

"My emotional stability was called into question, and he was there to give me an examination," Brad said.

Brad said he paid more than twelve thousand dollars for the assessment, and while the final report was still not in, Gould found him to be a truthful, nonviolent person.

One thing Stubbs felt Brad was not being truthful about was his level of cooperation with the Cary police. He said he had answered all of their questions and had spent at least nine hours with them since Nancy's murder.

"What's your primary focus?" Stubbs asked Brad pointedly.

"Getting, being able to see my girls again," Brad responded.

"Is that all?" Stubbs countered sharply.

"And helping out with the investigation of Nancy," Brad said awkwardly.

"Are you currently assisting in the investigation?" Stubbs asked as her tone transitioned from lamb into lion.

"I've answered every question the police have, yes," Brad replied.

Stubbs wanted to know if Brad had been to the Cary Police Department to give a formal statement. He said he had not, but still, he had been cooperative and answered their questions. He said his initial reluctance in going to the police station was leaving the children. Stubbs countered that he could go to the Cary Police Department now, since the children were in Canada and that was no longer an issue.

"Are you still willing to go down to the police station and answer any questions?" Stubbs asked assertively.

Brad's attorney, Debbie Sandlin, objected and asked Stubbs to "move on." Stubbs said Brad could not take the Fifth Amendment, even as it related to the criminal investigation. Judge Debra Sasser had made it very clear that if Brad sat for a deposition, everything, including his wife's murder, was fair game. At 2:37 P.M., after more than three and a half hours of questioning, the lawyers agreed to call Sasser at the judges' conference on her cell phone and let her sort out the debate.

"If she wants to ask questions around the situation that's fine, but to ask that kind of blanketing question to Mr. Cooper in an effort to try to pin him in to commit himself to make a statement to Cary Police or to any other police department is inappropriate," Sandlin argued.

After speaking with the judge, Sandlin ultimately gave in and told Brad to answer Stubbs's question. He answered it by saying that he would have to consult with his attorneys before making a decision about whether or not to go down to the police station and make a statement.

"Are you going to continue to cooperate with the police and answer all of the questions they have?" said Stubbs, still trying to pin him down.

"To the best of my knowledge, I don't see why I wouldn't do that," Brad replied evasively.

JUNE 28, 2008

Stubbs clearly had a strong working theory of the murder case. While she didn't share it during the deposition, her pointed questions about very specific issues made it obvious that she believed Brad had tried to cover up Nancy's murder and had made some very serious mistakes along the way.

Stubbs decided to hone in on the issue of the mysterious gas spill and the subsequent cleaning of Brad's car trunk, which had raised a red flag for police.

Brad began by saying that on Saturday, June 28, he cleaned Nancy's car just before she departed for her family vacation to Hilton Head with the girls. He said that after she left, he decided to also clean the trunk of his car.

"I emptied the trunk, yes," Brad said. "I emptied it and vacuumed it."

Stubbs asked him in detail about the circumstances of the gasoline spilling in his trunk that had prompted him to do such a thorough cleaning. He said that several weeks earlier, he had put a gas tank filled with fuel for his lawn mower in his trunk and that it had spilled on the way home.

"I could still smell it even a month later," Brad said.

Investigators, however, had smelled no such odor of gas in the trunk when it was searched in July of 2008. Surely not even a thorough cleaning would have removed such a powerful odor.

Stubbs wouldn't let the issue go. She kept circling back to the gasoline spill until the normally unflappable Brad Cooper became visibly agitated for the first time in the deposition.

"I'm trying to answer your question, but I'm not sure I'm answering it to your approval here. I'm trying to say I spilled some gas, or some gas spilled over, but it wasn't lots," Brad said defensively.

On that day, June 28, 2008, Brad claimed that he'd also cleaned the garage, which was so full of toys they couldn't park a car inside. He said he organized the toys, took some upstairs to a storage area, and cleaned the garage floor. This was how the Cary police found the garage on Saturday, July 12, when they first came to the Cooper home to investigate Nancy's disappearance.

However, an affidavit from a local exterminator, Gary Beard, said he had been to the Cooper home on July 8 and found the garage messy and cluttered, which meant it must have been cleaned not on June 28, as Brad had stated in the deposition, but on a later date, sometime after the exterminator's visit but before the Cary Police Department searched the home.

JULY 6, 2008

Nancy Cooper and her daughters returned from their vacation in Hilton Head with Garry, Donna, Krista, and Jim on Sunday, July 6. Nancy told her friends and family that when she returned the house was a wreck, nothing had been cleaned. She said that the house was so dirty and disgusting that it had become infested with bugs, hence the need for the exterminator. She also said there was not a bit of food in the house.

Yet Brad, in his deposition, said he had done his best to make sure the house was clean when his family returned and that there was food in the refrigerator.

"Was she upset with you?" Stubbs asked, playing the empathy card again.

"When she came home? I'd say she was upset, yes," Brad responded. "She was upset that the playroom wasn't clean."

"Was that all?" Stubbs asked.

"She thought that I didn't take the garbage out, but I had," Brad said.

"Anything else?" Stubbs continued.

"She was upset that I didn't wash the floors. She said that was the hardest job of cleaning the house, and I didn't do that," Brad said.

"How did that make you feel?" Stubbs asked sympathetically, as if she were suddenly on his side, understanding how his nagging wife must have forced his hand.

"I was a little disappointed. I thought the house was pretty clean," Brad said.

"Did you and she argue about it?" Stubbs asked.

"She expressed her unhappiness with me. I simply said I would try to get to it that week," Brad said.

JULY 11, 2008

On Friday, July 11, Brad said he and Nancy had had an argument about his not giving her the three hundred dollars he normally delivered to her on Fridays.

"She called me in the afternoon asking me why I forgot to drop off the money. I offered to leave work and return home and make sure she had the money," Brad said.

Brad called Nancy on his way home from work around 6:15 P.M., and she told him to bring some beer to the neighborhood party they were attending. He said he stopped at the Lowe's grocery store, the closest store to his home, and picked up some beer on the way to the party, which was directly across the street from the Coopers' home.

Brad said that when he arrived at Diana and Craig Duncan's house, Nancy immediately put him to work.

"When I got to the party, Nancy indicated to me that I was on child duty and to watch the girls while she could take a break," Brad said.

As a result of the dispute over the money earlier in the day, Brad said he felt as though Nancy was punishing him by forcing him to be on child duty while she socialized.

"I wouldn't say we argued. I would say she was cold and maybe short with me, and I spent most of my time with the girls," Brad said of Nancy's behavior at the party.

"Had Nancy told you that day that she hated you?" Stubbs asked.

"I don't recall. She may have. I don't know," Brad replied.

"Do you recall her telling you that she hated you on any

occasion?" Stubbs asked.

"I don't remember if she's ever said that. It doesn't stick in my mind," Brad said, appearing bored with the line of questioning.

"You don't recall if your wife's ever said that she hated you?" Stubbs asked incredulously as she morphed back into the lion from the lamb.

Brad again denied remembering if Nancy had ever said that. Brad said after playing with the girls at the party for a while and feeding them, he took them home to go to bed around 8:00 P.M. He said that around 8:30 P.M. Nancy called from the party and handed the phone to Mike Hiller who asked him to play tennis Saturday morning at 9:30 A.M. Hiller said that Nancy had already given her blessing.

Brad said after the telephone call and the girls' regular bedtime routine, he fell asleep between Katie and Bella around 9:00 P.M. He said it was normal for either him or Nancy to fall asleep with the girls. Brad said the couple had officially stopped sharing a bedroom in early 2008, and he had moved into the guestroom.

Brad said he didn't see Nancy again until she returned from the party several hours later.

"Nancy came home about 12:25, 12:30," Brad said. "When she opened the door, and I heard her come up the front stairs, it woke me up."

But Brad said he didn't speak to his wife even when she opened the girls' bedroom door and peeked in. This timeline of events from that night would later become critical in the murder investigation.

"She opened the door just to check on the girls is my assumption. She just kind of poked her head in, saw that I was sleeping between the girls, then closed the door and walked down the hall," Brad said. "I just saw the silhouette of her."

JULY 12, 2008

Brad said he was awoken by Katie a little after 4:00 A.M. Saturday morning because she wanted some milk. He said he took her downstairs to the kitchen to keep her from waking up Bella and Nancy and discovered there was no milk, so he first tried to placate Katie with water. About twenty minutes later, Brad said Nancy woke up and joined them downstairs in the kitchen.

"Nancy asked why we didn't have milk, and if we were out of milk, why didn't I get any the night before," Brad said.

"Was she upset about that?" Stubbs asked.

"She wasn't happy about it," Brad replied, starting to sound annoyed at the way Stubbs was drilling him.

Brad said that for the next hour and a half the couple tag-teamed taking care of Katie. He said they also cleaned up the kitchen and started getting several loads of laundry together. But Katie could not be consoled.

"It was probably 5:45 or something, and we'd both had kind of had enough, and we were getting frustrated with Katie not going [back to sleep], so Nancy told me to go to the store and get milk," Brad said.

Stubbs asked Brad if he recalled what he wore that morning. He said he could only remember by looking at the surveillance video from the grocery store.

"It looks like I wore jeans and a thin running top," Brad said.

"Do you typically wear long sleeves in the summer?" Stubbs asked pointedly.

"If I get up early with the girls, and I have to go downstairs, [it can be] a little bit chilly coming out of bed, I'll usually throw a long-sleeved shirt on, yes," Brad said.

Brad said he left the house a little after six in the morning and drove directly to the Harris Teeter grocery store, approximately two miles away. Stubbs asked him in detail the route he took and asked him to draw a map. He said he took Lochmere Drive to Cary Parkway, a route Stubbs knew that, with just a slight detour, would have allowed him to swing by Fielding Drive where Nancy's body was found.

Brad said he went straight home from the grocery store and was there just a few minutes when Nancy told him they were out of laundry detergent and that he would have to go back to the store again.

"Was she upset with you about that?" Stubbs asked with empathy in her voice.

"Yes, she was upset that one, we ran low on milk, ran low on laundry detergent, and she was gone the week prior so she kind of felt it was my fault that I hadn't restocked with milk and laundry detergent," Brad said playing on the sympathy card Stubbs seemed to be offering him. "She indicated that it was my fault and therefore my responsibility to hop back in the car and go to the store and pick up laundry detergent."

So Brad said he did just that.

"Just like every other request that Nancy asked me to do, I did," Brad said sounding once again like the perfect henpecked husband.

"You complied with all of her requests?" Stubbs asked.

"If she asked me to do something, I normally did it, yes," Brad replied.

The second time he went to the Harris Teeter grocery store, Brad said he remembered going a different way. He said he recalled taking a call from Nancy on his cell phone at the intersection of Tryon Road and Kildaire Farm Road, which meant he must have taken Cary Parkway to Tryon to Kildaire this time. This route would have taken him right by the Lowe's grocery store less than a mile from his home, the store he had stopped at the previous evening to buy beer on his way to the neighborhood party, another store that opened early on Saturday mornings.

He said in that phone call that Nancy asked him to also pick up some Naked Green Juice for Bella, which he did and then returned straight home.

Brad said after he returned he took Katie upstairs and had her on his lap while he worked on the computer. Around 7:00 A.M., he said Nancy yelled up to him from downstairs that she was looking for her running shirt. Brad said she then said "Never mind" and left the house. He said he was unaware of any plans Nancy had made for the weekend—including plans to paint Jessica Adam's house.

"Either she said good-bye or the door closed," Brad said.

Stubbs wanted to know if it was Nancy's habit to drink coffee before she ran—something friends had mentioned in their affidavits. Caffeine had been found in Nancy's body during the autopsy, so it was clear that sometime before she died she had had something caffeinated to drink.

"I don't know if coffee was part of her regular routine to drink before she ran," Brad said.

"Did you live in the home with her?" Stubbs asked incredulously.

"I did, but I wasn't usually downstairs as she got dressed and walked out the door. I was usually sleeping with the girls," Brad replied. Again, this was something Nancy's family and friends had categorically denied. They said the girls either slept with Nancy, or alone, not with Brad.

Brad said he knew Nancy was going for a run that morning but did not know with whom she was going with, if anyone, where she was going, or what she was wearing at the time she left the house. He had assumed she was probably running with Carey Clark because they had been running partners for some time now.

"Did she run on July 12?" Stubbs asked.

"Yes. She left the house at about 7:00 A.M.," Brad said.

"Did she have on her running clothes?" Stubbs asked.

"I did not see her. I was upstairs with Katie at the time," Brad replied calmly. Bella was still asleep.

Brad said Nancy left her cell phone and keys at home—items that, despite what her friends said, he claimed she never took with her when she ran.

Around 8:30 A.M., Brad said Bella woke up, and he brought her downstairs and made her some breakfast and let her watch cartoons. At this point, he said he was not worried about Nancy's whereabouts because it was not unusual for her to go for a long run and to return later than expected.

Brad said Nancy did know he had a tennis game scheduled with Mike Hiller at 9:30 A.M. that morning because she had been part of the phone call from the party the previous evening. When she didn't return in time for him to play, he said he called Hiller to reschedule.

Throughout the morning, Brad said he tried to make up for not cleaning the house to Nancy's satisfaction while she was on vacation. He said he scrubbed the kitchen and hallway floors and the bathrooms and also vacuumed.

"I thought she may have been punishing me by not coming back because the floors weren't clean, and they weren't washed. So she knew I was supposed to be playing tennis at 9:30, so I figured that maybe she, you know, was getting back at me. So I washed the floors just with hot water and vinegar, just the floors downstairs. I just kind of cleaned up trying to make her happy as best I could," Brad said contritely.

Brad said he also did more laundry while he was waiting for Nancy's return.

"Did you wash any of her dresses?" Stubbs asked as if it were a trick question. Everyone knew that most women didn't wash their dresses. They had them dry-cleaned. Surely, someone as fashion-conscious as Nancy would not put her dresses in the dirty clothes hamper.

"If it was in the laundry hamper, yes," Brad replied.

"Did you wash the dress that she wore to the party the night before?" Stubbs asked cryptically.

"I'm not too sure if we washed that dress or not because we couldn't clarify which dress she had on that night," Brad said.

Brad said he thought she had worn a light green or orange dress, but he couldn't say for sure. Brad said that he did, however, remember that Nancy had spilled wine on her dress the previous evening at the party. He said when he got to Diana Duncan's house on Friday night, Nancy had a big water stain on her dress where she had tried to get the wine out. Brad said he overheard Nancy telling someone else about the spill.

Nancy Rentz and Brad Cooper rushed to get married in Alberta, Canada, on October 13, 2000, in a small ceremony, attended only by Nancy's family. Brad had been offered a job in North Carolina, and the couple needed to be married for Nancy to go with him. *Courtesy of Donna and Garry Rentz.*

Krista Lister, left, and her identical twin, Nancy Cooper, were as close as two sisters could be. Nancy's death left Krista feeling like a part of her had died as well. *Courtesy of Donna and Garry Rentz.*

Nancy and her daughters, Bella, left, and Katie, loved the beach. The three spent part of their last trip with Nancy's family in Hilton Head, South Carolina, shortly before she was murdered. *Courtesy of Donna and Garry Rentz.*

Twin sisters, Krista, left, and Nancy shared many things—except motherhood, though Krista became especially close to her nieces. Nancy always said that if anything ever happened to her, her two sisters were to raise her children. *Courtesy of Donna and Garry Rentz.*

Days before her disappearance on July 12, 2008, Nancy Cooper and her family finished up their vacation, without Brad Cooper, at High Rock Lake in Charlotte, North Carolina. On that trip, Nancy had talked about her plans to leave her husband. *Courtesy of Donna and Garry Rentz.*

As a child, Nancy Cooper's younger sister, Jill Dean, looked up to her big sister and wanted to be just like her. When Nancy's marriage became troubled, the roles reversed, and she counseled Nancy through the emotional turmoil of trying to leave Brad Cooper. *Photo by Amanda Lamb.*

Friends and volunteers posted more than 2000 missing-person fliers in and around Cary, North Carolina, after a friend reported Nancy Cooper missing on Saturday, July 12, 2008. *WRAL-TV / Capitol Broadcasting Company, Inc.*

Having suspected Brad Cooper was responsible for his wife's death, Nancy's sister, Krista, and parents, Donna and Garry Rentz, put on a brave front for the local media—on more than one occasion—in an effort to help find Nancy. *WRAL-TV / Capitol Broadcasting Company, Inc.*

Cary Police Chief Pat Bazemore, at the first of seven news conferences, often referred to her as "our Nancy" and took a personal interest in the search and the subsequent murder investigation. *WRAL-TV/Capitol Broadcasting Company, Inc.*

After pointed questions from the media about why Nancy Cooper's husband wasn't speaking publicly about his wife's disappearance, Brad Cooper briefly spoke at a Cary police news conference on July 14, 2008. He thanked those searching for his wife and reiterated pleas from her family to help bring her home. *WRAL-TV/Capitol Broadcasting Company, Inc.*

Investigators cordoned off the Cooper home in the upscale Lochmere subdivision of Cary, North Carolina, shortly after a man found Nancy Cooper's body while walking his dog. They spent days taking potential evidence out of the house, while also keeping tabs on their prime suspect, Brad Cooper. *WRAL-TV/Capitol Broadcasting Company, Inc.*

A police officer in Canada, Nancy Cooper's older brother, Jeff Rentz, helped his family navigate the complexities of the criminal investigation into his sister's death. *WRAL-TV / Capitol Broadcasting Company, Inc.*

An anxious Brad Cooper waits in a Wake County, North Carolina, courtroom on October 8, 2008, minutes before attorneys for his late wife's family argue that he was an unfit father and should not have custody of the couple's two daughters. *WRAL-TV / Capitol Broadcasting Company, Inc.*

Visibly confident, Krista Lister, Garry Rentz, and others enter the courtroom on October 8, 2008, to argue before a judge that Brad Cooper was distant and mentally abusive to his wife and children in the months before Nancy's death. *WRAL-TV / Capitol Broadcasting Company, Inc.*

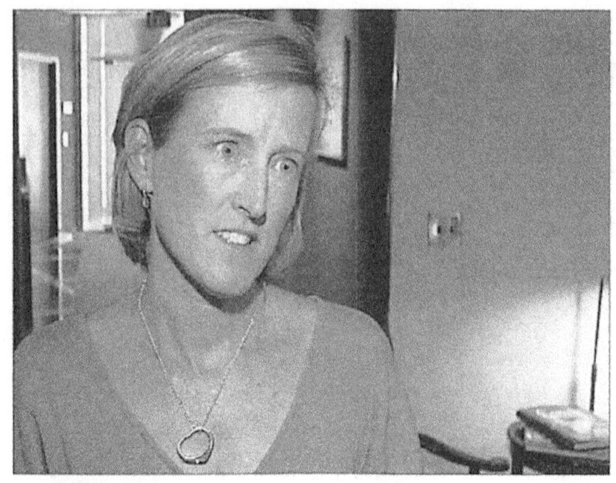

Alice Stubbs, a high-powered attorney in Raleigh, North Carolina, was instrumental in helping Nancy Cooper's parents and sister gain custody of the Cooper children. Her aggressive line of questioning during a deposition of Brad Cooper in early October 2008 gave police fuel to charge him with murder several weeks later. *WRAL-TV / Capitol Broadcasting Company, Inc.*

Minutes after a Wake County, North Carolina, grand jury handed up an indictment of first-degree murder on October 27, 2008, police arrested Brad Cooper at his Cary home. He appeared stunned by the turn of events as investigators led him to jail before a flock of reporters covering every little detail of both the custody case and murder investigation. *WRAL-TV / Capitol Broadcasting Company, Inc.*

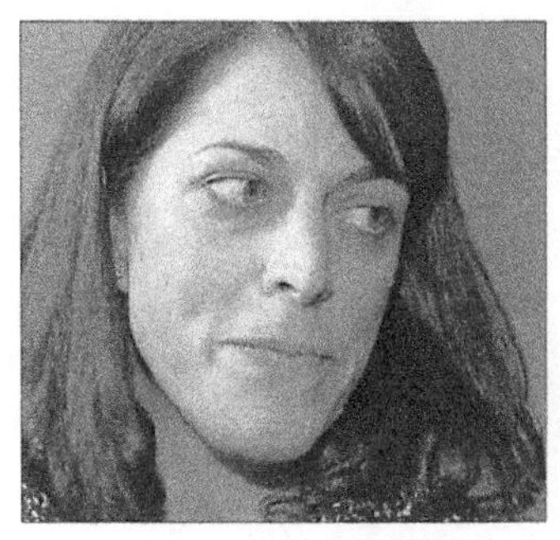

Fearful Brad Cooper might have done something to his wife, Nancy Cooper's close friend, Jessica Adam, called 911 to report Nancy missing when she failed to show up at her house the morning of July 12, 2008. *WRAL-TV/Capitol Broadcasting Company, Inc.*

Another of Nancy's close friends, Hannah Prichard, also suspected that Brad Cooper had killed his wife. *WRAL-TV/Capitol Broadcasting Company, Inc.*

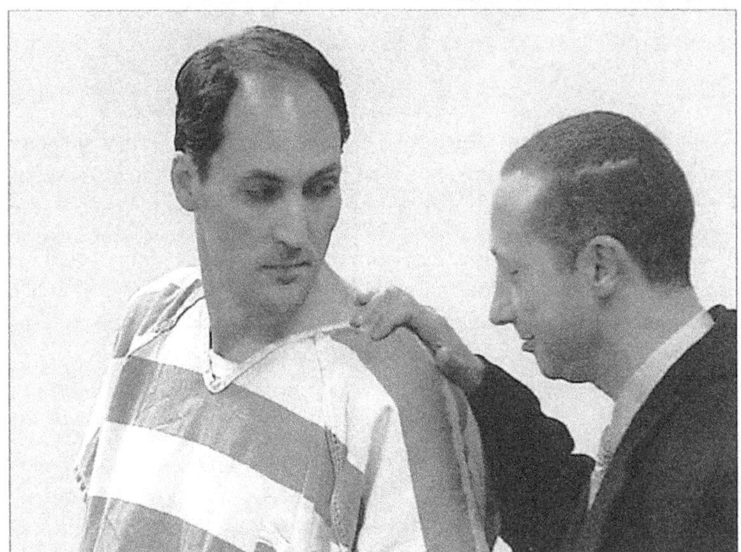

Brad Cooper consults with attorney, Howard Kurtz, during his first court appearance. Kurtz unsuccessfully defended Brad in his 2011 murder trial. Brad was convicted of killing his wife, Nancy, on May 5, 2011. *WRAL-TV/Capitol Broadcasting Company, Inc.*

Nancy's family and friends dedicated a bench in her memory at Regency Park in Cary, North Carolina. Some of Nancy's favorite moments had been spent running the trails around the park's lake. *WRAL-TV/Capitol Broadcasting Company, Inc.*

Their first Christmas without her, Nancy Cooper's family remembered her in a private ceremony at their vacation home in Alberta, Canada. Although it was an emotional holiday, the family celebrated gaining custody of Nancy's girls. *Courtesy of Donna and Carry Rentz.*

Nancy Cooper's parents, Garry and Donna Rentz, are the glue that has held their family together in the wake of an unfathomable tragedy. Years later, they are still slowly learning to live without Nancy. *Photo by Amanda Lamb.*

"Did Nancy ask you to wash her dress?" Stubbs asked again relentless in her pursuit.

"Not specifically. I just washed whatever was in the laundry," Brad said again.

"And did you wash the dress that she wore to the party?" Stubbs asked again, clearly trying to break him into submission.

"I don't know exactly which dress she was wearing to the party. I washed whatever was in the laundry hamper," Brad again replied. If he was offended by Stubbs's badgering, he was doing his best to sound nonchalant. Later, Cary police would share a very different version of the dress story that did in fact include Brad washing the dress that partygoers confirmed was the dress Nancy wore to the Duncans'.

By 10:00 A.M. that Saturday morning Brad said Jessica Adam and Hannah Prichard had both called. He told them Nancy was out for a run, and he expected her back soon. He said they did not seem alarmed, but by 11:00 A.M., they had called several more times and were obviously getting worried, as was he.

Brad said he called the women asking them if they had Carey Clark's number, which they did not. Eventually, he said he told Adam that he was going to put the kids in the car and go look for Nancy.

"It was kind of a blur at that time. I was getting worried. I was kind of driving, driving kind of like a madman not knowing where she was," Brad said.

He said that he drove around Lochmere, looking in the places where he knew Nancy liked to run. He said that he even went to the gym, Lifetime Fitness, to see if maybe she had checked in there and was working out. Finally, he said he drove around Carey Clark's condominium complex looking for Carey's car to see if Nancy might be with her. Brad knew where Clark lived because he had driven her home one night after the women had been out drinking together and had called him for a ride.

Sometime after 2:00 P.M. that afternoon, Brad got a call from the Cary police telling him that Jessica Adam had reported Nancy missing and that they were waiting for him at his house, so he returned home.

Brad said when he got home there were several police officers, neighbors, and friends waiting for him. He said he quickly handed off the girls to neighbors, Clea and Mike Morwick, and started talking to the police. Stubbs repeatedly asked Brad if he had contacted Nancy's family to tell them about her disappearance.

"Did you call anyone in Nancy's family?" Stubbs asked.

"Not at the time. I was focused on talking with the police pretty much the entire day," Brad said.

"Did you ever call Nancy's father?" Stubbs asked.

"No. I was kind of a wreck and a mess at that time," Brad said. "I asked our neighborhood friends to call because I just wasn't functioning right at that time. I was very distraught."

JULY 14, 2008

It was a little after 5:00 P.M. on October 2, 2008, when Stubbs moved into the homestretch of the deposition. At this point, Brad's bored look had transitioned into one of weariness. He was fiddling with a white pen in his hands as he continued to answer Stubbs's pointed questions.

"Where was Nancy's body found?" Stubbs asked.

"From what I understand, it was in a new subdivision, I guess east of the home," Brad said.

"Do you know what street it was on?" Stubbs asked.

"I believe the report said it was off Fielding Drive," Brad said.

"Do you know where that is?" Stubbs asked.

"I've seen it on a map, yes," Brad said, appearing to choose his words carefully.

"Have you ever driven there?" Stubbs asked.

"No," Brad said.

Brad said in his opinion it was not a place Nancy would have gone running. To do so, she would have had to have crossed Holly Springs Road, a very busy curvy two-lane country road with no breakdown lanes on either side.

Stubbs asked Brad to draw the location of the body on the map that he had already started.

"How do you know that?" Stubbs retorted.

"I saw a map in one of the news articles," Brad said.

"Did you have any interest in seeing where the location was?" Stubbs asked, clearly implying that any normal person would be curious about where his wife's body was found.

"No. I haven't driven past it. I have no interest in driving past it," Brad said.

Later, these statements would prove to be the most telling part of the more than six hours Brad spent in front of a video camera.

THE EMPEROR HAS NO CLOTHES

"He was very nonplussed and very calm, always very calm, very staid emotionally and very careful about what he said. He was just always that guy," Nancy's brother Jeff said after watching Brad's taped deposition.

But as a police officer, Jeff saw something else. He saw a man in the hot seat who was telling a story that wasn't making sense. By the time Stubbs was done with him, Jeff felt that Brad looked like a "deer in the headlights."

"If you don't lie, you don't have to remember what you said, and for him, it just looked like he was struggling to remember what he said on some things. In some cases, he just clearly forgot," Jeff said.

On October 9, 2008, DVDs of Brad Cooper's deposition were filed in the Wake County Clerk's Office for all to see. Frenzied representatives from all of the local media outlets ran to the courthouse and uploaded the DVDs onto their laptops in order to post them on their websites as fast as possible.

There were also two telling affidavits filed on the heels of the deposition's release. The first one was from Detective George Daniels with the Cary Police Department. He was the lead investigator on the case. The seventeen-year veteran of the department had watched the deposition and come to some startling conclusions.

"Bradley Cooper has not fully cooperated with our investigation into the murder of Nancy Cooper and has not been willing to come to the police department to assist in the investigation and provide information despite formal requests from the Cary Police Department that he do so," said Daniels.

It was the first time anyone in the Cary Police Department had publicly said anything negative about Brad.

"The testimony given under oath by Bradley Cooper during his video deposition is inconsistent with the statements made by Bradley Cooper to the Cary Police Department at his residence on July 12, 13, 14, 2008," Daniels said.

The other affidavit was from Jennifer Windsor Ball. She said she had been in a relationship with Brad from September 1997 to December 1998. During that period, she lived with him, and they were briefly engaged. She said she was the "Jennifer Wilson" Brad had referred to in the deposition, and she believed he had purposely misstated her name so that no one would be able to contact her.

"I am certain he remembers my real name," Ball said.

Ball had since moved to Hawaii, but thanks to the power of the Internet, a friend in Calgary told Ball about the deposition. She then called Stubbs on Saturday, October 11, 2008. On October 12, she sat for a deposition in Hawaii.

"Throughout our relationship Brad Cooper was emotionally abusive towards me," Ball said. "He constantly belittled me to other people. He frequently berated me about my weight and my physical appearance. He would make derogatory comments about me to others, even telling people I looked pregnant when I wasn't. I have never before, and have never again, been in a relationship with someone who treated me so poorly."

"He was emotionally detached and mentally cruel."

Ball shared anecdotes about times when she would be waiting to pick Brad up at the airport after a business trip, and he simply wouldn't show—never calling to let her know there had been a change of plans.

"At the end of our relationship, I became fearful for my physical safety," Ball said.

They had agreed that she would stay in the apartment, and Brad would leave. Ball said he took many of her personal belongings with him when he left. Brad then moved into another apartment in the same building. Ball said a neighbor told her that Brad had been secretly accessing her apartment when she was not home, long after he had moved out.

"Brad's behavior was creepy, and I was so disturbed by it that I broke my lease agreement and moved away so that I would not have to remain in the same building with him," Ball said.

Ball was the last woman Brad dated prior to meeting, dating, and marrying Nancy Cooper.

CHAPTER FOURTEEN

CUSTODY COUNTDOWN

OCTOBER 12, 2008

No battle plan survives contact with the enemy.
—Colin Powell

Brad Cooper wasn't the only person who sat for a deposition in the custody case. Nancy's family and friends also went through the same process. On each occasion, Garry and Donna Rentz were present, as was Brad. These made for uncomfortable encounters as those who loved Nancy had to sit across from the man they felt took her life, all the while keeping their emotions in check.

Diana Duncan, Jessica Adam, Hannah Prichard, and Donna Rentz were the first four people to be deposed. Garry was supposed to be next, but Brad's attorney, Debbie Sandlin, spent so much time with Donna that they never got to Garry.

During Donna's deposition Sandlin asked her if there were any moments in Brad's deposition where she could prove he was lying. Donna said yes, and the next thing Sandlin knew, they were going line by line through the transcript of Brad's epic deposition.

"That's when I talked about Brad, and I was very emotional because, you know, at one point I did love Brad. I did. I think most of us, although a lot of us won't admit it, did because he was my daughter's husband. He was the father of my grandchildren. I couldn't understand his behavior at this point," Donna said.

Donna sensed that Sandlin saw an opening in her, that she might just be the only person in the family who still had a shred of sympathy for Brad. She might be the only person from the plaintiffs' side that they could get to say a few moderately kind words about Brad.

"Donna, would you consider sitting in a room with Brad and discussing the future of his children?" Sandlin asked Donna.

"Yes, I would, but it would depend upon whether or not he had anything to do with my daughter's death," Donna replied, looking Brad directly in the eyes. He refused to meet her gaze. "I think you did."

Donna went on to say that much of the furniture in Nancy's home had been purchased by her and Garry, or Nancy, prior to the marriage, that Brad's stories about Nancy's penchant for buying expensive art were greatly exaggerated. At one time Nancy had owned a clothing store in Canada next door to an art gallery and had bartered for some artwork. Another expensive painting in the Cooper home had been a gift from Donna to Brad.

"One of them was a painting commissioned by me, paid for by me, and it was presented to you on your graduation," Donna said directly to Brad across the deposition table.

In Donna's opinion, Brad's deposition was full of lies and half-truths, twisted to make Nancy look as though she had spent the family into financial ruin while Brad sat by helplessly and watched.

"They were little things, but they were all lies, and that's what they wanted. They wanted to go with the lies," Donna said. "I think the biggest lie was the money—that he said all the debt they had was based on Nancy from her use of credit cards was just plain not true."

Donna said that their credit card bills were so high because Nancy had no access to cash and was forced to purchase everything, including food, on a credit card.

"A lot of things were household things because that was the only source she had to buy anything," Donna said.

As far as money went, Donna said she and Garry had given

the couple roughly twenty-five thousand dollars to help with debt. This was also used to pay for the eight-thousand dollar painting that Brad had referred to in his court filings. The Rentzes had purchased the girls' bedroom furniture and a dining room table and paid for some home repairs. Brad never acknowledged any of this help from Nancy's family in his deposition.

During one of the breaks in the session, Donna found herself alone in the kitchen at Sandlin's law firm. She turned around to see Brad standing there, smiling at her. Everyone else had vanished.

"Donna, you do understand that everything Jessica Adam and Hannah Prichard and Diana Duncan said were all lies," Brad said to her.

Donna looked at Brad, said nothing, and turned around and walked out of the kitchen and right back to her seat at the deposition table.

"They felt like I was going to be the one that was going to give him some room. They were searching for that, and they sent him in there to give it one more shot," Donna theorized.

PHANTOM JOGGER

At this point in the criminal investigation, few people actually believed Nancy Cooper ever went jogging on July 12, 2008. Cary was considered to be one of the safest places to live in the country. It seemed unlikely that a bogeyman had been waiting in the bushes on a bright sunny Saturday morning hoping to prey on an unsuspecting jogger with so much foot traffic in the area.

Dozens of people had been out in Lochmere exercising on that beautiful summer morning, yet no one had reported a definite sighting of Nancy to Cary police. No one, that is, until Wednesday, October 15, 2008, when Brad Cooper's attorneys filed an affidavit from Lochmere resident Rosemary Zednick, who claimed that she had seen Nancy Cooper jogging on the morning in question. According to the court filings, Zednick had contacted Brad's attorneys in October 2008 after she said she had repeatedly tried to contact the Cary Police Department about what she'd seen, but had gotten no response.

Zednick, who was in her sixties, said she had been out walking her dog around 7:10 A.M. on the sidewalk that July morning along Lochmere Drive toward Cary Parkway when she saw Nancy running along a bike path toward Kildaire Farm Road. Zednick said she had stopped to untangle her dog's leash when the woman, whom she did not know at the time, but recognized later from photographs, jogged by. Zednick said she made eye contact with Nancy and even spoke to her briefly.

"I said, 'Hi.' She turned her head and said 'Hi' back to me. We were almost close enough to touch," Zednick said in her affidavit.

Zednick said Nancy was wearing a light-colored top and running shorts and that her brown hair was pulled back in a ponytail behind her "long face." She also said the jogger was wearing an iPod.

"I am positive the woman I saw was Nancy Cooper because I saw her picture on a flyer either that very day or the next. It was a photocopied picture, but I could clearly tell that it was the woman I saw jogging," Zednick said.

Zednick said on Sunday, July 13, she called Cary police to report what she had seen. After a series of messages, she finally spoke to an officer by phone, but no one ever came out to her house to take her statement. She said on two subsequent occasions she told police officers at roadblocks in her neighborhood about what she had seen, and again, there was no follow-up.

But when she called Kurtz and Blum, the law firm representing Brad Cooper, their investigator not only came out and took a statement from her in person but walked the route with her and took photographs in the location where she said she had seen Nancy. *They* took her seriously.

It was clear to anyone reading the affidavit that Zednick was not happy with what she perceived as a lack of attention from the Cary Police Department and felt vindicated when Brad's attorneys believed her.

"There is no question in my mind I saw Nancy Cooper jogging at 7:10 A.M. on July 12, 2008, on Lochmere Road heading toward Lilly Atkins Road," Zednick said.

The affidavit got a chilly reception from Nancy's family and friends. If Nancy had been jogging on that day, then it meant Brad Cooper was telling the truth. It also meant that it was unlikely he killed her, and more likely that she was killed by a stranger.

Lilly Atkins Road was on the way to Fielding Drive where Nancy's body was found. If Zednick's story checked out, this information had the potential to derail the entire criminal case, or at least be enough of a red herring to create reasonable doubt.

CHAPTER FIFTEEN

GAME ON

OCTOBER 16, 2008

You may have to fight a battle more than once to win it.
—Margaret Thatcher

On the day of the custody hearing, October 16, 2008, both families walked into court ready to do battle. Brad walked in flanked again by his much smaller attorneys, Deborah Sandlin and Howard Kurtz, but even his crisp white dress shirt and cheerful pastel tie couldn't mask the anxiety etched across his face. He fidgeted and paced around the defense table as the attorneys unpacked and prepared their files for the trial.

Nancy's family, by contrast, strode into the courtroom confidently. Garry, Krista, Jim, Jill, and Chad came in with two of Nancy's friends, Jessica Adam and Susan Crook, along with attorneys Alice Stubbs and Wade Smith. Garry's nephews, Casey and Kelly also joined the family. They all had reserved smiles on their faces, and while they didn't stop to talk to the media, they took their time getting down the hallway, giving everyone a nice long shot of their cautious optimism as they entered the courtroom.

Alice Stubbs then began her opening argument in the custody case. "Bella and Katie have been in a very stable, loving environment," Stubbs said referring to the children's being with

Nancy's family in Canada.

Stubbs went on to say that "substantial evidence" existed linking Brad to the murder.

"We maintain that not only is he a suspect, he is the only suspect," Stubbs said with urgency.

She pointed out that Brad never called the police to report Nancy missing, nor did he call Nancy's parents or any other member of her family. Stubbs also said Brad had not cooperated with police, despite his attorneys' statements to the contrary.

Stubbs then called her first witness, Nancy's father, Garry Rentz.

Garry told Judge Debra Sasser that he had been very close to his daughter Nancy and had spoken with her often by phone about her marital troubles and her concerns. Garry testified that just before her death his daughter had been "fearful and angry." She told her father about being cut off from access to credit cards and bank accounts and about being restricted in her movements by the amount of gas in her car.

"Brad's behavior became more controlling," Garry testified.

As a result, Garry said he'd loaned Nancy money to hire Stubbs in order to get the separation agreement on the table. He said his other twin daughter, Krista, had also lent Nancy money, as had some of Nancy's friends. Garry said Krista had become increasingly concerned about Nancy's safety in the weeks leading up to her murder.

"Krista asked us to get Nancy out of North Carolina," Garry said, his voice laden with remorse.

The last time he saw his daughter was Sunday, July 6, at the Charlotte Douglas International Airport just before he and Donna flew back to Canada after their family vacation.

"Her demeanor was very sad. She was hugging her mother and crying," Garry said. "Nancy said she wanted to come home."

Stubbs played the portion of Brad's video deposition where he claimed to have cleaned the house in preparation for his family's return. She then played a voice mail Nancy had left for her father directly after she returned home to Cary from the family vacation.

"I've been furious," Nancy's voice said on the tape creating an eerie silence in the courtroom as the dead woman seemed to be speaking from the grave. "I came home, and the house was so dirty. The plates that the girls ate on were still there covered in food and ants. I had to call the exterminator. There were even these wormy things. I didn't even know what they were," Nancy said with growing frustration in her voice. "I'm so furious at how disgusting my house was when I got there."

When Stubbs turned off the tape you could hear people quietly weeping in the audience as they listened to Nancy's voice, many of them for the first time since her death. Stubbs had one final question for Garry.

"Do you believe that Brad murdered Nancy?" Stubbs asked.

"Yes, I do," Garry said without reservation. "He is the only person I think of with motivation like that and access."

Then it was Debbie Sandlin's turn to cross-examine Garry. She asked him if, to his knowledge, Brad had ever been violent toward Nancy during their marriage. Garry said no, that he had seen them argue but nothing beyond that.

Sandlin asked if Garry had ever given the couple money. He said he had on occasion. She pointed out that in 2007 Nancy spent thirty thousand dollars on the couple's credit cards when Brad was making just fifty-four hundred dollars a month. Garry responded that clearly they'd needed to budget better.

Sandlin had just one more question. She asked him if Bella and Katie loved their father.

"Yes," Garry said honestly.

Then it was Krista Lister's turn to take the stand. Not only had she become a new mother to Katie and Bella, but she was a living reminder to everyone in the courtroom of what they had lost. She was Nancy's spitting image.

"She was amazing. She would do anything for her kids," Krista said, beginning to tear up already. "She was my one and only," Krista said, fighting back the tears again. "She was my best friend, my soul mate."

Krista said she'd spoken to Nancy by phone at least three to five times a week, sometimes multiple times in one day, and had come to North Carolina twice in 2008. Her visit in March was aimed at getting the house ready to sell so that Nancy and the girls could move back to Canada. But Krista said that shortly after her trip Brad had taken the girls' passports and told Nancy that he had changed his mind about her leaving. Krista said Brad's change of heart was because he'd learned from his attorney that he would have to pay alimony.

"I couldn't imagine a husband, someone who loved you, treating her so awful. I was scared for her. She had no money. She felt helpless and useless, and that's not Nancy," Krista said, describing a woman who was a far cry from the strong, gutsy sister with whom she had grown up. "I phoned my parents and begged them to come back and get Nancy," Krista said, referring to the call she'd made to Garry and Donna when they were on a trip to China. "I was really worried about her, and she was unsafe."

Krista said by the time Nancy went on the family vacation to Hilton Head in June 2008, she was happy again because she had made peace with the fact that the marriage was over and, one way or another, she was planning her literal escape.

Stubbs then asked Krista what she had asked Garry—whether or not she thought Brad had killed Nancy. Krista answered yes and listed the reasons why she believed her brother-in-law had murdered her sister.

"Motive, access. His attitude. He didn't contact the family. He didn't contact me. Gut feeling," she said with a concentrated stare in Brad's direction as he looked down at the defense table in front of him.

Stubbs went on to ask about the children, about how they were doing in their new home. Krista said they were enrolled in school, ballet, and gymnastics and had already made many friends, but that they still had a lot of questions about their mother's death.

"Bella constantly asks me where she is. Why did she die? If she could still see her mother? Why would she leave her? Why she had to talk to her dad without her mom there? If she still loves her?" Krista said, with a rising level of anger in her voice.

Krista said a psychologist was working with the girls to help them deal with the loss of their mother. She said her husband, Jim, had been a great source of support to the girls and that "they adore him."

She said the girls had had two visits so far with Brad in Raleigh, and that they spoke with him by webcam several times a week, during which the girls behaved very badly. She said they refused for the most part to sit in front of the camera and interact with Brad, making the entire situation stressful for everyone.

And then it was Sandlin's turn to cross-examine Krista. The grieving sister was no shrinking violet. She made no bones about her animosity toward Brad and his attorneys.

Sandlin probed Krista about whether or not she and her husband had been following the court order about allowing Brad access to the girls.

"I feel like Brad had murdered my sister, and I deem it extremely inappropriate for the girls to be around him," Krista said incredulously.

"How often do you think they should see their dad?" Sandlin asked.

"Never," Krista said through clenched teeth.

Sandlin then asked about the allegation that Nancy had had an affair. Krista testified that her sister did in fact have an affair in the first year of her marriage to Brad. Krista said she and Nancy had talked about it, and she was disappointed in her sister for straying outside of her marriage. She said Nancy wanted to work things out with Brad, and Krista had promised to support her.

"When the murder is solved, when do you think Brad should get his children back?" Sandlin asked.

"He'll be in jail," Krista said with an almost smile at the corners of her mouth.

Krista's husband, Jim, took the stand next. Like Krista, he was angry about the predicament in which Brad had left the girls.

"Those kids didn't do anything wrong," Jim said angrily.

Jim said he loved them as his own children and was prepared to care for them over the long term. He also described the difficult webcam visits between the girls and their father.

"It's heartrending. It is very unnatural," Jim said of the calls.

Stubbs called Jessica Adam to the stand next. She looked serious in a black dress with her long jet-black curly hair pulled back in a severe pony tail. Unlike the others who had testified, Adam appeared visibly nervous as she sat down in the witness box to the right of the judge.

Stubbs then played the tape of the call Adam made to 911 on the day Nancy disappeared. Stubbs asked her to explain why she implied during the call that she thought Brad might have something to do with Nancy's disappearance.

"Brad and Nancy's marriage was increasingly tense. My understanding, he had taken control of the finances, and she was extremely limited in her movements," Adam testified.

"She said she would be doing specifically as he instructed because she didn't want to rock the boat and didn't want him to get angry," Adam said.

Adam said when Nancy failed to show up at her house and she called the Cooper home on July 12, 2008, she tried not to act like she was worried, but she was. When Brad returned her call at 1:30 P.M. that day, she ran to the phone excitedly, hoping that it was Nancy, but it was not.

Stubbs then asked the money question: "Do you think Brad killed Nancy?"

"I do, yes," Adam said with confidence.

After Nancy was reported missing, Adam said Brad was not acting normally. He sat on the curb in front of his house with his head in his hands and did not interact with anyone.

Then it was Sandlin's turn to take a crack at Jessica Adam. From the moment she made the 911 call, Adam had been out on a limb with her very public allegations against Brad. She was the first person to imply that he might be a murderer. She now had plenty of company, but her status as the person who got the ball rolling clearly didn't sit well with Sandlin. Sandlin said Adam had been inconsistent about the times of the phone calls, about whether or not she thought Nancy was running with Carey Clark, and about their plan to paint Saturday morning, which had not been noted on the calendar that Adam had turned over to the court during the discovery process. Sandlin also pointed out that it would have been impossible for Nancy to be at Adam's house to paint at 8:30 A.M. when she knew Brad was playing tennis at 9:30 A.M.

Sandlin also asked Adam if she had ever witnessed Brad being violent.

"I've seen tension between them, but I can't recite an actual argument," Adam replied.

In addition to Adam, another one of Nancy's close friends, Hannah Prichard, also took the stand. Like Krista, Prichard could not hide her animosity toward Brad. She glared in his direction as he hung his head and stared down at a yellow legal pad on the table in front of him.

Prichard testified that she had watched as her friend's relationship with her husband began slowly to crumble. She said that on New Year's Day 2008, Brad had confirmed to Nancy that he had slept with Heather Metour. Nancy had also shared with Prichard the notes Brad had written regarding wills, insurances policies, and the children's likes and dislikes. It had made her even more worried that her friend was in deep trouble.

"I was very concerned. I told Nancy I thought he was crazy, and you never know what a crazy person is going to do next," she testified.

Prichard said she was also concerned because Brad had initially agreed to let Nancy and the girls move to Canada, but when he took the girls' passports, he essentially held them hostage in North Carolina.

"He was saying how they should each take a girl and be done," Prichard said incredulously. "At one point Nancy told me Brad was going to spend as much time with them until they left, and then was never going to see them again."

Prichard said that on the morning of July 12 she talked to Brad on the phone several times about Nancy's whereabouts.

"I walked around panicking for a little while," Prichard recalled.

Then Stubbs asked Prichard the question: "Do you believe today that Brad Cooper murdered Nancy?"

"Yes," she responded, adding that there were "so many reasons" she felt this way, including that had Nancy been attacked by a stranger during a jog, she would have fought hard—yet she had no defensive wounds on her body.

"She was such a strong lady, I believe she would have fought like hell if someone tried to attack her, and I believe she was caught by surprise," Prichard testified.

Prichard said in the days following Nancy's disappearance that she, Jessica Adam, and Krista Lister had all tried to help Brad by taking care of the girls, but he kept changing plans at the last moment. Prichard said that when Krista finally got a visit with the girls, they were reluctant to leave her when it was time to go back to Brad.

"Bella did not want to leave Krista. She was clinging to her and crying. Bella would not go with Brad. It was heartbreaking," Prichard said.

Sandlin went after Prichard the same way she had Adam—with cool, detached professionalism, trying to paint the women as exaggerators who had unfairly portrayed Brad as a murderer. Sandlin asked Prichard if Nancy's married neighbors Mike Morwick and Craig Duncan had ever expressed romantic interest in Nancy. Prichard admitted there had been some incidents when the two men had independently told Nancy they had crushes on her.

"I'm not saying these people killed her. I'm just saying there are other people that could have done this," Sandlin said throwing the two men under the bus.

Stubbs then called Donna Rentz, Nancy's mother, to the stand. Donna told the court that Nancy was her third-born child. Krista had beaten her identical twin into the world by just five minutes.

"I love her desperately. We had a lot in common. She was a good friend, an exceptional mother," Donna said.

Donna said she felt so fortunate to have spent time with her daughter on vacation in July 2008, just before Nancy was murdered. The last time that she saw her daughter was in the airport as Donna and Garry prepared to fly back to Canada.

"She said to me that she did not want to go home. She wanted to go home with us," Donna said, breaking down in tears. She paused and wiped her eyes and then continued. "She was sobbing, and she said 'Mom, I just want to come home.' But she couldn't because Brad had one of the [girls'] passports."

Sandlin clearly knew that she had to use kid gloves so as not to appear to be beating up on the grieving mother. Donna told Sandlin that Brad never called them after Nancy disappeared. While she never saw Brad do anything inappropriate with the kids, she said he handled stress by withdrawing, and as a result, she was concerned about his being around the children.

"I feel the children were not safe with him any longer," Donna said.

When the judge recessed the hearing for lunch, all of the players wearily paraded out of the courtroom ignoring the television cameras. It was clear that the experience was emotionally draining, and it was far from over.

ROUND TWO

The Coopers' exterminator, Gary Beard, was the first witness up for the plaintiffs in the afternoon. He talked about how he had made a visit to the Cooper home on July 8, 2008, at Nancy's request. Nancy had called Beard after she returned from Hilton Head and found bugs infesting the house.

Despite Brad's testimony in his deposition that he had cleaned the garage on June 28, 2008, the day Nancy left for vacation, Beard testified that it was full of clutter on July 8. Yet when Cary police arrived on July 12 to investigate Nancy's disappearance, they said the garage was clean. This meant that Brad must have cleaned the garage in between July 8 and July 12, something he'd adamantly denied during the deposition.

Stubbs then called Dr. James Hilkey, a forensic psychologist who had examined Brad for the plaintiffs. Not only had he administered multiple tests to Brad, but he'd also watched and evaluated the entire deposition.

"I think Mr. Cooper is a very complex man," Hilkey said. "He is in a very complex situation which makes the evaluation challenging."

Hilkey said while Brad was a very intelligent person, he had issues with anxiety.

"Mr. Cooper presents as someone who is somewhat anxious and somewhat angry," Hilkey testified.

Hilkey said Brad was able to keep his anger in check most of the time, especially in social situations, but that when it came out, it was usually directed at family members. He said that because Brad was not good at reading social cues and nuances, he came across to others as arrogant and detached. Hilkey said it was clear that Brad had trouble with long-term intimate relationships. He specifically referred to Jennifer Windsor Ball's affidavit in which she talked about Brad's abusive behavior toward her.

"Reviewing the affidavit, it confirmed some of the things I observed in my testing and my contact with Mr. Cooper," Hilkey said. "My opinion is that this is a longstanding anger that has been with him for a fair amount of time."

Sandlin took her time cross-examining Hilkey. She knew that in many ways the entire case came down to this. It was the expert testimony the judge would weigh most heavily.

Hilkey said Brad was not defensive when he answered questions. He said Brad came from a high achieving family—his father was an organic chemist who expected a lot from his sons. While Brad said there was no abuse in his family, he told Hilkey there was not a lot of real communication among the family members. Sandlin asked Hilkey why her psychologist, Dr. Jonathan Gould, had gotten such different responses from Brad during his examination.

"I can't rule out the fact that there was some deception," Hilkey replied.

Hilkey added that Brad had a problem with memory lapses, for example, forgetting the name of his nephew or the correct name of his former fiancée, Jennifer Windsor Ball.

"Mr. Cooper should not benefit from being untruthful in his deposition," Stubbs said as she rested her case.

Sandlin than called her own psychological expert, Dr. Jonathan Gould of Charlotte. He had examined Brad at his attorneys' request. Unlike Hilkey, who examined Brad on behalf of the state, Gould found that Brad was acting normally given the circumstances.

"When he is confronted with emotionally powerful experiences, he tends to kind of withdraw," Gould said. But he went on to say that Brad's recent behavior was not out of the norm for someone experiencing a crisis. "He's not a guy that is typically anger based, but under current circumstances, he's feeling very frustrated."

Gould said he simply had a different interpretation than that of Dr. Hilkey, and that in his opinion, Brad should not be denied the right to care for his children.

"I didn't see anything that there had been historically any risk to the children," Gould testified.

When it was the plaintiffs' turn to cross-examine Gould, Stubbs's boss, attorney Wade Smith, got up to ask the questions. Smith and his brother, Roger, were senior partners in Tharrington Smith, one of the Southeast's most powerful and reputable law firms. An unfailingly polite gray-haired southern gentleman, Smith looked like a grandfather, not the daunting litigator he really was in the courtroom.

Smith asked Gould whom he'd talked to in order to get more information about Brad for his evaluation. Besides Brad, Gould said he'd interviewed Brad's friend, Scott Heider, Heather Metour's ex-husband. In that interview Smith pointed out that Heider had said Brad was a workaholic and that Nancy, for the most part, took care of the children. Smith was just warming up with Gould. The next witness would make or break the case—at least the murder case, and no matter what anyone said, this case was as much about the murder as it was about child custody.

Rosemary Zednick took the stand almost gleefully, dressed for the occasion in a colorful floral top along with a string of beads and bright red lipstick. She was the woman who claimed to have seen Nancy jogging the morning of Saturday, July 12, along Lochmere Drive.

"I saw that gal," Zednick said with a strong New York accent as she leaned into the microphone on the witness stand. In person, Zednick came across as almost too eager to be a part of the unfolding drama. This only fueled the skepticism of Nancy's family and friends in the courtroom who believed she was wrong.

Zednick said she had tried to contact the police as many as nine times to let them know that she'd seen Nancy that day. She said she wasn't sure how far Nancy was from her when they passed one another and that she thought Nancy might have been wearing an iPod. Zednick said she didn't know Nancy but later identified her from photographs in the news.

Smith played off Zednick's growing frustration that the police were ignoring her story. He got her to admit, that was why she finally turned to Brad's attorneys, because she wanted someone to listen to her. He implied she was someone who wanted media attention, someone who had made comments about the national media finding out who she was.

"All I said to the police was, 'I don't want Nancy Grace at my doorstep,'" Zednick said with a wide grin. The entire courtroom broke out in a much-needed chuckle. But while she provided much-needed comic relief, Zednick's story still came across more like wishful thinking than actual fact. She seemed nervously eager to please and willing to say whatever she had to say to make her version of the story sound credible.

Next up was Mike Hiller, Brad's friend who was supposed to play tennis with him the morning of Saturday, July 12. Hiller had been very defensive in his affidavit filed on behalf of Brad. In it he said that Cary police had tried to coerce him into saying that he'd tried to help Brad by supplying a false alibi. On this day, Hiller's body language radiated his defensive posture as he took the stand. He appeared to have so little respect for the proceedings that he hadn't even bothered to dress up. Instead of a sport coat and tie, like all of the other men in the courtroom, Hiller wore a plaid button-down shirt with the shirt sleeves rolled up like he was about to go work in the yard. His face seemed taut with anger.

Hiller confirmed that he had been at the neighborhood party the night before Nancy disappeared and that he did have a tennis date lined up for the next morning with Brad. He said he knew the couple socially, mostly from parties and an occasional tennis game.

Hiller repeated the story from his affidavit about when both couples had been looking at a house for sale on the lake. Nancy had heard that Hiller said something about her and Brad's not being able to afford the property, at which point he said Nancy called him and attacked him about his statement.

"Nancy was tough. She wasn't a pushover," Hiller said.

Hiller said that as far as he could tell, Brad was a good, normal father, and his daughters loved him.

"I never saw him do anything bad to the kids, or inappropriate to the kids," Hiller said.

When it was time for closing arguments, Sandlin went first and told the judge point blank that nothing that had been said in the courtroom was enough to take away a father's rights.

"I have not heard any evidence that Mr. Cooper had anything to do with his wife's death. These children need to be with their father. These children have an attachment to their father," Sandlin said.

She said Nancy had been financially irresponsible and that she seemed to have had a full social life, which contradicted the allegations that she was being controlled by Brad. But Sandlin did admit that Brad worked a lot and was often absent from his children's lives in the past.

"That does not make him a killer, that does not make him a bad parent," Sandlin said. "That should not take away his constitutional right to parent."

Stubbs then got up to handle the rebuttal and said the girls needed to be in a stable, loving environment like the Listers' home. She chided Brad for not taking the stand and fighting for his children.

"I find it incredulous that Brad Cooper didn't take the stand," Stubbs said. "You need to hear from the father. We didn't hear from a single relative. I don't get it."

But it was attorney Wade Smith, Stubbs's boss, who refused to dance around the elephant in the middle of the room.

"The Colon Willoughby express train is coming," Smith said referring to the Wake County district attorney who would ultimately take the criminal case to a grand jury seeking an indictment. Smith looked directly at Brad as he spoke. "It may not be next year. It could be in two years, but [it's] coming."

The judge ended the draining eight-hour hearing, saying she needed more time to review the deposition and the web chats between Brad and his children before making her decision.

Nancy's family looked weary as they left the courtroom, but there was still a glimmer of hope in Garry's eyes. He knew the end was near, one way or another.

O CANADA

Garry, Donna, Krista, and Jim were permitted by the court to take the girls back to Canada while they waited on the judge to make her ruling. They left with the knowledge that they had done all they could to make their case, and it was now in the judge's hands. Alice Stubbs told them they had every reason to feel confident.

Their patience paid off. Four days later, on Wednesday, October 22, 2008, Judge Debra Sasser made her decision, granting temporary custody of the children to Nancy Cooper's family.

"This is a very good day for Nancy, her children, and our entire family," Garry said in a statement. "We are extremely grateful to Judge Sasser for her careful and thorough attention to our case.

We could not have asked for a more fair or deliberate process and are confident that she acted in the best interest of not just our grandchildren, but all children who may be in a similar circumstance."

Criminal attorney Seth Blum spoke on Brad's behalf.

"He's extremely disappointed. He misses his daughters. He would like to have them back in his arms," Blum said with his typical dramatic flair.

"Brad has been put in a position where he's required to prove his innocence, which is a very difficult thing to do, given we don't have the police file, and we don't know the details of the investigation up to this point," Blum said.

As it turned out, they wouldn't have to wait much longer.

CHAPTER SIXTEEN

CAPTURED

OCTOBER 27, 2008

There's nothing in the world more shameful than
establishing one's self on lies and fables.
—Johann Wolfgang Von Goethe

There was a buzz at the Wake County Courthouse on the afternoon of Monday, October 27, 2008. Word among the press corps was that something big was about to happen. The grand jury was hearing testimony that day, so everyone assumed there was going to be an indictment in a major case, but which one?

Brad Cooper wasn't even on the media's radar. Everyone assumed it would take a while after the custody case was resolved before the district attorney would make a move. Plus, cases from the Cary Police Department were usually heard on Tuesdays. But the district attorney had other plans. He had decided to move swiftly and slipped the case in at the end of Monday's agenda.

One witness, Detective George Daniels, testified in front of the grand jury, laying out the case for the panel.

Late that Monday afternoon, the district attorney confirmed for reporters combing the hallways of the courthouse that Brad Cooper had been indicted in his wife's murder. Almost simultaneously, just about twelve miles away, police armed with the fresh indictment were arresting Brad at his home in Cary.

Brad looked casual in a gray V-neck sweater and jeans as three Cary detectives led him down the stairs in front of his home and across the lawn to a waiting patrol car. He wore the same impassive expression as always, but the rigid way he held his mouth foretold more going on inside.

Brad's neighbors stood in the street and watched the spectacle. Craig Duncan, who lived across the street from the Coopers, clapped loudly as Brad was put into the patrol car. The tension in the neighborhood over the murder had grown so deep that for many people Brad's arrest was a relief.

Brad was taken immediately to the Wake County Jail to be booked. Then Brad had his first appearance in front of a Wake County magistrate. He said nothing as he appeared in the tiny windowless courtroom in front of the magistrate who informed him he was charged with murder and would be held without bond. Through a thick glass partition, the television cameras zoomed in on his expressionless face.

VINDICATION

"The police were really good about keeping us in the loop without hindering their investigation," Nancy's brother, Jeff Rentz, said.

By the time Brad was arrested, the family knew that the Wake County's first assistant DA, Howard Cummings, had intended to take the case to the grand jury, but they hadn't known exactly when.

Jeff and his wife, Shannon, were out to dinner when Captain Michael Williams of the Cary Police Department called him on his cell phone to tell him the good news.

"I just want you to know we've got him, and he's under arrest," Williams said. Jeff didn't have to ask who "him" was.

"It was awesome. It was a great feeling," Jeff said.

Nancy's parents were still at their office in downtown Edmonton when they got three calls in a row, one from Cary police spokesperson, Susan Moran; one from their attorney, Alice Stubbs; and one from a television reporter telling them about the arrest.

"There was cheering in our office," Donna said, remembering the moment.

"A great relief," Garry said. "We were ecstatic with the fact that [we] had the indictment and then the arrest that quickly."

Krista got a call from Nancy's friend, Hannah Prichard, about the arrest. For her, it was more than just relief that Brad would finally be locked up. It was about keeping Nancy's daughters safe.

"Huge weight lifted. I was elated. Oh man, we were so happy we felt like we won. It was good. Closure, now we have the kids. We're good," Krista said with jubilation. "I felt that all of my suspicions were correct and that I was finally allowed to grieve and say, okay, now I know that what I was feeling was right. It was great. It was so good."

Jill Dean also had an initial feeling of elation, but it was quickly replaced with sadness and regret. Of all of Nancy's siblings, her younger sister had related to Brad the most. With Nancy's death and Brad's arrest, Jill was not only mourning the loss of her sister, but the loss of the brother-in-law she'd once loved.

"When I saw him being arrested, the first time I saw him in the stripes, at first I had this euphoric 'Thank God.' I felt like, 'You're not so smart. Ha-ha, you got caught. You're going to pay for it,' but then immediately, within an hour I was crying," Jill said.

VICTORY DANCE

That night the Cary Police Department held its final press conference on the case. Chief Pat Bazemore came to the podium in uniform, looking much more relaxed than she had in previous appearances. She even managed a slight smile for the throngs of reporters and photographers.

"Today, based on the evidence provided by the town of Cary Police Department, the Wake County grand jury indicted Bradley

Graham Cooper for the murder of his wife, Nancy," Bazemore said.

Bazemore explained that Brad was being held in the Wake County Jail without bond and would have his first appearance in Wake County District Court the following afternoon.

"With the possible exception of saving a life, I can think of no more important work than investigating the taking of a life," Bazemore said. "With this arrest, it should be clear to everyone that Cary citizens have been and are safe. This has really never been the case of a jogger being randomly attacked. It has been a case of domestic violence of the very worst kind."

Bazemore then introduced Nancy's father, Garry, who was on the speakerphone from Canada ready to make a statement to the media.

"Today our family needs to say thank you very clearly to all of those people who stood with us, led us, and supported us in the most complex 108 days of our history," Garry said with his trademark grace-under-fire tone. He went on to thank specifically the chief, her investigators, and the Wake County District Attorney's Office. He also thanked the lawyers who helped his family get custody of his grandchildren.

"Nancy's memory has been kept alive by a family who loved her, by a group of incredible friends who were always there for her and for our family," Garry said.

Bazemore wrapped up the press conference by thanking all of the other law enforcement agencies that assisted in helping her police detectives make an arrest. She also thanked Nancy's family for their dignity throughout the investigation.

"They have changed our lives," Bazemore said speaking of Nancy's family, "and we are better for having to get to know them even under these terrible circumstances."

Bazemore said that this would be her last statement until the case was decided in court. After the press conference, Hannah Prichard and Jessica Adam joined the media in the hallway of the police department to make brief statements.

"She was the kindest, most generous, loving friend I have ever had," Prichard said. "She was definitely once in a lifetime."

While they looked weary from grief, both women had smiles on their faces for the first time in weeks.

"It's been hard to really grieve for our friend without some sort of resolution," Prichard said. "We're one step closer to a conclusion and justice for Nancy."

FIRST APPEARANCE

"Mr. Cooper, I need to advise you that you've been charged with first-degree murder," Judge Jane Gray said as Brad Cooper stood silently in front of her bench in a Wake County district courtroom. He was clad in a bright orange and white striped jumpsuit, a sharp contrast to the comfortable sweater and jeans he'd had on when he was arrested.

Gray told Brad that if he was found guilty he would face life in prison or the death penalty. Brad, as always, stood blank-faced as the judge spoke.

In a surprising turn of events, Howard Kurtz and Seth Blum, the criminal attorneys who had been representing Brad up until this point, asked the judge to appoint a public defender to represent Brad because he could no longer afford to pay for his own attorneys. Clearly, the custody case had wiped him out financially. The Office of the Capital Defender agreed to appoint Kurtz to be one of Brad's public defenders, which meant the state would now be paying Kurtz what Brad could not.

Brad's mother, Carol Cooper, also attended the court appearance. She sat silently behind her son in the courtroom and then rushed past reporters, waving away their questions.

Nancy's friends, Hannah Prichard and Jessica Adam, sat in the courtroom with barely concealed grins on their faces. They stopped and spoke with reporters in the hallway after Brad's court appearance.

"I think everyone is feeling good that we have taken a step in the right direction," Prichard said.

RULE 24

On December 5, 2008, a Rule 24 hearing was held to let the court know whether or not the state intended to seek the death penalty against Brad Cooper. Brad was permitted to wear a jacket and tie, delivered to him by his attorneys, instead of the regulation orange and white striped jumpsuit. The time in jail looked to already be taking a toll on Brad. His long face was puffy and pale, and he had gained weight on his formerly athletic frame.

"Based on the investigation our office is aware of working with the Cary Police Department, we don't believe at this time there are any aggravating factors to proceed capitally," Howard Cummings, the Wake County first assistant district attorney, said in superior court to Judge Donald Stephens.

Stephens ruled that the state would not be seeking the death penalty. Howard Kurtz then asked Stephens to set bond in the case saying that Brad's job at Cisco hung in the balance if he was not released from jail pending the trial.

"Mr. Cooper's employment may be important to him, but frankly, sir, it is of little consequence in the scheme of things in light of the charges he is facing," Stephens said sternly as he peered over the top of his wire-framed glasses.

After a few moments of consideration, Stephens set the bond at two million dollars.

"It's a bond almost no one can make," Kurtz said incredulously. "Our focus here is to clear Brad Cooper's name."

Nancy's family, who had flown in from Canada for the hearing, said that they were in agreement with the state's decision not to seek the death penalty. They were ready to move on with their lives.

"We've been through a horrendous five months. We're really pleased that there's some light at the end of this period. We're lucky a lot of things have gone right," Garry said in the hallway as he stood smiling with his arm around Donna in front of the television cameras. Donna had always seemed frail. She was the one who cried at press conferences, always the grieving mother. But on this day, Donna beamed as she described their upcoming plans for the Christmas holidays.

"It's a time when we're going to take time for Nancy, and we are having our own private family memorial for her, and we're expecting that to be very special," she said with a glimmer in her eye instead of tears.

THE LITTLEST VICTIMS

The girls had been in therapy since soon after they returned to Canada with Nancy's family, but the process of assimilating in their new life was still challenging even with professional help. It was more challenging for Bella, who had vivid memories of her mother, while Katie seemed to have few, if any.

Per the court order, the girls still had phone contact with Brad. Many days Bella didn't feel like talking on the phone to the man she called "Daddy Brad." Jim had become "Papa" to the girls, and Krista had graduated from "K-Mum" or "Krista-Mum" to simply "Mama."

"I've got two mommies, one's in heaven, one here, two daddies, one's always working, and one lives with me," Bella said of her family's situation.

For Krista, no matter how much she loved the girls, the transition was still daunting.

"I'm a mom. I never thought I'd be a mom. I've got challenges in that way because Nan was such a good mom," Krista said.

One thing Krista refused to lose herself in was her grief, no matter how palpable it was. For the girls' sake, she knew she had to put on a brave face even though Nancy was still part of her daily thoughts.

"I do feel empty," Krista said. "I'll be walking in a mall, and I'll stop and say, 'Oh my God, there's Nancy.' It's just weird."

Per the court order, Nancy's family was not to speak negatively about Brad or talk about the murder. They worked hard to abide by every single guideline the judge had prescribed. When Bella didn't want to talk to Brad on the phone, Krista would try to come up with topics and encourage her to stay on the phone.

Krista made sure the girls would not forget Nancy. She kept pictures of Nancy around the house and would constantly refer to things they had done together.

"Oh my God, this is our favorite song," Krista would say when she heard a certain song on the radio.

"You and Nan?" Bella would say.

"Yes," Krista would say.

"She always thinks about Nancy, and I just want it to continue. That's why I have all the pictures of Nancy up. I think it will be more detrimental if they don't remember her," Krista said.

The psychologist told Krista and Jim that the girls would only ask about things or talk about things they were ready to confront.

In February of 2009, a little girl at Bella's school drew a picture of a woman in a pool of blood and said, "This is Bella's mama." When Krista found out about it from another parent, she went immediately to the school to confirm that it had happened. The psychologist told Krista only to answer Bella's questions about the picture in simple language that the child could understand. She cautioned Krista to tell the truth without giving Bella too much information that she was not yet ready to handle.

"I know that Mama Nancy did not hurt herself running, she was too strong, and I knew that she would have to have been killed by a bear or a man," Bella said pointedly to Krista one evening as they sat together on the bathroom floor.

"Honey, it wasn't a bear, it was a man. And you're right. She was killed. You're right," Krista said as she put her arms around Bella and held her tightly.

"Do you know who?" Bella said pulling away from her aunt's embrace to meet Krista's eyes.

"No, but the police have a suspect and one day, there's going to be a court case, and the police are working really hard to figure out who would do this," Krista said as her heart started to beat rapidly. She so wanted to give this child the whole truth, but she knew it wasn't the right time. She had to be patient. She had to wait until

Brad was convicted.

"Will I be able to meet this man?" Bella asked.

"Do you want to?" Krista responded curiously.

"Yes," Bella answered without hesitation.

"Why?" Krista asked.

"Well, I want to ask him a couple of questions," Bella said in a voice that was wise way beyond her five years.

"I'd ask him why he would ever hurt the best mommy on the planet," Bella said.

"You know what, that's a very good question. If you want to ask that, you can," Krista said, regaining her parental confidence and composure.

"Will you tell me who it is?" Bella asked.

"If I ever know for sure, yes," Krista answered honestly.

THE BUTTERFLY FUND

With Brad Cooper behind bars, Nancy Cooper's family and friends finally had the time and the energy to focus on Nancy's memory. They wanted her legacy to be more than just that of a murdered woman who was dumped in the woods like a piece of trash.

They decided that a natural way to honor Nancy's memory was to start a fund to help the victims of domestic violence get out of their impossible living situations. They decided to call it the Butterfly Fund, because after Nancy's death big, beautiful butterflies started appearing to her loved ones.

"A butterfly, both large and vivid, seemed to be a constant guest in our neighborhood," Garry said.

Bella and Katie drew the logo for the fund, and Nancy's friends in Cary busily started preparing for a gala on June 13, 2009, and a run on July 11 to raise money for the fund. At the same time, in Canada, Nancy's family and friends started planning similar events there to raise money for the same cause.

After the frustration of watching the investigation unfold over a three-month period, Nancy's friends were eager to do something proactive for other victims rather than focusing on the murder case.

"We believe that Nancy would be very proud and is probably looking down on us. She would be happy we are doing something positive with our grief and our love for her," Jessica Adam said in an interview with WRAL. "If we can save even just one life, we feel we've accomplished something."

CUSTODY WAR

On April 27, 2009, Brad Cooper's attorneys filed a motion asking that the final custody decision be delayed until after the criminal trial. The temporary custody order was coming up for review in June.

The Motion to Maintain Status Quo suggested that the girls should stay with Krista and Jim Lister under the guidelines of the original custody order until after the criminal trial. Only after the trial would it be revisited. This meant that the custody of the girls could potentially hang in legal limbo for years.

"It is Mr. Cooper's desire to shield his children from as much publicity as possible within his control. Mrs. Cooper's murder has drawn international press attention and has been closely followed by the media locally, nationally and internationally," the order read.

What the order didn't say was that Brad was obviously pretty confident he wouldn't be convicted of Nancy's murder. He believed that he was going to walk away from this a free man and fight to regain custody of his children.

A hearing on the motion was scheduled for Friday, May 15, but to everyone's surprise, instead of a hearing, both sides entered into a consent order granting Nancy Cooper's family permanent custody of Bella and Katie Cooper. Brad's custody attorney, Deborah Sandlin, walked the order over from the Wake County Courthouse to the Wake County Jail so that Brad could sign it.

"Certainly, while Brad's awaiting trial, he's not able to care for the girls, and he did not want another disruption in their lives," she said. But she added that if he was found not guilty, he would have an opportunity to come back to court and petition for custody again.

Garry and Donna were almost giddy as they walked out of the courtroom.

"We're very happy to achieve a decision that was in the best interest of our grandchildren, for stability," Donna said to reporters assembled in the hallway outside the courtroom.

"You want to be sure you can say to your children, here's where you live, and here's where you go to school, and here's the future. It's easier to do that today," Garry said.

FOR THE LOVE OF NANCY

As Donna got off the plane at the Raleigh-Durham airport on the weekend of the first fund-raiser for Nancy's Butterfly Fund, she was suddenly reminded of exactly where Nancy used to stand, just outside the security checkpoint, when they came to visit her. For just a moment, she closed her eyes and imagined her beautiful daughter awaiting her arrival, but when she opened them, Nancy was, of course, not there.

"Every day we think of Nancy," Donna said through tears in an interview with WRAL. "And what we're doing here really helps."

As the gala to honor the Butterfly Fund approached, Nancy's family wanted to shift the focus again from the criminal trial to what they hoped would be their daughter's legacy—helping the victims of domestic violence.

Their mission was to help women get out of abusive situations, especially educated women in upper-middle-class neighborhoods who might not realize they were in danger and might be less likely to reach out for help because of embarrassment.

"We felt that maybe there's a chance to help somebody who's in a situation and doesn't recognize the seriousness of the situation they're in, and we might be able to do something for someone," Garry said in an interview with WRAL. "That made us feel good."

"So many times there are no signs," Donna said. "Domestic violence is a topic that people don't discuss."

FINALITY

Since Nancy's death, her family had had more than ample time to think about Nancy and Brad Cooper's relationship, to turn over every little moment, every little milestone and examine it for the red flags that upon reflection had been there from the very beginning. But Nancy had seemed to love Brad, so her family had loved Brad, too. Now, however, they saw the past in a very different light, and they saw Brad as a very different person than the man they thought they knew.

"I just think I didn't want it to be Brad because I didn't want to think that that was a possibility at first, but all signs in my head were leaning toward Brad. In the beginning, I was trying to think of excuses why it could not be him," said Nancy's little sister, Jill.

"It was so surreal thinking he was capable of doing something like that. I didn't think of him that way. I didn't really think he had it in him. Based on that, it kind of shakes your belief about everything else," said Nancy's brother, Jeff.

When Jill saw Brad on television in that first press conference on July 14, 2008, everything suddenly came into focus for her. *You're a liar. You are a compulsive liar*, she thought.

"He thinks he's better than everyone. He thinks he's smarter than you. He thinks he's better than you, and he has this way to undermine people," Jill said.

Regarding Brad's not contacting her family after Nancy's disappearance, Jill said this fell right in line with the man he had become.

"Of course he didn't call us. He didn't feel bad. He still doesn't feel bad," Jill said angrily. "I think in his mind he's a more important person than her. It makes me sick to my stomach. He treated her as a disposable good."

CHAPTER SEVENTEEN

ANATOMY OF MURDER

Hateful to me as are the gates of hell, is he who,
hiding one thing in his heart, utters another.
—HOMER

Everyone in Nancy's family had their own theory of how she was killed. In the months after Brad was arrested while they waited for the trial to take place, they mulled over various hypotheses. Although they all agreed that Brad Cooper did it, they had differences of opinion about the way the crime was committed.

"From the time she came home, it was within a couple of hours when she walked in the door. It was all done at that point, and then he panicked," Nancy's brother, Jeff Rentz, surmised. And after Nancy was dead, Jeff imagined that his type-A brother-in-law went into a panic, trying to literally clean up his tracks. He had to get rid of the body, clean the house, and try to keep the fact that Nancy was gone under wraps for as long as possible.

Almost all of the family members agreed that whatever happened when Nancy returned to the house that night, it started at the party. Nancy was already mad at Brad for not giving her the agreed-upon allowance that day. He arrived at the party late from work, and she immediately put him on kid duty. At some point Katie started to fuss, and according to witnesses, Brad looked to Nancy for help.

"You're going to be a single dad soon. When you have these kids you need to learn how to watch the signs. I'm not going to be there to be your housewife anymore, so you better learn how to do this yourself," Nancy reportedly said to him.

Nancy wielding her sharp tongue in front of their friends embarrassed Brad, no doubt. It wasn't the first time she had put him in his place, but in her sister Jill's mind, he likely vowed to make it the last.

"Her making him feel like that? He probably left with those kids, and he brooded," Jill said. "He probably went home by himself and sat in a dark room and thought about all of the things she just said, and he probably felt angrier and angrier and angrier."

For Jill there were two possible scenarios—one in which Brad jumped Nancy as soon as she walked in the door and killed her and another in which they got into an argument when she got home and he killed her in the midst of a fight.

"I think he's sick, and he sat there and waited for her to drink. He waited for her to have a couple glasses of wine and hid, turned the lights off and hid. Then there's another scenario where she comes home, and they get into it. She tells him he's a jerk, she hates him, and she wants to leave," Jill said, shaking her head.

But given either version, Jill said the most terrifying fact in her mind was that, as Nancy was dying, she surely thought of her precious little girls asleep upstairs.

"The most heartbreaking thing for me is being a mom and knowing the kids are upstairs. This person is doing that to you. What's going to happen to your kids? I know that's all she cared about," Jill said. "She would have been so panicked, thinking, 'This person is insane, and my children are in this house.'"

Jill imagined that Brad must have blocked the girls' bedroom door to keep them from coming out, especially when he took his trip to dump the body. She surmised that leaving his young daughters alone in the home was the least of his worries after he murdered his wife.

"He's calculated. I have to totally disengage the person I cared about from the person who did this horrible thing," Jill said.

Jill said Brad may have panicked, but he would have pulled himself together and tried to come up with a plan to cover his tracks. The one thing he didn't count on was Nancy's friends trying to locate her.

"I think he had everything planned, and the person who saved Nancy is Jessica. If she hadn't made that call, he might have gotten away with it. I think he had everything planned up until that point. As soon as she called, everything was out of whack," Jill said.

Like Jill, Krista thought the altercation that ultimately was the tipping point that led to her sister's murder must have started at Diana and Craig Duncan's party.

"Nancy had berated him at the party, made fun of him at the party," Krista said. The partygoers had told the family about Katie being fussy and how Brad had asked Nancy for help.

"What do I do?" Brad said to Nancy.

"Be a dad, and figure it out. This is how you can tell you're never around," Nancy responded.

"Everyone kind of laughed," Krista said.

Like Jill, Krista imagined that Brad left the party quietly infuriated and went home and stewed about it. When Nancy got home, Krista said she believed Brad was waiting for Nancy and they would have immediately gotten into an argument in the kitchen.

"I think Brad approached her about making fun and being mean to him in front of people because he was embarrassed. And I think that's when Nancy's like 'Get over yourself.' She had been drinking so she's lippy and feisty, and she just probably said whatever came to her head that just pissed him off, and then I think she walked away from him," Krista said.

Krista believed Nancy went into the den and laid down on the couch to watch television, and Brad followed her.

"I think he came in and strangled her on the couch," Krista said.

And then, like Jill and Jeff, Krista said she thought Brad

probably panicked, doing things that he had never done before.

"He has never cleaned, ever. Laundry, you've got to be kidding me, never," Krista said. "He wouldn't even clean a plate off. He was a pig."

And as for washing the dress Nancy wore to the party, Krista said she knew for sure Nancy would never have put a dress in the hamper. It was a dress that needed to be dry-cleaned or hand-washed. Krista believed Brad's goals were to get rid of the body, clean the house, and then take the kids out somewhere for the day like to the science museum in Durham. That would have delayed the search for a full day because he could have waited to report Nancy missing until Saturday evening when they returned. Curiously, the car seats that were always in Nancy's car had been moved to Brad's car. If he really had been panicking and looking for his missing wife that afternoon, wouldn't he just have jumped into Nancy's car with the kids instead of taking the time to move the seats?

What he didn't anticipate, said Jill, was that Nancy had made plans with a friend in the morning and that her absence would be noticed early in the day.

"I don't think he knew that Nan had made plans to go to Jessica's house because they weren't talking," Krista said.

Garry and Donna, like their children, pored over the details of the night Nancy died a hundred times. They, too, felt that Nancy probably said something to Brad at the party in front of their friends that caused him to finally snap.

"She belittled him in front of people," Donna said.

Around midnight, Nancy made the short walk alone from the Duncans' house across the street to her house. Diana Duncan shared with Nancy's parents that she wished she had walked Nancy home that night. But they have told her more than once that it would not have mattered. No one could have predicted what was waiting for Nancy on the other side of her front door.

Once Brad killed Nancy, the Rentzes agreed, he had a big problem on his hands. He only had a few hours of darkness left in which to dispose of the body.

"You've got a very narrow window of time," Garry said.

"He knew where to go. Brad didn't just accidentally find that," Donna said.

They believed that Brad dumped the body in between his two grocery store runs, changing his shoes on the second grocery store trip because his sneakers would have gotten covered with mud on Fielding Drive. They felt that the two grocery store runs made no sense other than to give him an alibi for being out driving so early on a Saturday morning.

Nancy's parents also believed Brad washed the dress Nancy had been wearing that night.

"I think he ended up with either blood or vomit on the dress, and he had to clean it," Garry said.

Brad said in his deposition that he washed the hardwood floors with vinegar and hot water, a technique that most men wouldn't know. But Garry said Brad knew about this process because just a few months prior Garry had cleaned their floors himself on his hands and knees on a visit to his daughter's house after he noticed how disgusting the hardwoods had gotten.

"The reason he did that is because I did their floors on the second to last visit when I was there. Brad was embarrassed that I was washing his floor," Garry recalled.

Like their daughter Krista, Donna and Garry also believed Brad had not really planned on searching for his missing wife Saturday afternoon, but was actually taking off with the girls for an extended period of time.

"He was heading out," Donna said, as she imagined he planned to get the kids out of the house for the day and return sometime in the evening. "He didn't expect this to happen, to have the response and support. He didn't expect Jessica to call 911."

CLOSURE

For Nancy's entire family, getting Brad convicted was an important step in their healing process. It was not just something they wanted; it was something they desperately needed in order to put their lives back together.

"It's extremely, extremely important for I think all of us to sleep at night," Jill said. "I can't imagine living a life where I know he's out there. It would drive me quite literally insane."

"I know he's guilty. I think other people should know he's guilty," Jill said. "He is guilty no matter what you think could have, should have, might have happened. It didn't. The most obvious person is *the* person."

"I would never get over it if he got out. I would never get over it if he got the kids back. You don't want to turn into a bitter angry person from a thing like this, and I would. I can't see myself being able to say that's okay, because it's not," Jill stated.

Jill also said that since Nancy's murder, she had developed a different perspective on women in domestic abuse situations. She realized that so many women in Nancy's situation were reticent to seek help because of their social status. Well-educated, professional, upper-middle-class women not only didn't label themselves as abused, they were concerned about what people would think if they reached out for help.

But now, Jill said, she thought, "Your pride doesn't matter, it just doesn't. It doesn't matter what your neighbors think. It doesn't matter what your high school friends hear about you. At the end of the day if you leave, you're going to be safe, and your kids are still going to have you," Jill said. "Who cares [what people think]. Get out of the house with the kids. Do it. Even if you never got a dime from him, it doesn't matter."

Garry and Donna also learned from Nancy's death that domestic abuse could be dangerous even when there's no actual history of violence.

"I think you get yourself out and don't worry about the dollars,"

Garry said. "The danger heightens the closer you get to walking out the door."

They also agreed that it's harder for women of higher socioeconomic status to admit that the abuse is taking place and to walk away from their lives.

"Very, very difficult for people of status and background to walk away. They say, 'This shouldn't be happening to me,'" Garry said.

For Krista, making sure that Brad was convicted was about more than just keeping him off the street; it was about protecting the futures of Nancy's children.

"It's the ending that needs to happen. It is also the permission to finally be truthful with the girls when they're ready because right now I hate keeping it from them," Krista said. "If he's found guilty, please God, may he disappear."

For Nancy's brother, Jeff, the trial was more than just having Brad locked up. It was about getting answers.

"I want to find out what happened when she came home," Jeff said. "I want to know a play-by-play. I want to know everything that happened. Right now there are so many loose ends that need to be tied together, and I want them to be tied together."

CHAPTER EIGHTEEN

TRIAL BY FIRE

Some say the world will end in fire, some say in ice.
—Robert Frost

The legal wrangling continued into the summer and fall as the initial trial date of October 25, 2010, quickly approached. A special judge was assigned to go through the voluminous number of e-mails taken off Brad Cooper's computers and decide if they were relevant to the case.

Prosecutors challenged Brad's attorney, Howard Kurtz, and implied they might call him as a witness because he had posted detailed information on his firm's website about the murder investigation months before Brad was arrested. If the state called him to testify, he would have to withdraw as Brad's attorney, which could cause a serious delay for the trial.

Kurtz also filed a motion asking for a change of venue, claiming his client couldn't possibly get a fair trial given all of the pretrial publicity. Three motions from the defense also requested the state to turn over specific evidence from the July 2008 and October 2008 searches of the Cooper home. The court filings asked for everything from scientific information about Nancy Cooper's body decomposition to her dental records. But there was another element to these motions that caused Nancy's family and friends new pain: Brad's attorneys suggested that Nancy had had multiple extramarital affairs.

"There was the possibility that this was Nancy Cooper reaching out for relationships," Howard Kurtz said of an allegation in the motion that Nancy visited dating websites on her computer. They also pointed to an April 2008 receipt police found for a sexually transmitted disease screening. Although Nancy might have been concerned about Brad's sexual exploits and whether or not she had been exposed to anything, that was not how defense attorneys were spinning it.

Although no one ever had pretended Nancy was an angel, there was no doubt from anyone who knew her that the defense's tactics amounted to muckraking. They were going to throw everything at the wall and see what stuck. Krista had admitted during the custody hearings that Nancy had had one affair in the first year of marriage, but no one in her family expected allegations like this to surface. It was going too far in their opinion, but it set the stage for the battle about to come.

Brad Cooper was fighting for his freedom, and it was clear his attorneys would use any means possible to win.

Due to the enormous volume of discovery, the trial was ultimately moved to the spring of 2011, almost three years after Nancy's death. It seemed like an eternity for those who had been waiting for justice.

OPENING STATEMENTS

"It was a beautiful July morning," prosecutor Amy Fitzhugh began her opening statement on Thursday, March 9, 2011, as she took jurors back to July 12, 2008, the day Nancy Cooper was reported missing. Fitzhugh, the young attractive blond assistant district attorney, had worked on the case since the beginning, and had sat at the state's table throughout all of the previous hearings, but this was the first time she had spoken in open court since the case had started. She sounded a bit unsteady initially, but slowly gathered steam as she methodically unveiled the story of Nancy's death, which she hoped would convince a jury that Brad Cooper had murdered his wife.

But Fitzhugh didn't want the jury to focus just on that day—she wanted to take them back in time, to show them how Nancy ended up facedown in that ditch in the woods three miles from the home she had shared with her family. She told them that initially the couple's decision to divorce had been "amicable." It was agreed upon that they would sell the house, and that she and the girls would return to her native Canada. But then, Fitzhugh said, Brad got wind of the separation agreement that Nancy was working on with her attorney, Alice Stubbs, and realized he would have to pay child support. That, Fitzhugh said, was when everything changed.

"She was not free to leave anymore," Fitzhugh told the jury. That's when she said Brad took the children's passports and started to exhibit extreme financial control over his wife.

Fitzhugh said that Brad learned of the separation agreement because he had gotten into Nancy's e-mail without her permission.

"From April of 2008 until she died, the defendant was secretly intercepting all of her e-mails," Fitzhugh said, "from her friends, from her lawyer."

She told the jury that Nancy had been at a party at Diana Duncan's the night before she died, and that she and Brad had been arguing. Fitzhugh said Brad had refused to pay her weekly allowance because he learned that Jessica Adam was giving her money to paint her house.

"[Nancy's] angry, she's angry with the defendant," Fitzhugh said. "She told him on the phone that day 'I hate you' three times."

Fitzhugh said when it was time for Nancy to go home, Diana Duncan walked her to the door, hugged her, and told her she loved her.

"It's the last time Diana Duncan sees her friend alive," the prosecutor said.

When police arrived at the Cooper home, Fitzhugh said they noted many strange things, including that Brad had been doing copious amounts of cleaning. He'd done laundry, washed the floors. After obtaining search warrants, they discovered that the trunk of Brad's car had recently been cleaned, as had the garage. Brad told police he'd spilled gasoline in the trunk of his car, but officers smelled no such odor.

Police asked Brad for an item of Nancy's clothing to give the canine a scent to follow as they continued to look for her. They asked for the dress she had been wearing the night before. Fitzhugh said Brad told police he couldn't find the dress, but then produced it the next day—after putting it through the wash. He said it had gotten stained at the party, but Fitzhugh said no one remembered Nancy spilling anything on her dress.

Police asked Brad to come down to the station and give a statement as the search continued for Nancy. Yet, Fitzhugh said, he refused.

"He said he was not charged with anything and he was not going," Fitzhugh said. "And this was *before* the body was found." In other words, it was still just a missing persons case, not a murder investigation, but Brad was already talking about charges.

Fitzhugh described how, on July 14, 2008, Nancy's naked and partially decomposed body was found by a dog walker in an undeveloped area of a subdivision not far from the Cooper home.

"She died of homicidal violence," Fitzhugh said.

She went on to claim that the nearly seven-hour deposition that Brad sat for in the child custody case in October 2008 provided many inconsistencies in his story, enough to lead police to charge him with his wife's murder.

As she finished her opening statement, Fitzhugh had just one more thing to tell the jury. She turned away from the podium and pointed directly at Brad as he sat at the defense table between his attorneys, looking confident. Since the beginning of the trial, Brad had occasionally appeared smug, often leaning in to his attorneys and smiling, or laughing at something they had said. Gone was the pale, solemn Brad who had graced all of the previous pre-trial hearings.

"You will be convinced that Nancy Rentz Cooper never went

for a run on July 12, 2008," Fitzhugh told jurors. "You will be convinced that Bradley Graham Cooper killed his wife and is guilty of first-degree murder."

DEFENDING BRAD

On Friday, March 10, 2011, defense attorney Howard Kurtz came out of the gate swinging with an opening statement that lasted more than two hours and dropped new bombshells at almost every turn.

Kurtz told the jury that the state had ignored any evidence that didn't fit their version of the crime. He said there were sixteen people who told police they saw Nancy Cooper out jogging on the morning of July 12, 2008, but that police never followed up on this information.

"This didn't match up with the Cary Police Department's Brad-Did-It theory," Kurtz said.

Kurtz told the jury that one witness, Curtis Hodge, had been on his way to work that morning when he'd passed Nancy jogging along Kildaire Farm Road. Kurtz said Hodge also claimed to have seen an older model Chevy van with two Hispanic males in it turn around and follow Nancy.

Kurtz said that, by disregarding evidence that didn't fit with their rendition of events, the police had essentially carried out an "inept" investigation.

"Chief of Police Bazemore was concerned about Cary's reputation as a safe city," Kurtz said. "There was pressure for this to be an isolated incident, and it was their job to put the public at ease."

Kurtz admitted that the Coopers had a troubled marriage, that they were close to "financial ruin," and that Brad had had an affair with Nancy's one-time best friend, Heather Metour. But, he said, Brad was committed to saving the marriage and had agreed to go to counseling. It was Nancy, Kurtz said, who didn't want to fix things and instead went around airing the couple's "dirty laundry" and "embellishing as only Nancy could" to her friends.

The biggest piece of "dirty laundry" Kurtz revealed that had not been publicly aired was an affair he claimed Nancy had had with her neighbor and friend, John Pearson—the same married man whom court filings said had also had an affair with Heather Metour.

He contended that, while Pearson initially denied the affair to police in his first interview, he later admitted to it in a subsequent one. Yet the investigators never followed up on the information.

"Nancy and John had a history, and one that John was very reluctant to share with police," Kurtz said. He went on to detail how, in 2005, Pearson walked Nancy home from a neighborhood Halloween party while Brad was out of town on a business trip.

"John remembers showering, and he remembers winding up naked with Nancy on the couch. He could not recall if they had intercourse," Kurtz said. "Though later police say that Mr. Pearson has since admitted to having sex with Nancy."

Kurtz said Nancy and Pearson agreed never to speak of the incident again.

At the time, Nancy and Brad had been trying to have a second child. To that end, she was on the fertility drug Clomid. Kurtz then dropped the biggest bombshell of his opening statement: "Katie was born eight months and twenty-four days after Nancy had sex with John Pearson."

Kurtz said that, despite repeated attempts, defense attorneys for Brad Cooper were never able to get a DNA test from Katie, and that it was unclear whether one had ever been performed.

Kurtz claimed Nancy and Pearson met for coffee at a bakery in Cary one morning shortly before she was killed. Nancy had Katie with her. Pearson told police she had asked him to run on several occasions, but he had declined her invitations. Kurtz said there was also a pattern of phone calls between the two in the weeks leading up to Nancy's death. Kurtz said Pearson told police Nancy had made him angry about something during that period of time, but he couldn't recall exactly what they had fought about.

It was clear that Howard Kurtz was pointing the finger at a potential murder suspect, and that man was *not* Brad Cooper.

THE BURDEN OF PROOF

The state started its case on the night of July 14, 2008, the night a man walking his dog found Nancy's decomposing body in a drainage ditch in the woods near his home and called 911.

Deputies with the Wake County Sheriff's Office, including Deputy Karen Harper, were dispatched to handle the investigation.

"We raised the emergency blanket up and looked at the body," Harper said. "The only clothing that we could see at this point was either a tank top or a sports bra that had been pushed up underneath her arms."

Next on the stand was Diana Duncan, Nancy's longtime friend and neighbor. The women had met in 2001 at a neighborhood Super Bowl party and maintained their friendship until Nancy's death. Duncan and her husband, Craig, had hosted the party Nancy and Brad had attended the evening prior to her disappearance.

"I felt she was a sister, and she felt the same way," Duncan said. Duncan appeared confident and credible on the stand, although she did at times break into a nervous laughter.

But Duncan said something changed in their friendship after it became clear to her that Brad didn't like her. The families had had a falling-out after her son accidentally broke Bella's nose when the kids were roughhousing one day. Nancy got over it, and the women eventually reconciled, but not Brad, she said.

"He looked at me like I was mud," she testified, recalling a time she'd knocked on the door and asked if Bella could play with her son.

Duncan said eventually it also became evident that Nancy and Brad's marriage was in trouble. She said Nancy confided in her at a party in 2007 that Brad had had an affair with Heather Metour.

"I just found out that Brad had an affair, but we are going to work on it. He's coming over, and I want you to treat him just like it hasn't happened," Nancy told her.

But Nancy was not able to move past the affair, and the marriage continued to deteriorate.

"Brad did admit that he had had the affair, and also admitted that at least at one point he had thought that he was in love with Heather," Duncan said, testifying that that was the last straw for Nancy, who started plans to leave Brad and move back to Canada with the girls.

"She decided she was pretty much done," Duncan said. "She said she wanted to get divorced."

That, Duncan said, was when Brad tightened his grip on her friend, cutting her off from access to credit cards and bank accounts. Initially, Nancy told her that Brad only wanted to give her eighty dollars a week for household expenses and items for the children. After much negotiation, Duncan said they settled on three hundred dollars a week.

"She was pretty upset and angry. She felt like he had no idea what it took to buy groceries," Duncan said.

Duncan also testified about the time the water was shut off to the home, and Nancy didn't have a credit card to get it turned back on. She told the jury about Nancy finding the strange note in Brad's handwriting with a list of Bella's and Katie's favorite things plus notations about bank accounts and life insurance. She became concerned for her friend's safety. "It felt creepy, kind of wrong," Duncan said of the note. "It showed planning."

"'Would you like to come stay with me or do you want to get away for a little bit?'" Duncan recalled asking her friend. But Nancy turned down the offer.

"I don't think he would ever hurt me," Nancy told her.

Plans continued for Nancy and the children to return to Canada, Duncan said. She testified that a going-away party for Nancy was scheduled for Saturday, April 19, at Laura and Mike Hiller's house. In lieu of gifts, everyone had planned to give Nancy cash to begin her new life in Canada as a single mother. It had been aptly dubbed "The Saddest Party Ever" because Nancy had made so many good friends in Cary who were going to miss her terribly. Duncan was planning to drive with Nancy to Canada, and had made a one-way flight reservation to return to North Carolina from Toronto on

Monday, April 28.

But on Friday, April 18, Nancy called Duncan to tell her the party was off.

"She sounded like she had been crying," Duncan said.

Nancy told her that Brad had gotten hold of the proposed separation agreement sent to her by e-mail from her attorney, Alice Stubbs, and that he now realized he was going to have to pay alimony and child support.

"She thought he was upset about the money," Duncan said. "She said that it seemed like he had hired a lawyer and that his demeanor changed fairly abruptly."

Nancy, who had worked in Canada in information technology and had once owned a retail store, decided she wanted to get her visa and start working again. Duncan said Brad seemed publicly open to the idea of Nancy working, and even started paying more attention to the children and attending the neighborhood social gatherings, which he had previously eschewed for many years.

Even with these positive changes, however, Duncan said Nancy confided to her that she still did not trust Brad. She locked important papers in her car, and kept the keys with her at all times. Duncan testified Nancy told her she even went so far as to bring her keys, her purse, and her important documents with her into the bedroom at night and locked the door—sometimes she even put something in front of the door to block Brad from coming in. "She felt very nervous and scared that he was going to come and get those things from her," Duncan said.

The fact that Nancy's keys had been found left in the front hallway of the Cooper home when she disappeared had always been a red flag to Duncan.

At a festival in the nearby town of Apex one weekend, Nancy told Duncan that Brad had asked her for the keys to her car. Because she was distracted with the kids, she gave them to him. Soon after, she told Duncan that she realized that Brad had removed all of the important documents from her car, including the children's passports.

The women talked mostly on cell phones because Nancy didn't trust the phones in their home, which Brad had installed. They worked through the Internet. Nancy told Duncan she was always hearing clicks when she was on the home phone, and calls often dropped out. She was convinced that Brad was monitoring her calls.

Duncan said Nancy even went so far as to go to a local jeweler to have him redesign the stones from her wedding and engagement rings into a new ring, which she planned to wear on her right hand. She told her friend that she loved the diamonds, but couldn't bear to wear them in their original form because they were a painful reminder of her failed marriage. To pay for the cost of the new ring, she was selling the store the platinum wedding band itself.

When Nancy returned from her trip with her parents to Hilton Head in July of 2008, Duncan said the house was a disaster. Nancy told her that Brad had done nothing while she was gone to clean up, even leaving dirty dinner dishes that were there prior to the vacation molding in the sink. Nancy told Duncan she was starting to feel very run-down by the whole situation. But despite her continuing sadness, the women planned a barbecue on Friday night, July 11, at Duncan's house.

Duncan said Nancy was the first person to arrive that night and that she was upset because Brad had learned that she was getting money from Jessica Adam to paint her house. Nancy said he told her that she would therefore not be getting an allowance from him that week.

"This was an 'I hate Brad day,'" Duncan said, recalling Nancy's demeanor. "She was kind of in a state, but she was still talking to people and putting on a good party face."

But when Brad arrived at the party, everything changed. Duncan said the couple went out onto the porch and could be seen and heard arguing about his inability to read necessary cues from his one-year-old child, Katie.

"I remember she was sort of pointing at him," Duncan said. "Just very angry body language."

A short time later, Duncan said Brad left with the girls and that's when Nancy finally relaxed, drinking several glasses of wine and socializing with her friends.

"Nancy shined in social situations," Duncan said. She recalled that her friend was wearing a teal-green sundress with a black pattern on it and flip-flops that night. Around midnight the women hugged, exchanged "I love yous," and Nancy walked across the street to her dark house.

"Everyone must be asleep," Nancy said to Duncan as she peered out at the dark windows across the street before leaving.

The next morning Duncan and her family slept in. At about noon, Duncan got a call from Jessica Adam asking her if she had seen Nancy.

"I was dazed, not knowing what's going on, worried," Duncan said. A crowd of friends and police began to gather outside the Cooper home just steps from Duncan's door.

At one point that afternoon, Duncan testified, she saw Brad in the street in front of the house and went up to him. "I remember seeing him, going up to him and patting him on the back and saying, 'Don't worry,'" Duncan recalled. She said he refused to look up, refused to meet her eyes. "His reactions looked very false. They looked acted."

The next thing that Duncan remembered was that Brad asked her to help him find the dress Nancy wore to the party the previous evening so that the police could use it to give the search dog a scent to track. In her confused state, Duncan could not immediately recall what Nancy had worn. She said Brad told her it was a black dress, so that's what she helped him look for; but there was still a part of her that doubted her own shaky memory. While she couldn't remember the exact dress, she didn't recall it being black.

"Are you sure it was a black dress?" Duncan said to Brad. He told her he was sure.

The day after Nancy's body was found, Duncan was in the Cooper home and saw a teal-green V-neck sundress with black accents draped over the back of a dining room chair. It had been washed. At that moment, she knew exactly what dress Nancy had worn to the party. It was *that* one, *not* a black dress.

"I felt that Brad did it on purpose," Duncan said regarding his telling her that the dress was black.

In court, prosecutor Amy Fitzhugh handed Duncan a sealed brown paper bag. She asked Duncan to open it and pull out the dress. As Duncan pulled out the dress and held it up in front of her, she had tears in her eyes. It was a green v-neck summer dress with cap sleeves and a black lacy design overlaid on the green cotton material.

"I don't have a good picture of her in my head anymore," Duncan said struggling to get the words out. It was clear that Duncan was not just talking about a picture of Nancy from that night, but also in general. The further away she got from her friend's murder, the harder it was for Duncan to remember the exact details of the way Nancy appeared to her when she was living, how she looked, how she sounded, how she moved.

Shortly after Nancy's body was found, Brad asked Duncan and her husband for help with the children. Brad asked them to get the kids dressed and take them to preschool one morning. They agreed, not realizing what a challenge it would be. Duncan testified that both children were fussy and the house was completely disorganized. During that time she popped her head into the Coopers' garage, looking for some shoes for Bella, and realized it was immaculate. She found this strange, considering that in all the years she had known the Coopers their garage had been so messy they couldn't even fit one car inside. Finally, after much stress, they got the girls fed, dressed, and into the car.

"Bella really, really, really got upset and angry and started screaming for her daddy and screamed for her mommy," Duncan said. "We got them to preschool late, and they didn't want us to leave."

The next day, after this gut-wrenching experience, Duncan said she called Brad and told him the girls needed a consistent caregiver instead of being shuffled around from one friend to another. She said he hung up on her after she told him what they really needed was their mother back.

Duncan went to the local memorials for Nancy. She said Brad did not attend either service.

"He said he stayed away to keep the focus on Nancy," Duncan testified. While Duncan was grieving, she said Brad seemed strangely relaxed and happy, "Like a huge weight was off his shoulders."

On cross-examination, defense attorney Howard Kurtz brought up John Pearson. Duncan testified that in October 2005 she and her husband had attended a neighborhood Halloween party with Nancy. When they left, Duncan said Pearson had accompanied them, presumably to walk Nancy home because Brad was out of town on business. Duncan testified that she just saw Nancy and Pearson go up to Nancy's front door. But Kurtz said Duncan had told police in an earlier interview that she saw Nancy and Pearson actually enter the house together. As Kurtz probed, Duncan admitted that upon more reflection she now saw that night differently than she had when she first spoke with police about it. After Kurtz asked her how she now saw the situation, Duncan said, "That he hit on her and that they probably fooled around."

But even with this epiphany, Duncan could not be rattled by Kurtz. She had brought one very important observation home to the jury—that Brad Cooper hadn't acted like a worried husband when his wife was missing, or like a grieving husband when her body was found.

"It seemed very wrong," Duncan said of Brad's reaction to Nancy's death.

A MOTHER'S BURDEN

In the first day of jury selection, overwhelmed by the magnitude of what was about to happen, Nancy's mother, Donna Rentz, had broken down once. But with her husband Garry's help, she was somehow able to compose herself and sit stoically until the trial officially got under way, and then suddenly all of those feelings she'd had on that first day came flooding back to her. She couldn't bear to look at Brad as he sat at the defense table, appearing confident and almost jovial at times with his attorneys.

The pain of losing Nancy was almost too much to bear, but she had also lost a son-in-law, someone she had loved like a son. This combined grief made it even more difficult for her to put on a brave face day in and day out. During the pre-trial motions, photographs of Nancy's body were shown to the judge as he decided on their admissibility.

"I put my head down," Donna said. "I will not be there when they read the autopsy either. I have never read it. I never will."

Behind Brad sat his parents, Carol and Terry Cooper, who, like the Rentzes, had flown in from Canada to be there for the trial. Donna noticed that while she and Garry were always surrounded by a group of people, the Coopers were usually alone, standing in the corner in the courtroom lobby area during the breaks, looking weary and timid.

At one point, Donna decided to go over and speak to her daughter's former mother-in-law. "She's a mother like me. She's a grandmother like me. It's hard on all of us. I told her that," Donna said.

FRIENDS

On Monday, March 14, a steady stream of Nancy's friends took the stand to talk about the Coopers' troubled relationship as well as the events leading up to, and just after, Nancy's death.

Neighbor Ross Tabachow and his wife, Damia, were close friends of Nancy's and casual acquaintances of Brad's. Tabachow testified that he and his wife had been at the Duncans' party on July 11, 2008, the night before Nancy was reported missing. Tabachow said Nancy's mood was "subdued" when he first saw her that night, but she soon evolved into her usual social self, playing with the kids in the yard. He said Nancy had told him it was Brad's turn to take care of the kids that night at the party once he arrived, and that's exactly what he did. Tabachow said Brad pushed the kids on the swings while Nancy socialized.

"Katie started to get fussy as it started to get closer to her bedtime. Brad asked Nancy what to do. Nancy responded along the lines, 'You can figure it out,'" Tabachow testified.

A short time later, Brad left and took the children home to put them to bed. That's when Tabachow said he had an opportunity to sit down with Nancy. He recalled that they talked for about thirty minutes.

"Nancy had told me she was living in a separate bedroom from Brad, they were headed towards divorce," Tabachow said. "Nancy said their relationship was like a pendulum. Sometimes it was tolerable. Other times it was in hate mode. On the night of the party it was in hate mode."

Tabachow recalled Nancy wore a blue-green summer dress to the party. He said to his knowledge nothing was spilled on it. Tabachow said he overheard Nancy talking to Mike Hiller about Brad playing tennis the next morning.

The next day, when Tabachow heard about the fact that Nancy was missing, he joined his neighbors in searching the woods in his subdivision. One of the people he searched with was Heather Metour, the woman with whom Brad had had an affair.

"I was aware that Heather had had an affair with Brad Cooper, and Heather and Nancy had a strained relationship," Tabachow said.

On cross-examination, Tabachow was asked whether he had ever seen Brad Cooper act violently towards his wife. He hadn't.

"Nancy never said anything about being afraid of Brad Cooper?" defense attorney Robert Trenkle asked.

"That's correct," Tabachow replied.

Next on the stand was Tabachow's wife, Damia. Damia Tabachow first met Nancy at a baby shower in 2004. Their children attended the same preschool. Over the years, they developed a close friendship and Nancy eventually started opening up more and more to Damia Tabachow. Heather Metour had also told Tabachow about her affair with Brad. Tabachow knew that Nancy knew about the affair as well, but waited for her friend to broach the subject.

"She knew that Heather had told me, and she expressed that she was very upset about what had happened," Tabachow said. "She was very disappointed that this [was] how things had turned out."

At first, she said, the couple seemed to be trying to work through their differences by going to counseling, but it soon became clear to Nancy that she could not get beyond her husband's infidelity.

"She said they had been in counseling, and that she recently found out there had been additional affairs," Tabachow testified.

Tabachow talked on the stand about Brad's financial control of his wife and how he put her on an allowance and followed her to the gas station to put gas in her car so she couldn't get cash from the credit card. Tabachow said the final straw was when Brad found out he would have to pay Nancy alimony and child support.

"He wouldn't agree to the separation agreement because he didn't want to pay the money," Tabachow said on the stand.

The last time Tabachow saw Nancy alive was at the party at the Duncans' house. Like her husband, she noticed the couple had been fighting.

"I asked her how things were going with Brad and she said they were back in hate mode," Tabachow said.

The next day, Diana Duncan called Tabachow to say that Nancy was missing. Tabachow came to the neighborhood and helped with the search. She remembered approaching Brad outside his home.

"I said I am sorry you're going through this," she told him.

Despite having offered those words of comfort, on cross-examination the defense attorney asked Tabachow why she hadn't reached out to Brad after his wife was found dead, why she and her husband didn't call or send him a card.

Her answer was simple: "I didn't think that anyone else would have killed Nancy."

The third friend of Nancy's to take the stand that day was Craig Duncan, Diana Duncan's now ex-husband. Duncan said he and his wife had met the Coopers when they were newlyweds, shortly after they moved from Canada to Cary. They had socialized together a great deal in those early days. They both had children around the same time, and their son, Caelen, and the Coopers' oldest daughter, Bella, became playmates. But then there was a shift in the relationship. His ex-wife had said the shift happened after Caelen accidentally broke Bella's nose while roughhousing. But he had a very different take on the situation. He said Brad had made a pass at his wife, Diana.

"He hit on her one night in the kitchen," Duncan said. The incident caused a rift between the Duncans and Brad that Craig said was never truly repaired.

But eventually, the couple continued their friendship with Nancy. She started confiding in them about the problems in her marriage, and specifically about Brad's affair with Heather Metour.

"There was a great deal of strain in her face. She was not crying, but she was nervous, anxious. I gave her a hug to comfort her," Duncan testified.

And that wasn't the only affair of Brad's that Duncan said he learned about. He said one night a group of men from the neighborhood went to a bar to play pool. Brad was invited to join them. Duncan said everyone was trying to one-up each other with their exploits, and Brad topped them all.

"Brad quite happily said he had fucked his boss's wife," Duncan testified. "We found this distasteful and did not want to hear any more."

Craig and his wife, Diana, hosted the party on July 11, 2008, the night before Nancy was reported missing. Duncan recalled Nancy and Brad fighting vociferously in the kitchen over Brad's inability to understand his daughter's needs.

"I think Brad didn't know how to interact with the kids and would get easily frustrated," Duncan said. "It was out of character for her or Brad to have a commotion like that in public."

But after Brad left the party, Duncan said Nancy went back to being her usual self, "a social butterfly" who made everyone laugh and feel comfortable in her presence.

The next day, his wife, Diana, received a call from their friend Jessica Adam that Nancy was missing. While running errands, they saw police cars and neighbors gathered in front of the Cooper home.

"Jessica was in a panic," Duncan said.

Duncan noticed that no one was talking to Brad, who was sitting alone on the front steps of his home. He decided to go over and speak to him.

"He told me the police kept asking him the same questions over and over again," Duncan said, recalling Brad's words. "He was sitting there clasping his hands. Looking forward."

"It was not a natural conversation," Duncan testified. "It was almost like a rehearsed statement."

Later that same day, Duncan had the opportunity to walk with Brad to Mike and Clea Morwick's house a few streets away to pick up Bella and Katie. Again, he said something didn't seem right to him about how Brad was acting.

"His demeanor was crouched over, shuffling his feet, a very unnatural walk," Duncan said. "You don't forget how to walk no matter what state of mind you're in."

On cross-examination, Howard Kurtz tried to discredit Craig Duncan by claiming that Duncan himself had once made a pass at Nancy, a pass that she thwarted and then talked about to her friends.

"You expressed to Nancy that you were interested in having a sexual relationship with her," Kurtz stated.

"Never," Duncan said.

"She told other people that you had hit on her, and she was repulsed by that," Kurtz responded.

"I did not," Duncan said coolly.

Kurtz also said that, according to his information, another friend had also made a pass at Nancy.

"Mike Morwick made a comment to his wife that he wanted to fuck Nancy," Kurtz said.

"The comments that Mike made were during an argument with his wife," Duncan replied, adding that the Morwicks, who were also now divorced, had had a very volatile marriage.

When Brad was arrested, Diana and Craig Duncan stood in the street and watched him being led to the police car in handcuffs.

Craig had clapped and cheered. Kurtz wanted to know how Duncan was so sure that Brad had killed his wife.

"I did not simply believe it, I knew it in my heart," Duncan said. "I knew Brad had killed Nancy when I went over and sat on the stoop with him. I knew it when I walked with him to the Morwicks."

The next witness, Donna Lopez, had never met Nancy Cooper until the night of the Duncans' party. Her husband was a colleague of Diana Duncan. Yet, when she entered the party, Nancy had greeted Lopez's family warmly and immediately wanted to know everything about her three children. The two women eventually found themselves alone outside on the deck, where Nancy confided in her about her crumbling marriage, the affairs, the financial control, and her failed plan to return to Canada with her children.

"'No, you're not going anywhere,'" Nancy said Brad had told her.

She told Lopez, a perfect stranger, intimate details about her marital problems, including the fact that Brad had had an affair with someone from his MBA program, as well as with her best friend. Lopez recalled Nancy saying that "she would babysit for her best friend while [Metour] and Brad would go out on dates."

As the night wore on, Lopez became increasingly concerned about Nancy's well-being.

"It seemed a bit like she was nervous," Lopez said after Nancy looked out the Duncans' front window multiple times to see if the lights were out in her house across the street. "I was worried for someone I didn't know," she said on the stand as she began to cry. "I knew something bad was going to happen."

JESSICA SPEAKS

Gone was the anxious housewife who by a tragic stroke of luck had been pulled into a murder investigation. More than two and a half years after Nancy's death, Jessica Adam was a confident, poised young woman who seemed totally prepared for what was about to come as she took the stand on Tuesday, March 15, 2011.

There was no doubt that Adam would be one of the star witnesses in the case, since she had not only made the initial call to police to report Nancy missing, but she was also the first person to imply to investigators that Brad might have something to do with it.

Since Nancy's death, Adam had gone down a new path, going back to school to become a nurse. While the demands of graduate school and parenting were grueling, she was surer of herself than she had ever been, and it showed in her no-nonsense demeanor on the stand. Her once long, full mane of thick black hair was now cut in a flattering layered cut just at her shoulders. Instead of the nervous answers she gave in the civil custody hearing, this time she spoke without hesitation.

Adam explained that she had met Nancy at the Triangle Academy Preschool, which Bella and Adam's son, Max, attended. The women became fast friends.

"She immediately embraced me and introduced me to a lot of her friends," Adam said.

Eventually, Adam met Brad as well, but between his work and training for his many races, Adam said she rarely saw Nancy's husband.

"She was the primary caretaker for the children and had the children with her at all times. She was a really, really good mother," Adam said, briefly smiling.

Nancy helped Adam, a novice runner, train for upcoming races. The pair had done a 5 K in November of 2007, and planned to do a half marathon in August of 2008. It was around this time that Nancy started to share her marital problems with Adam.

"I heard from Nancy herself that she had been told of an affair," Adam testified. "That it was with Heather Metour. She was very sad."

At this point, Adam said Nancy told her the marriage was over. A going-away party for her was planned, and Nancy was making arrangements to move with the girls back to Canada.

"Things had gotten increasingly tense. Brad had told Nancy

about the affair," Adam said on the stand. "Once he finally admitted it, she was clear that she wanted to move and separate."

But then something changed. Adam said Brad refused to let Nancy go. At that point, Adam said Nancy was having a hard time making ends meet. She had no visa, so she could not work. Brad was giving her an allowance that she said was not enough to live on.

"Nancy always put on a smile, but I know that she was definitely stressed out," Adam said.

The women started communicating only by cell phone because Adam said strange things were going on with Nancy's home phone.

"There was a period of time when our calls would be disconnected," Adam said. "She had concern that Brad was somehow controlling the phone."

Adam said things between the Coopers continued to deteriorate. In order to help Nancy with her finances, Adam agreed to allow Nancy to paint her living room for $250.00.

"That sounds great. Let's do it," Nancy said to her.

One evening, Nancy was over for dinner at Adam's house with the children and got a call from Brad telling her that she had to leave because they already had plans to eat at the Morwicks' house.

"She got a call from Brad saying he was not happy she had made these plans, and that she needed to leave immediately," Adam said. "She was upset, irritated, frustrated."

Nancy left Adam's house, took the children to the Morwicks, left them with Brad, and returned to Adam's by herself for dinner with Jessica and her husband, Brett.

The week Nancy was killed, the women decided Adam would help organize Nancy's house, and that Nancy, in return, would paint another room in Adam's house for her. They spoke about the plan on Friday, July 11. Later that day, Adam went to Nancy's house and walked through the rooms, looking for ways she could help her friend organize.

That day, like every day, Adam recalled that Nancy was wearing her diamond stud earrings and her signature diamond pendant necklace. Adam said Nancy never took the necklace off for any reason—not to swim, shower, sleep, or even to go running.

"There were absolutely no times when I saw her that she didn't have it on," Adam said on the stand, reading from her original statement to police. Later in the trial it would be revealed to the jurors that the pendant Nancy never took off was found in the home during a police search, *not* on Nancy's body. She was found wearing just one diamond earring.

On that Friday, the day before Nancy disappeared, the women made plans to organize Nancy's house Sunday and to paint Adam's house Saturday morning.

"Why don't I come first thing tomorrow morning at eight o'clock and paint your dining room?" Nancy said.

"You don't have to do that. It's early. You might want to sleep in," Adam told her.

"No, that will work out well. I have plans with Hannah later," Nancy said.

The next morning, Jessica and her husband, Brett, woke early and moved furniture out of their dining room in preparation for the painting. When Nancy didn't show up, Jessica called her cell phone, and then finally called the home phone.

"I asked Brad if she was there, he said no, she was out for a run with Carey [Clark]," Adam testified.

Adam said that she didn't tell Brad at that time that she had expected Nancy because she didn't want to cause more tension between the two of them. They had plans, and it was not like Nancy to change plans without calling. A short while later Brad called back.

"I immediately had goose bumps. Something felt wrong. He called to ask me if I had Carey Clark's phone number. I said: 'I'm worried, Brad.' He acknowledged and said: 'I am, too,'" Adam recalled.

Adam then contacted Hannah Prichard, and the women decided it was time to start calling hospitals. When she didn't have any luck, Adam called the police. In her call to the Cary police to report Nancy missing, Adam implied that Brad may have had something to do with her disappearance.

"About her husband. I mean if he's done something. God forbid," Adam said to the emergency dispatcher.

Adam was too upset to drive, so she had her neighbor, Mary Anderson, drive her to the Cooper home. A short time after they got there, the police arrived. Brad was not home yet. Adam walked around outside the house with a police officer. Soon, more police officers, neighbors, and friends started to show up. By the time Brad returned, there was a small crowd in front of his home, but Adam said Brad ignored everyone except for the police.

"I remember thinking it was odd that he kept his distance from everyone. He had his baseball hat pulled down," Adam said.

In the days following Nancy's disappearance, whenever Brad came to pick up Katie and Bella from Adam's home, she said he acted uncomfortable and refused to meet her eyes. She described his behavior multiple times from the stand as "avoidant."

On Monday, July 14, Krista Lister, Nancy's twin sister, was at Adam's home and Bella had fallen asleep on her aunt's lap. Adam said when Brad came to pick her up, Bella started crying and did not want to go.

"Did she want to leave Krista?" prosecutor Amy Fitzhugh asked.

"No," Adam testified through tears.

"Did she want to go with the defendant at that point?" Fitzhugh countered.

"No she didn't," Adam replied.

On cross-examination, defense attorney Howard Kurtz brought up a fight Adam had had with Mike Hiller in front of the Cooper home on the day Nancy was reported missing. He said that his tennis plans with Brad contradicted Adam's painting plans with Nancy. Adam testified she had known nothing of the tennis plans.

"He was suspect of me having plans with Nancy," Adam said.

RUNNING SCARED

The next witness for the state was Carey Clark, the woman with whom Brad had told Adam and police that he believed his wife was out running on the morning of Saturday, July 12.

Police had talked to Clark throughout the investigation, but she had kept a very low profile. She submitted an affidavit, but did not testify in the custody hearing.

"She was my friend and running partner," Clark said of Nancy, who she had been jogging with for about a year. But she quickly confirmed that the two had no plans to run on the morning of the twelfth. "We were tentatively making plans to run Sunday. She already had plans Saturday morning."

The women had planned to run on Friday morning, July 11, but Nancy had called Clark at 5:20 that morning to say that she had to take a rain check. That's when they discussed possibly running Sunday instead.

The day that Nancy disappeared, Clark's husband called her and told her the police needed to speak with her at the Cooper home. She went right away. When she got there, there was a crowd of friends and police officers gathered outside the Cooper home. That's when Clark came face-to-face with Brad.

"He looked drawn and a little panicked," Clark said. "He said: 'Nancy's not with you? You haven't seen her today?'"

Clark's testimony was the key to poking holes in Brad's assertion that Nancy went jogging that morning. It was starting to look like she may have never left home that day.

CHAPTER NINETEEN

THE TRUTH OF THE MATTER

The truth is rarely pure and never simple.
—Oscar Wilde

Patrol Officer Dan Hayes of the Cary Police Department had been the first police officer to arrive at the Cooper home on July 12, 2008. Brad was not home at the time, but Jessica Adam was there waiting for help to arrive.

"She was upset. She was very concerned. She said she didn't know where to turn, so she called us," Hayes recalled.

Hayes then tried to call Brad several times on his cell phone. Finally, he was able to get in touch with him. Hayes said Brad told him he was in the Regency Park area looking for his wife. Hayes asked Brad to return to the house, which he did. They went inside together.

"He was calling Nancy's name several times," Hayes testified about Brad and he entering the house and walking up the stairs toward the bedrooms.

Once upstairs, Hayes noticed some cleaning supplies on the bathroom sink. He also noticed that the house seemed to be in general disarray—toys, clothing, and other items were strewn around haphazardly.

Hayes testified that Brad told him that his daughter Katie had woken up early, and that when he and Nancy could not console her, he went to the grocery store to get milk. When he returned home, Brad said Nancy asked him to go back to the store and get laundry detergent. After returning a second time, he said he took Katie upstairs with him to his home office. Brad told Hayes that Nancy called up and asked if he knew where her T-shirt was. Brad said Nancy then said, "Never mind," and he heard the door close behind her and assumed she had gone running.

Brad then told the officer that he became worried when Nancy didn't come home, because she knew he had a tennis game planned for 9:30 that morning. He started calling her friends and then went out with the kids to look for her.

"I didn't get a sense that he was upset," said Hayes.

The next officer on the stand was a canine handler, Officer Jeremy Burgin. At Burgin's request, Brad had given him one of Nancy's running shoes to see if the police dog, Max, could pick up her scent. The ultimate goal was to track her scent from the front door when she left to go running, and see where it took them. But each time the trainer tried to get the dog to locate Nancy's scent from the front door, he got nothing. Burgin testified that the dog kept trying to get back inside the house instead of heading away from the house.

Up next was Cary Police Detective Adam Dismukes. Dismukes had been the first detective called to the Cooper home. He'd arrived around 3:30 that Saturday afternoon. Soon after arriving, he met Jessica Adam, who told him that she'd expected Nancy at her house early that morning. She also told the detective about Nancy and Brad's marital troubles.

Dismukes took a brief walk around the outside of the house. In the passenger seat of Nancy's car he noticed a purse, some cash, a pair of children's jeans, and a prescription for Bella. He also noticed a rubber floor mat lying in the driveway between Nancy and Brad's cars. It appeared to belong to Brad's car, the BMW sedan.

Dismukes introduced himself to Brad and told him he wanted

to have a few words with him inside the house.

"I got the impression at first that he didn't want to talk to me," Dismukes said. "He asked what we were doing to locate his wife."

Brad reluctantly agreed to go inside and speak with the detective. Immediately, Dismukes started taking note of things he felt were unusual.

"I noticed that Mr. Cooper had a Band-Aid on the middle finger of his left hand," Dismukes said.

As Dismukes passed the den with the big flat-screen television on the wall, he noticed something else that he found strange.

"The TV was on, and there was a golf match going," Dismukes said. "That struck me as odd given the nature of the call."

Detective Dismukes, along with Officer Dan Hayes, sat down with Brad at the dining room table. Brad again told Dismukes the story that would become the backbone of the case: waking at 4:00 with Katie, the two trips to the store, hearing Nancy downstairs leaving for a run.

"Mr. Cooper asked us again what we're doing to locate Nancy," Dismukes testified. "He also asked me if there were any police canines in the area."

Dismukes said Brad seemed very interested in the techniques used by canines to track people. He wanted to know if they could be used on trails and around lakes.

At the officers' request, Brad gave Detective Dismukes Nancy's cell phone, which he retrieved from the table in the front hallway, as well as her address books.

After interviewing others at the scene—including Carey Clark, who confirmed that she hadn't been running with Nancy that morning—Dismukes teamed up with Detective George Daniels, who had just arrived. Daniels, who was part of the Major Crimes Unit, would ultimately be assigned as the lead detective in the case. He told Dismukes he wanted to talk to Brad again.

"Mr. Cooper seemed a little bit annoyed" as well as weary, Dismukes recalled. Nonetheless, Brad led the detectives back inside his house to the dining room.

"Daniels pointed out that Mr. Cooper had some red markings on the back of his neck," Dismukes said. "I did see some red markings."

Brad then told the detectives the story of his morning, also backtracking and telling them about going to the Duncans' party the previous evening and how he had left early to put the kids to bed, but Nancy had stayed and arrived home sometime after midnight. He told the detectives he was asleep with the girls and that he'd heard his wife come upstairs, but that they did not speak.

They asked Brad what Nancy was probably wearing when she went jogging, even though he'd told them he hadn't actually seen her leave the house, and he said she usually wore a black jogging bra that also had a little red and white on it, a T-shirt, and running shorts.

Detective Daniels then asked Brad if they could take some pictures of the house. Brad agreed, and Detective Dismukes went to his car to get his camera.

"Mr. Cooper began to inquire as to why we needed to take pictures of his house," Dismukes said. "He made a comment about my camera that he thought I would have a more high-powered camera. It struck me as bizarre due to the nature of this being a missing person case."

On Monday, July 14, Dismukes got a call that a body had been found on Fielding Drive. He was asked to pick up Chief Pat Bazemore and take her to the hotel where Nancy's family was staying so that they could inform them about the situation. While the body had not been officially identified yet, investigators told the family they believed it was most likely Nancy.

After he dropped the chief back off at the police station, Dismukes headed to the Cooper home to meet with Detective Daniels and speak with Brad a second time. Once again, the three men found themselves sitting around the Coopers' dining room table. The detectives told Brad a body had been found on Fielding Drive.

"Mr. Cooper began to rub his forehead with his right hand, he held his head with his left hand," Dismukes said.

They again asked Brad what he thought his wife would have been wearing to run. He started to describe the black and red sports bra and then stopped in mid-sentence, Dismukes said. At that point detectives knew that Nancy had in fact been found in the black and red sports bra.

The children were in the other room watching television. Suddenly, in the middle of this rapidly unfolding tragedy, Bella wandered into the dining room looking for her father. He told her to go back in the other room and watch television.

"Mr. Cooper was holding his head and groaning, but I did not see him cry," Dismukes testified. "The groaning seemed a little strange and a little forced."

Dismukes said Brad then clutched his hair and said he didn't think Nancy ran in the area of Holly Springs Road. The detectives cautioned that they were not yet positive the body was Nancy's.

"It can't be her. It just can't be," Brad said to the police.

The next day, July 15, Dismukes said he got a call around 2:30 in the afternoon from Detective Daniels confirming that the body was Nancy Cooper. Once again, Daniels asked Dismukes to meet him at the Cooper home. By the time Dismukes arrived, Daniels had already given Brad the news.

"He (Brad) asked how do we know it was her?" Dismukes said on the stand. He told Brad that the dental records had confirmed her identity. Dismukes then asked Brad if he would sign a form allowing them to do a complete search of the home. By this point Dismukes said investigators strongly felt that Nancy may have been killed in her own home.

Brad obviously picked up on that feeling. "He commented that we already think he's a suspect," Dismukes recalled. He also told the detective that he did not understand the consent to search form. Dismukes began to read it to him. Brad then cut him off after the first paragraph. "He said he did not agree with the form and told us he wanted his lawyer."

The yellow crime scene tape went up around the Cooper home that night as patrol officers secured the property in preparation for the search that would take place as soon as a judge signed off on the warrants. Dismukes left and then came back to let Brad know that if he chose to leave his home during the search, he could not take his cars because they would be searched as well. Dismukes offered to take Brad to his lawyer's office. His job was to keep tabs on Brad.

Detective Daniels had said Brad could take a few personal items from the home for himself and the girls. While he packed, Brad told Dismukes that he did not need a ride because Scott Heider would be picking him up. Dismukes was aware that Heider was the ex-husband of Heather Metour, the woman Brad had had an affair with. Given what he knew, Dismukes considered it to be a strange arrangement for Brad to be getting a ride from Heider. When the men left the house, Dismukes, along with Detective Brisco Gasperson, was right behind them.

"We needed to make sure we followed Mr. Cooper and keep eyes on him," Dismukes said.

Heider and Brad's first stop, surprisingly, was Heather Metour's house, where they switched out the minivan Heider had been driving for a silver Honda Element. Dismukes watched Brad briefly speak to Metour. He said Brad and Metour shared a quick hug before Brad and Heider got into the car and left. Dismukes then followed the men downtown, where they parked the car and left for approximately two hours to meet with Brad's attorneys.

On Wednesday, July 16, police finally arrived at the home with signed search warrants around 4:00 in the morning. Dismukes gave the crime scene investigators from the City/County Bureau of Identification a tour of the home and background on the case as they prepared to conduct their search. After the CCBI agents finished, Cary police then also searched the house.

Prosecutor Amy Fitzhugh showed the photographs Dismukes had taken in the Cooper home on July 12 and asked him what he understood had changed since Jessica Adam had toured the house the previous day in preparation for her organization job.

One photograph depicted a large empty red vase in a nook at the base of the stairs. Adam had told police that on the day before Nancy's disappearance the vase had been filled with tall bamboo sticks. Another photograph showed the chest of drawers in the entrance hall by the front door with nothing on top of it. Adam said there had been a line of decorative duck figurines on the chest the previous day. In the photographs, the kitchen counter was clean. Yet Adam said it had been completely covered with dishes just prior to Nancy leaving for the Duncans' party. A photograph of the den showed a recliner facing the television, which Adam said had been in the kitchen the day before, facing away from the den and piled high with laundry. There was also a photograph of the top banister of the stairwell covered in clothing that had obviously been put there to dry after it had been washed. Adam said there had been no laundry on the banister the previous day.

When it was time for cross-examination, Howard Kurtz used the same photographs. After he displayed each one on the large projection screen in front of the jury, he would then disdainfully ask Dismukes the same question: "What in this photograph goes to show that a homicide was committed in this house?"

Cary police took nearly one hundred photographs on Saturday, July 12. Because at the time they didn't know what they were looking for, some of the pictures had little or no significance. Dismukes answered honestly that some of them did not have any connection to the murder. But when Kurtz showed him the photograph of the front hallway minus the bamboo in the red vase and the ornamental ducks on the side table, Dismukes replied with confidence.

"Possibly a struggle ensued there," Dismukes testified.

Kurtz pointed out that other items in the hallway were not broken and that there were no scuffs on the walls. With every subsequent photograph, he pointed out the items that were not broken.

"Nothing needs to be broken for someone to be murdered," Dismukes repeated multiple times in response to Kurtz's observations.

In the photograph of the children's bedroom, a television set on a rolling cart that Jessica Adam said had been against the wall the day before was pulled out into the middle of the room, partially blocking the doorway. Kurtz asked Dismukes what he believed this meant.

"That the TV was there to occupy the children," Dismukes

said. "It's directly in front of the doorway," he added, implying it may have even been meant to keep the children in the room by barricading their only exit.

In several of the photographs there were cleaning supplies visible. In the picture of the master bathroom, there were two bottles of cleaning solution on the sink surrounded by toiletries. In Brad's bathroom, there was a jumbo-sized container of Clorox wipes. Kurtz asked Dismukes what he made of this.

"The cleaning supplies being out could have been used to clean up something," Dismukes said. "Could have been body fluids, could have been blood."

There were several photographs of Nancy Cooper's bedroom. There were packing boxes stacked high against one wall. The bed was unmade and laundry baskets full of clothing, including the green dress she wore to the party, sat at the foot of the bed. Kurtz asked him the significance of the photo, and Dismukes told him that any of the items in the bedroom could have been used to suffocate Nancy.

"Could have been a pillow, could have been one of those sheets, could have been a clothing article," Dismukes testified.

Kurtz then started to get sarcastic and asked Dismukes if every home that had bedding, or a bathroom where someone could clean up after committing a crime, had the potential to be the scene of a homicide.

Kurtz showed the jury photographs of the garage, which Dismukes said had been significantly cleared since Jessica Adam saw it on the evening of Friday, July 11. He asked Dismukes what he thought this meant.

"On July 12 a car could fit in there. That told me something happened that a car needed to be put in there," Dismukes said on the stand.

There were multiple photographs of Brad and Nancy's cars—her BMW SUV and his BMW sedan, parked side by side in the driveway. One picture was a close-up of Brad's license plate that looked slightly askew and tilted down on the right lower corner.

Dismukes said a bolt was missing from Brad's plate. Kurtz asked him what conclusion he had drawn from this.

"It is a possibility he removed it," Dismukes said, "so as not to be identified, at least his vehicle."

Kurtz was clearly trying to make it look like the Cary police had jumped to erroneous conclusions based on slim circumstantial evidence. Kurtz asked Dismukes what he believed had happened in the house.

"I believe Nancy Cooper came home in early morning hours of July 12, and Mr. Cooper murdered her," Detective Dismukes said calmly. It was the first time anyone from the Cary Police Department had ever publicly called Brad a murderer. He went on to say that he thought Brad had put Nancy's body in his car and then drove the body to Fielding Drive and dumped her on the side of the road.

Kurtz's major attack involved whether or not Dismukes had followed up on the more than a dozen people who'd said they thought they'd seen Nancy jogging on the morning of July 12.

Dismukes said that, after gathering leads from all of the officers involved in the investigation, he followed up on every possible sighting of Nancy but was not able to confirm a single one. He said most of the people were well-meaning citizens who had seen the posters with Nancy's face on it during the search and only made a connection after the fact.

"They thought they saw her jogging. It was someone who resembled Miss Cooper, but they couldn't say for sure it was Nancy Cooper," Dismukes replied to Kurtz's inquiry.

"Do you believe you did your best to leave no stone unturned?" Kurtz asked.

"Yes I do," Dismukes responded.

KRISTA

Krista Lister had come from Vancouver to North Carolina to attend the trial. She had left the girls back home in the care of her husband,

Jim, who was getting help from his family. Krista sat in the front row of the courtroom every day, right behind the prosecutor's table, next to her mother. She was just a few feet away from the jury box and served as a living reminder of the victim—the spitting image of Nancy sitting in the courtroom in judgment, waiting for her twin sister's murder to be avenged.

Krista would also eventually be a witness for the state, but for now, she was just a member of the stoic grieving family who sat attentively and listened to the testimony. During some moments, it seemed like the weight of it all was too heavy for Krista. She would bow her head and let her long brown hair cascade down, obscuring her face.

During breaks, she and her family gathered in the courthouse restaurant to share a coffee, a snack, and sometimes even brief laughter, despite the heaviness that was swirling around them. Krista shared photographs of the two growing girls, Bella and Katie, just like any other proud mother. But clearly, she was not like other mothers. She was a woman who had become an instant mother on the heels of tragedy in a way that no one would want to enter parenthood.

One morning after a break, Nancy's family edged into the crowded elevator that would take them back to the courtroom. As they exited, a man in the corner of the elevator had obviously recognized them from the news reports. "God bless you," he said. For the first time that day, Krista smiled.

ON TAPE

It started to become clear that both the prosecutors and the defense attorneys intended to use the surveillance video of Brad's two trips to the grocery store on July 12 to support their separate theories of the case.

On Detective Dismukes's third day on the stand, defense attorneys questioned him about a 6:40 A.M. phone call that Brad received on his cell phone from his home. Brad had said that phone call came from Nancy as he was making his second journey to the Harris Teeter grocery store that morning about two miles from their home. Cell phone records showed that the call lasted thirty-eight seconds. Brad said Nancy was asking him to get Naked Green Juice, which he said was a favorite of Bella's, as well as the laundry detergent he had originally set out for. Defense attorney Howard Kurtz asserted that this was proof that Nancy was still alive at this time.

Kurtz said in his opening statement that the state would argue that Brad, an expert in Internet phone technology at Cisco Systems, was able to set up an automated call from his home in order to give himself an alibi. That possibility had already been stated by investigators in a recent search warrant that said that Brad Cooper had the technology to make this type of automated call happen. But Kurtz refuted this, saying Brad *did not* have this technology in his home and that there was no evidence that an automated call took place.

Kurtz then asked Dismukes if he had considered any other suspects during his investigation.

"We conducted several interviews, but no other suspects were developed," he testified.

"Do you recall doing two interviews with John Pearson?" Kurtz asked.

"Yes," Dismukes replied in reference to the man Kurtz had said in his opening statement that Nancy had had a one-night stand with in 2005.

"And did his stories change substantially?"

At this point the state objected to this line of questioning, and Judge Paul Gessner sent the jury out again so the lawyers could hash out the issue. Gessner was clearly fed up with the defense attorneys going down a road that not only involved hearsay, but a serious potential for libeling a man who had not been charged with a crime, let alone investigated for one.

"If you want to call Mr. Pearson, then you can call him and

have him," Gessner said. "We've wasted a lot of time arguing these," he added. "We have wasted a phenomenal amount of time chasing these rabbits. I'm tired of it. I'm watching the jury get tired of it and this needs to stop!"

MEDICAL EXAMINER

In many murder cases the medical examiner provides the smoking gun that solves the mystery not only of how someone died, but also of who the killer was. But in Nancy Cooper's case, the autopsy left as many questions as answers, mainly because her body was already so badly decomposed and infested with bugs when it was found.

The retired chief medical examiner for the state, Dr. John Butts, took the stand on Friday, March 14, 2011. He described Nancy as a 5'10", 132-pound woman who'd been found wearing just a jogging bra that was pulled up over her breasts and a single diamond stud earring. He said that she was positively identified with the help of her dental records.

As Butts showed the autopsy photos in court, Brad Cooper kept his head down. He looked like he was furiously taking notes. He would occasionally draw his attorneys' attention to something he had written down on his pad or even rip off a piece of paper with writing on it and hand it to them.

Butts explained in his testimony, as he had in his autopsy report, that Nancy's right back hyoid bone (found just above the Adam's apple in the neck) was fractured, indicating that she had likely died from asphyxiation by strangulation. There were also three marks on her neck that Butts said were likely a result of manual strangulation. He said her neck was clearly pressed, but there was no sign of a ligature mark.

Because her body had been lying for at least three days in a muddy area through periods of heavy rain, the decomposition made it hard, if not impossible, to tell if there were other injuries or trauma to the body. He said it appeared that she had died on or about July 12. Butts also testified that there were no obvious signs of sexual assault.

Butts said there was nothing but caffeine and a small piece of onion in her system at the time of death. Defense attorneys said Nancy often ran after drinking just coffee. But Butts pointed out that the caffeine could have been from even earlier, since it lingers in the body. No one saw Nancy drinking caffeine at the party, but she was seen eating avocado salad with onion in it, as well as a piece of lemon cake and some chips. As for the presence of just a small piece of onion and nothing else, prosecutors asked if this might be because she had vomited up the contents of her stomach when she was strangled. Butts said he didn't know for sure, but couldn't rule out that possibility.

EVIDENCE AT THE SCENE

Next on the stand was Agent Christopher Hill with the City/County Bureau of Identification. Hill was tasked with documenting the scene where Nancy's body was found on the evening of July 14, 2008, off of Fielding Drive. He first took video and photographs of the area in and around where Nancy was found lying facedown in a shallow puddle of water next to an undeveloped cul-de-sac.

Hill described how there were some shoe impressions and multiple tire tracks, and although they photographed and measured everything they found, the treads from both the tires and the shoes were impossible to read because the rain had turned them into a muddy mess. Plus, the shoe prints were more than likely made by the first emergency responders on the scene who'd tended to Nancy prior to the arrival of law enforcement. As a precaution, the shoes of all of the emergency responders were collected in case they needed to be used to eliminate prints at a later date.

Hill did measure the distance between two of the tire tracks, which defense attorney Robert Trenkle pointed out was smaller than the distance between the tires on Brad's car, but the crime scene investigator added that he wasn't even sure the two tracks came from the same car because there were so many tracks in close proximity.

Two pieces of wire and a cigarette butt were also found near the body and collected, but Hill said this was clearly an area under construction, and it looked like a fair amount of traffic had been in and out of the cul-de-sac in preparation for the homes they were getting ready to build there.

"It is possible they were used to bind Miss Cooper's arms," defense attorney Robert Trenkle stated.

But Hill said the wires were picked up just to be on the safe side, even though he didn't believe they actually had anything to do with the case. He said they were faded in such a way by the sun that indicated they had been there for some time.

When the evidence turned to the video of the scene, Donna Rentz, Nancy's mother, and Krista Lister, Nancy's sister, left the courtroom, not wanting to see the watery grave where Nancy's body was discarded like a piece of trash. Brad looked down at the table in front of him instead of viewing the video that was playing just a few feet to his left on a large white screen for the jury to see.

When it came time to view the photographs of the scene, jurors watched intently for a few minutes until one woman became visibly overcome with emotion. Judge Gessner said he decided to take a break to allow her to compose herself. She told the sheriff's deputy in the courtroom that she thought she might throw up at the sight of Nancy's decomposing body. After receiving a note from the jury about their concerns, Gessner told attorneys that from this point on in the trial the jurors would need fair warning when they were about to see graphic photos.

A MOTHER'S LOSS

Nancy's mother, Donna Rentz, was terrified to take the stand in the trial. She was sure that defense attorney Howard Kurtz would push her into a corner, confuse her, and make her break down.

But everyone around her told her that it would not look good to the jury for the defense attorney to beat up on the mother of the dead woman. Still, in the late afternoon of Monday, March 21, she sat nervously in the courtroom waiting for prosecutor Howard Cummings to call her name after Hill was finished on the stand.

With her usual trademark Canadian politeness, Donna answered Cummings's questions with a great deal of care. She admitted that at first she had been very fond of Brad and had immediately welcomed him into their large, loving family. But she said trouble in the marriage started early when Nancy returned home to Canada in December 2001 and told them that things were not good. She had no car, no visa that allowed her to work, and she said that Brad spent all of his time at the office. He then came to Canada and convinced Nancy to go back with him to North Carolina and give the marriage another shot.

Donna testified that things started to go bad again after Nancy and Brad had children.

"Nancy was expressing ongoing concerns about Brad's lack of participation in family life," Donna said.

Nancy was also growing more concerned about her husband's faithfulness. After he returned from a trip to Europe, Nancy told her parents Brad was a changed man and kept talking about moving the family to France. Then she began hearing rumors that he had had an affair with her best friend at the time, Heather Metour.

"Brad was continuing to deny that he had a relationship with Heather, [even though] Heather had told Nancy she had had an affair with Brad. Brad had convinced her that he had not," Donna testified.

It was around that time that Donna and her husband Garry traveled to North Carolina to attend Brad's graduation from the MBA program at North Carolina State University. The night before the graduation, the family was making a meal together in Nancy and Brad's kitchen, as they often did, when the discussion turned to what Metour had said to Nancy about Brad.

"He said, 'I'm going to sue the bitch,'" Donna recalled. "We said, 'Go for it Brad.' He should sue her, Heather Metour. She was hurting his reputation."

Donna said her next memory of that visit to North Carolina involved Brad's graduation ceremony. They were in the auditorium where the event was being held, and Nancy got up to get the girls some treats. Moments after she left, Brad crossed the stage to get his diploma. In the distance, Donna heard her daughter cheering for her husband.

"We heard Nancy yell, 'Way to go Brad!' above everybody else," Donna said choking back tears on the stand.

But Nancy's affection for her husband didn't last. Donna said on New Year's Eve their daughter called them and said Brad had finally owned up to the affair with Metour.

"He finally admitted it. He said it was a one night stand. He said he phoned [Metour] the next day and told her it was a mistake and it would never happen again," Donna said. But she said Nancy and Brad went to counseling, and that was when Brad admitted that not only had he had the affair with Metour, that he loved her, and that it had been going on for years.

At that point, Nancy made it clear to her parents that the marriage was over and that she was making plans to get a divorce and return with the girls to Canada.

In February of 2008, when Garry and Donna were on a cruise to China, Donna said they got a frantic call from Nancy.

"She was totally distraught. She said to us that Brad was acting crazy," Rentz said. "He had cut her off from their banking sources. He had cut off all her credit cards, and she said he had cut off the water." Donna said her daughter was literally trapped. "She had no money, no access to money, no access to credit, no access to banking," she said. "She couldn't pay that water bill."

They were very concerned and upset, but Donna said neither she nor her husband really believed that Brad was dangerous. Donna didn't even have the heart to believe Brad would intentionally have the water turned off because she knew he loved his daughters and cared about their well-being.

"The very last question her father asked her on that telephone call was whether or not she was afraid for her life. She said no," Donna said letting the last word of her sentence quietly trail off.

Nancy's parents lent her money to pay for divorce attorney Alice Stubbs. Nancy told them she would repay them as soon as the house sold. Donna said there were strange negotiations going on—that Brad at one point told Nancy he wanted her out immediately, then he said he wanted to spend the summer with the girls and then he never wanted to see any of them again. Donna said he even suggested at one point that they each take one child. But by mid-April, Donna said all bets were off after Nancy told her mother Brad had gotten hold of the proposed separation agreement and realized he would have to pay alimony and child support. He would not let her leave.

As Nancy struggled with Brad over her desire to return to Canada with the girls, the Rentz family decided to take a vacation together to help cheer her up. Donna remembered the vacation as a joyous time where they all shared stories, sang songs, and tried to keep Nancy in good spirits. Donna recalled, as other witnesses had, that Nancy *always* wore her diamond pendant necklace in and out of the water, twenty-four hours a day on that trip. Donna said she and her husband paid all of Nancy's expenses on the vacation including putting gas in her car.

"Her financial situation was dismal," Donna said.

When it came time for the Rentzes to fly back from Charlotte to Canada, Nancy and her mother had a tearful good-bye in the airport, one that Donna could not talk about without completely dissolving into tears.

"It was time to go to the departure gate. I had Nancy in my arms. She was sobbing and she said, 'Mom, I just want to come home.' And I couldn't take her with us because Brad had the passports," Donna said, barely getting the words out in the courtroom.

That moment in the Charlotte airport was the last time Donna and Garry Rentz would ever see their daughter alive. On July 12, 2008, just about a week later, Garry got a call from his daughter Krista.

"Garry told me that Nancy had not returned from her morning

run and was missing," Donna recalled as her husband relayed a message he had received on his phone from Krista while the Rentzes were attending the funeral of a friend. "He told me that—we were walking out, and he turned to me and said, 'Donna, this story is not going to have a happy ending.'"

Donna testified that she and her husband quickly made arrangements to head to North Carolina to participate as much as they could in the search for their daughter. They never heard from their son-in-law at any point about Nancy's disappearance, or even in the aftermath of her body being found. It wasn't until Donna saw him at the vigil at the Lutheran Resurrection Church on Tuesday morning, July 15, that she confronted her newfound fears about Brad.

"I just didn't get it," Donna testified. "He didn't even look at me. This is a man I loved. He's my daughter's husband, and the father of my grandchildren," she said with sadness in her voice. "I couldn't understand. I walked across the circle, put my arms out."

Donna reached out to embrace Brad. She said he awkwardly accepted her embrace, but looked down beneath the brim of his baseball hat the entire time. She maneuvered to get a look at his eyes.

"I knew in my heart that he had murdered my daughter," Donna said without reservation.

The next morning, March 22, 2011, Donna looked frightened as she sat in the witness box again.

But surprisingly, Howard Kurtz stood up and told the judge that the defense had decided not to ask Donna any questions. Suddenly, it looked as if a weight had been lifted off Donna's shoulders. She had been hunched over, but she now sat up straight and looked in the judge's direction to make sure she understood him correctly. He looked at her directly and said, "The witness is excused." Donna practically leapt out of the box, lest someone change his mind, and headed back to her seat with her family in the audience.

CHAIN OF EVIDENCE

Thomas Como, an agent with the City/County Bureau of Identification, testified that he tested multiple items and surfaces in the house, but detected no blood. This included spots on Nancy's bed, a streak on the garage floor, and surfaces in the bathrooms and kitchen.

"No blood was found?" Robert Trenkle asked.

"No blood was found," Como replied.

Como also confiscated several pieces of potential evidence from the Cooper home, including some men's sneakers that were covered in mud; a pair of women's high heels, also covered in mud; a pink living room rug; some of Nancy Cooper's running clothes; seat covers to the BMW sedan, found in the garage; and a white Nike shirt belonging to Brad that contained three small rust stains near the collar, as well as some light tears in the chest area.

While videotaping and photographing the inside of the home, Como noticed there were stuffed animals in the sink of an upstairs bathroom that appeared to have been washed, which he deemed "peculiar." He also took soil samples from the rug and beneath the shoe rack in the laundry room.

Agent Michael Galloway of the City/County Bureau of Identification also examined Brad's BMW. Galloway said he noticed some reddish brown material on the outside of the car near the driver's door handle. He tested the car for blood, and the test came back negative. He also noticed vacuum cleaner streaks in the back of the trunk but did not smell an odor of gas, which Brad had said was the reason he'd cleaned the trunk. He did find a fiber attached to the lid of the trunk as well as one on the wheel well and some grass inside the car.

CSI

On Wednesday, March 23, members of the State Bureau of Investigation took the stand to talk about their analysis of evidence collected from Nancy Cooper's body and the Cooper home.

Agent Ivy McMillan analyzed the scrapings from beneath Nancy's fingernails.

"Scrapings from the left and right hand gave chemical indications for the presence of blood," McMillan testified. But, she said, no DNA analysis was possible due to the environmental conditions—extreme heat and rain—and the decomposition of the body.

She was also responsible for examining the rape kit that was done on Nancy's body.

"The examination of the vaginal swab failed to reveal the presence of semen," McMillan testified. "I did not find any evidence that indicated a sexual assault."

McMillan said no blood or DNA was found on the sports bra Nancy was wearing when she was found. She also tested the pink oval rug from the Cooper home, a pillowcase, and a child's nightgown and found no blood or bodily fluids on any of them.

Other agents testified that nothing was found in Brad's trunk—the trunk investigators implied had been used to transport the body. A fiber attached to the lid of the trunk turned out not to be a human hair as originally thought, but was actually a fiber from some material in the floor of the trunk.

In short, none of the physical evidence could be linked to Brad Cooper.

CYBER INVESTIGATION

Cary police officers took the stand that Wednesday afternoon. Detective Jason Ice had seized Brad Cooper's computers as part of the search of the home on July 16. On cross-examination, Howard

Kurtz tried to expose Ice's lack of knowledge about computers to assert that he was not in fact a computer expert—a contention that Kurtz had been voicing all along, that people who weren't experts had examined the computers, perhaps improperly.

Brad's Cisco laptop was not powered down when it was confiscated. It was left on for twenty-seven hours after it was taken from the Cooper home. This was a fact that would later play a major role in the defense team's strategy.

RED FLAGS

Detective Jim Young took the stand midday Thursday, March 24. He was called to the Cooper home on the evening of July 12, 2008, and asked to locate a piece of clothing for the canine officer to help track Nancy's scent. Young asked Brad Cooper for the dress Nancy had worn the night before.

"Brad advised that Nancy had worn a blue summer dress that was knee-length with thin straps across her shoulders," Young testified.

He said he and Brad then proceeded to search the house for the blue dress. Dismukes saw the green dress with the cap sleeves and black design in a laundry basket in Nancy's room, but didn't consider it as a possibility since Brad had described the dress so differently.

"I asked Brad Cooper, 'Are you sure about the color of the dress?'" Young said. "He said he was quite sure."

When their search came up empty, Brad left the house for a few minutes and came back with Diana and Craig Duncan. He said that Diana Duncan had told him the dress was in fact black. So they began searching for a black dress. But earlier, Duncan had testified that it was *Brad* who had suggested to her that the dress was black, not the other way around.

"Brad appeared to be getting frustrated with this search for the dress," Young said.

The next day, during an interview with police, Young said Brad jumped up from the dining room table and told them he had found the dress. He went upstairs to retrieve it.

"Brad stated that he located the green dress," Young said. "It took me aback because we had been looking for a blue or black summer dress the night before." Now it was *green?*

"He provided it to us and advised that it had been washed the previous day," Young said.

Detective Young's second interaction with Brad occurred on Sunday, July 13, when he and lead detective George Daniels went to the Cooper home to give him an update on the case.

"Brad advised they were trying to reconcile after [his] one night of being unfaithful with her friend Heather," Young said. "In the past two months things had improved between he and Nancy, and she was not going to proceed with the divorce."

The detectives asked Brad to walk them through the events in the early morning hours of July 12 leading up to Nancy's disappearance. Brad methodically told the same story again. He spoke about Katie waking early, about trying to comfort her to no avail with water. He said Nancy was awoken by the crying and got up to do laundry.

"He told us that Bella was asleep at this time," Young said.

Brad told the officers about his two trips to the grocery store, and how he took Katie upstairs to his home office, then heard Nancy leaving for a run, but didn't see her before she left.

Daniels then asked him how he was able to provide police with a clothing description of what Nancy was wearing running if he hadn't seen her before she left.

"Brad stated that he had guessed at her favorite tops when he provided the clothing description," Young recalled.

Brad told the officers that his older daughter, Bella, awoke at 8:30. When Nancy still had not returned by 9:00, he said he canceled his tennis game with Mike Hiller, then spent the next five or six hours or so cleaning the house.

"He did laundry, put dishes away, scrubbed floors, vacuumed, picked up around the house," Young testified. This directly contradicted the responding officers' observations that the house had been messy when they arrived.

Brad told the detectives about searching for his wife in the late afternoon of July 12—that he searched the areas in their neighborhood where she ran. He told the officers he was "hoping to catch her."

The officers then returned to the state of the Cooper marriage. He told them they had tried counseling, but once he admitted to the affair with Heather Metour, things continued to go downhill.

"Brad told us that Nancy desired to return to Canada to be closer to her sister in Toronto. Brad objected to this because he wanted to be close to Bella and Katie," Young said.

But Brad told the detectives that his wife had also caused problems in the marriage.

"After Nancy learned about the affair, she spent $40,000 to get even," Brad told them. Brad said $10,000 of that money was spent on a painting of a bear in the couple's living room. He called her a "shopaholic" who could spend three thousand dollars in one day. That's why he said he had put her on a three-hundred-dollar-a-week allowance.

Brad also said his wife had a drinking problem and that he'd suggested she go to Alcoholics Anonymous and try to stop drinking for at least thirty days.

"Nancy drank heavily to moderately in the past six to eight months," Young recalled Brad telling them.

Brad said he often stayed home with the kids in the evening so that Nancy could go out with her friends. He commented to the police that "there was always someone's birthday to celebrate."

He said Nancy also accused him of having affairs that he hadn't had, like once when he went on a trip to Europe with his MBA program. While he admitted to having sex one time with Heather Metour, "Brad denied to us that he had an affair with anyone in the MBA program," Young testified.

There was also the allegation of Brad having an affair with his former boss's wife. Brad said this did happen, but back in Canada, before he ever met Nancy.

Brad told detectives that he and Nancy had split up the passports to prevent one of them from taking the girls to Canada. He said one was at his office at Cisco, and one was in the home.

He said that when Nancy and the girls went on vacation with her family, he had worked fifteen to sixteen hours a day to catch up. Prior to the trip, he said he had been working just eight hours a day so he could spend more time with the girls. So when Nancy came home from her trip, he admitted there was no food, and she was upset with him for not cleaning the house.

On July 14, 2008, Young and Daniels spoke with Brad again at his home. As far as they were concerned, they were still investigating a missing person case. Nancy Cooper, they surmised, could easily have left of her own volition, and for all they knew, could be at a shelter for domestic violence victims.

They asked him to again go through his actions on the morning of July 12. Brad told basically the same story, but this time he added some new details, specifying that Katie had screamed for about ten to fifteen minutes before he got up with her at 4:00 A.M., and that when he got up, Nancy came out of her room and met them in the hallway. Previously, Brad had talked only about the three of them being in the kitchen together.

Immediately, something didn't seem right to Young about the story. He shared his concern with Detective Daniels off to the side when Brad went to take a phone call.

"I had a red flag that one child was crying," Young said, adding that it was loud enough to wake Nancy, who was sleeping down the hall. "However the older child, Bella, was not awakened by the ten to fifteen minutes of crying?"

Another red flag for Young was the fact that two pairs of Nancy's running shoes were found in the home in the pantry near the garage. Brad described one pair, a weathered pink pair of Asics as her "old shoes," and a blue and white pair of Saucony sneakers were her "new shoes." For Young, this didn't make sense if Nancy had really gone running; what was she wearing on her feet if both pairs of sneakers were at the house?

"The pair that Nancy would have worn to go running was not

mentioned," Young said.

As their suspicions grew, Brad appeared to become more agitated with the detectives' questions. Finally, Detective Daniels just came right out and asked him if he knew where Nancy was. Brad told them he didn't.

ALL IN THE DETAILS

Detective Jim Young testified again on Friday, March 25, and then again on Monday, March 28.

He continued to point out inconsistencies in Brad's story. For example, Brad had told police that he was helping Nancy with the children Friday morning, July 11, 2008, and that's why he was late for work. He said he left the house for his office around 10:00 that morning. But a receipt from Lowe's showed him buying a drop cloth at 9:30 that morning. The drop cloth was found in the garage at the Cooper home by police. Defense attorneys said he bought it for Nancy to use as she painted Jessica Adam's home, but Adam and members of Nancy's family had testified that Nancy never used a drop cloth when she painted.

Phone records also showed that Nancy tried three times to call her husband on July 11—one call went to voice mail, and two calls were unanswered. The records showed that Brad and Nancy didn't actually connect by phone until 2:30 that afternoon.

But Detective Young also admitted that he had accidentally erased the history from Nancy's AT&T phone, making it harder to isolate the exact call history. Young said he was simply following the instructions of an AT&T representative who was trying to walk him through accessing the password-protected phone. When he entered the incorrect password, he said he accidentally erased the information on the phone. Defense attorneys said this information could have helped them find the real killer. Once again, Kurtz used this as an example of what he saw as a bumbling investigation by Cary police.

On cross-examination, Kurtz tried to prove that Young, along with the rest of the Cary police force, never considered other suspects, thereby unfairly targeting Brad. Young adamantly stated that he was investigating a missing person case, and that he did not even consider suspects until the case became a homicide.

"Brad Cooper was identified as a suspect on July 14 after Nancy Cooper's body was found," Young testified.

Kurtz kept at him, badgering him, trying to get him to admit that no other suspects were ever even on the investigators' radar. But Young wouldn't budge, saying that based on the evidence they amassed the only conclusion anyone could come to was that Brad was *the* suspect.

"Brad Cooper is the suspect regarding the homicide of Nancy Cooper," Young said.

Young also pointed out several things about Brad's appearance in the surveillance video at the grocery store on the morning of July 12, 2008. In his first trip to the grocery store, Brad was wearing sneakers. In the second trip, just sixteen minutes later, he was wearing sandals. Young said the police never recovered the sneakers Brad wore on the first trip to the store. Young also pointed out that on the first trip Brad made a motion as if he was "wiping sweat from his brow" and then rubbed his hand on the right leg of his jeans.

Detective Young's testimony continued into Tuesday, March 29, when he talked about how investigators had confiscated several pairs of Brad's shoes from the Cooper home on October 29, shortly after Brad was arrested. The shoes were tested against soil samples found in the area where Nancy's body was discarded. But again, investigators never did find *the* pair of shoes they were looking for—the sneakers Brad was wearing in the first surveillance video.

Several items that *were* located by police included jewelry from a drawer in the guest room. The jewelry belonged to Nancy, yet it was in the room where Brad had been sleeping. By the time the police searched the home in October, Brad had moved back into the master bedroom, and his mother was occupying the guest room where the jewelry was located. The list included a pin, two necklaces, three rings, and a strand of pearls. One of the necklaces was the diamond pendant that friends and family said Nancy wore twenty-four hours a day and never took off for any reason. This bolstered the state's theory that Brad had taken the necklace off his dead wife's body.

On Wednesday, March 30, the cross-examination continued. This time, Howard Kurtz went after the fact that Young had erased Nancy's cell phone data during his attempt to retrieve it. He came close to implying the act was deliberate, but Young maintained it was an accident.

Kurtz also grilled Young about the two pairs of Nancy's sneakers that police had found in the first search of the Cooper home. Young had said it seemed odd to him because she had supposedly gone for a run, yet both her new sneakers and her old sneakers were found in the house. But on this day, Kurtz produced a photograph in court of Nancy running in a 5 K with Jessica Adam in the fall of 2007. She was wearing a pair of sneakers that did not appear to match either of the pairs that police found. In the photograph, she was wearing a pair of Saucony 3D Grid Hurricane running shoes purchased from the local Athlete's Foot store in September 2006. Investigators never located these particular shoes. Kurtz implied that it was possible that Nancy had been wearing the sneakers from the photograph when she allegedly went for a run on July 12, 2008. In the photo, she was also wearing a pair of red and black running shorts that Kurtz said matched the jogging bra she was found wearing near Fielding Drive. He questioned Young as to whether the shorts had ever been looked for or located in the Cooper home. Young said no.

This wasn't the only photograph of Nancy shown in court that day. Prosecutors also showed a picture of Nancy in the green dress she had worn to the party at the Duncans' the night before she was reported missing. In the photograph, she was also wearing the diamond pendant. Prosecutor Boz Zellinger said the picture was taken about a week before Nancy disappeared. Nancy Cooper, a woman with a reputation for bawdy, sarcastic humor, had a big smile on her face and was flashing her middle finger directly at the camera. The photograph was put up on the large white screen just a few feet from where Brad sat in the courtroom. For a moment, even Detective Young, who had sat solemnly in the witness chair for five days, cracked a small smile. It looked as if a larger-than-life Nancy was giving her husband the finger one last time.

CHAPTER TWENTY

THE NITTY GRITTY

Patience is the companion of wisdom.
—SAINT AUGUSTINE

When Hannah Prichard took the stand on the morning of Thursday, March 31, everyone was hoping the tide was beginning to turn in the trial. After days of tedious back-and-forth between the attorneys and Detective Jim Young, a civilian was finally taking the stand. The sentiment in the community was that the case against Brad Cooper was entirely circumstantial at this point. There were whispers, even from those who believed he was guilty, that he might walk. So far there had been no concrete physical evidence connecting him to the crime, just a lot of people talking about how bad the Cooper marriage was. *We get it already; show us the evidence*, people were saying.

Prichard looked more like a librarian—albeit a sexy librarian—than the sassy, bubbly blonde who, as one of Nancy's best friends, had taken the lead during the custody case. Her hair was shorter and pulled back into a conservative ponytail, and she wore minimal makeup, a button-down shirt and a cardigan.

Prichard had met Nancy at the gym in April of 2007, and the two women became fast friends, as they had children around the same age. Shortly after they met, Nancy confided to Prichard about her husband's affair with Heather Metour.

"She wasn't happy, she didn't know what she was going to do," Prichard said. "Brad was not admitting it."

After a brief stint in counseling, Prichard said Nancy was determined to get divorced and move with her children back to Canada.

"She was done, and those were her exact words," Prichard testified.

But Prichard said things really started to go downhill after Nancy hired a lawyer—that Brad became more aggressive about spending time with the children. On one occasion, Prichard said Nancy showed her the note she had found under the keyboard of Brad's computer that detailed the girls' likes and dislikes, and the list of "to do" items involving insurance, bank accounts, and wills.

"She found both of the notes very disturbing and during this time, we both believed, based on his behavior that Brad was suicidal," Prichard said on the stand. She reiterated how Nancy would lock her important documents in her car and would only talk on her cell phone because she was sure Brad was somehow monitoring the home phone. She even believed he was monitoring her e-mail communications.

"She probably told me that she hated Brad more times than I could count," Prichard testified.

On Friday, July 11, 2008, Prichard and Nancy went to Prichard's neighborhood pool together with their children and had lunch and swam. They were joined by their friend Susan Crook.

"She was teaching Bella to swim," Prichard said, her voice cracking under the weight of her last memory of her dead friend. The women made plans to go to the pool again the next day and talked that night on the phone before the neighborhood party to confirm.

When Prichard hadn't heard from Nancy Saturday morning as expected, she called the Cooper home. Brad told her he thought Nancy was probably running with Carey Clark. Around 1:00, Brad called Prichard back looking for Carey's number.

"I was very worried and had been panicked since one," Prichard said. She then called Jessica Adam and both women shared their fears that they were worried Brad had done something to Nancy.

While Adam called hospitals to see if Nancy was there, Prichard called Susan Crook to come over. Eventually, the women went to the Cooper house. A crowd began to gather outside the home. Brad finally returned and spoke only to police, not to his neighbors and friends. At one point, in the early evening, Prichard noticed Brad drinking a beer in the driveway. She decided to approach him.

"He was very, very, very pale and kind of swaying around. I told him he needed to get some sleep," Prichard said. She added that he was "just not with it."

On Sunday, Prichard came over to help Brad with the children after she spoke to him on the phone and he asked for her help.

"Bella heard me and started calling for Nancy," she said with tears beginning to form in the corners of her eyes.

That night, she recalled, Brad called her again to see if she had heard anything new. He asked her to call Captain Mike Williams of the Cary Police Department and see if there were any new developments. Prichard told him that he had a police officer stationed outside his house, and Brad should just ask him.

"I thought it was strange," Prichard said on the stand. "If anyone could get information fast, it would be him."

Brad also told Prichard that night on the phone that he was tired of police asking him the same questions over and over.

Police called Prichard on July 14 to inform her that a body had been found, and then again on July 15 when it was identified as Nancy. She was told what Nancy was wearing, and what she was not wearing. Prichard told police at that time that Nancy *always* wore her diamond pendant necklace. Because Nancy was not wearing it when her body was found, Prichard assumed the killer must have taken it.

On cross-examination Howard Kurtz grilled Prichard about an e-mail she had sent to another friend, Jennifer Fetterolf, asking her for any pictures she had of Nancy between October of 2007 and July of 2008 "wearing the necklace." Kurtz implied that Prichard was trying to "exclude" any photographs where Nancy was not wearing the necklace because they did not support her contention that Nancy always wore the necklace. Prichard said this was not the case at all; she simply wanted pictures where Nancy was facing the camera and the necklace was "visible."

THE NEIGHBOR

Susan Baughman had been Nancy's neighbor for years. While they didn't socialize much, Baughman often talked to Nancy and the girls while she was walking her dog, Ginger. She had chatted with Nancy enough in the months prior to her death to know that there were marital problems, and she had been invited to Nancy's going-away party. When Baughman saw Nancy shortly after the party, she was surprised that Nancy was still in North Carolina.

"She said Brad had the girls' passports, and she said she wouldn't leave without the girls, and it was all about money," Baughman said. "I asked her if Brad would do anything to the children. She said no, Brad was a good father."

But it wasn't what she knew about the Coopers' relationship that landed her as a witness in the case, it was what she *saw* on the morning of Saturday, July 12. Baughman said she went out to walk Ginger at about 6:00 that morning and didn't notice anything unusual at the Cooper home. But on her way back down the street, however, at around 6:45, she noticed that the Coopers' garage was wide open. She thought this was strange, considering she knew they did not park their cars in their garage because it was too cluttered.

"It was unusual in our neighborhood to have garage doors open," Baughman testified.

FORESHADOWING

Up next was Jennifer Fetterolf, a friend Nancy had met while walking in the neighborhood. Because Fetterolf worked during the day, she could only get together with Nancy in the evenings. Like many of Nancy's friends, though, their children were close in age, and the two women bonded quickly.

Fetterolf was privy to the marital problems between Brad and Nancy, as well as Nancy's desire to move back to Canada. She also knew that Brad had changed the plan, leaving Nancy in a sort of hellish limbo because she didn't think she could stay with him in the house much longer.

"Jennifer, he's breaking me, and I don't know how much I have left to fight," Nancy said to Fetterolf in the weeks prior to her death.

In May of 2008, Fetterolf had a party and invited the neighborhood families. Nancy asked if it was okay if Brad came, despite what was going on in their marriage. Fetterolf agreed. Nancy and the girls came early, but when Brad arrived later that evening, the couple immediately started arguing.

"I remember Nancy being extremely angry and frustrated at him," Fetterolf said. "She just kept yelling at him."

"He wasn't responding to her," she testified.

Ironically, the week before Nancy died, she and Fetterolf had several heart-to-heart conversations about Fetterolf's own marital problems. Nancy encouraged her friend to go to counseling and work it out.

"She said to hang in there, to give it all that I had," Fetterolf said.

The weekend Nancy disappeared, Fetterolf was away in California. On Saturday morning, July 12, 2008, she texted Nancy to tell her she was taking her advice and had decided to work on her marriage. Fetterolf was concerned when she didn't hear back from her friend. Later that day, she got a call from a friend in Cary telling her that Nancy was missing. She got the first flight home from California Sunday morning.

When Brad showed up at Java Jive wanting to help with the

search, Fetterolf enlisted her own husband, David, to search with him. The men combed the woods behind the Waverly Place Shopping Center and, later, as they were walking out of the woods together, Brad commented that his phone looked similar to Fetterolf's.

"'Could you tell me how to figure out what time somebody called me?'" David Fetterolf testified that Brad asked him. He was fighting off a smile on the witness stand. "I was surprised that he would be asking me something like that at that time."

Fetterolf was also surprised, as prosecutor Boz Zellinger pointed out, that Brad, a telecommunications expert specializing in phone systems, wasn't able to figure out such a simple task. Zellinger asked Fetterolf where he had last seen the phone. He said it was during one of the 2008 custody hearings; he saw Howard Kurtz hand it to Brad Cooper's mother, Carol Cooper. By the time police got a warrant to confiscate the phone and had it sent to the FBI, it had been wiped clean of all data.

A CRY FOR HELP

Susan Crook met Nancy through Hannah Prichard in the fall of 2007. Soon afterward, Crook was put on bed rest with her first pregnancy and didn't see Nancy again until the spring of 2008. By that time, the Cooper marriage had disintegrated to a point where Crook was very concerned for her new friend. As the former assistant director of the North Carolina Domestic Violence Commission, she knew that most women who were killed by their partners were in the process of leaving them. So she called Interact, Wake County's support organization for the victims of domestic violence. They told her to have Nancy call them and let them know what kind of help she needed.

Crook last saw Nancy at the pool in Apex with Hannah Prichard on Friday, July 11. They talked about the deteriorating situation between her and Brad. Nancy shared with Crook how dirty the house had been when she returned from her vacation with her family to Hilton Head. Crook remembered Nancy being beyond angry with Brad at that point.

"It seemed to be weighing heavily on her shoulders. It was what was really going on in her life at the time. Clearly she was very upset," Crook testified.

Crook also remembered Nancy drinking a Diet Coke at the pool, a possible contender for the caffeine found in Nancy's system during the autopsy. Defense attorneys had implied the caffeine proved Nancy must have had a cup of coffee before she allegedly ran on Saturday, July 12, 2008.

But maybe not.

THE EXTERMINATOR

Next on the stand was Gary Beard, the exterminator who'd serviced the Cooper home. He said Nancy called him after returning from her vacation and told him the house was full of ants. He agreed to come treat the house on Wednesday, July 8. He said when he arrived, Nancy told him Brad forgot to leave a check "again." He agreed to treat the house anyway, and said he would simply bill her.

Beard had done work for the Coopers since he was referred to them by a neighbor two years earlier. He had gotten to know Nancy on a casual basis. On one occasion, he told her that Heather Metour, who was also his client, had not paid her bill and he wondered if Nancy could speak to her about it.

"She proceeded to tell me that Brad had had an affair with Heather," Beard testified.

On July 8, 2008, he said Nancy was just leaving to paint at Jessica Adam's house when he pulled up. He used the key pad and a code Nancy had given him to open the garage door. He said the garage was cluttered, as it had been for the prior two years that he had worked for the Coopers.

"Could you ever during those two years fit a car in the garage?" prosecutor Amy Fitzhugh asked.

"No Ma'am," he replied.

A MATTER OF SCIENCE

On Monday, April 4, 2008, Heather Hanna, a geochemist with the North Carolina Program for Forensic Sciences, took the stand to talk about soil samples she evaluated in the case. Hanna had taken samples from Fielding Drive, where Nancy Cooper's body was found; Wallsburg Court, near the Cooper home; and from the area around the lakes in Lochmere, where the search had taken place.

Hanna was then given a pair of Brad's sneakers to see if she could find soil in the soles to compare to these locations. She discovered that the soil at Fielding Drive had a mineral called "mica" in a form called a "mass." The same mica mass was found on Brad's sneakers. However, there was no mica mass found in the soil from the area around the lakes in Lochmere, nor was there any found in the soil near the Coopers' home. While Hanna admitted she could not determine specifically that this mica mass on Brad's shoe had come from Fielding Drive, it was the first time there had even been a shred of forensic evidence linking Brad even remotely to the crime scene.

IN NANCY'S IMAGE

It is very unusual for a jury to see a living, breathing image of a murder victim in the courtroom. But that's exactly what they got when Nancy's sister, Krista Lister, took the stand on the afternoon of April 4. She looked weary from having sat in the courtroom for weeks, reliving her sister's murder.

Prosecutor Howard Cummings first asked Krista gentle questions about her relationship with Nancy, how often they had contact, and what they meant to one another. Krista described how she and her husband, Jim, had moved to Toronto from Edmonton partially so that she could be in the same time zone as Nancy and be able to hop on a plane anytime and visit her.

"Nan and I were inseparable," Krista said with a small smile.

Eventually, she said Nancy told her about Brad's affair with Heather Metour.

"Nan always thought she married the safe guy, the guy that wouldn't cheat on her, best friend, that would never hurt her. She was devastated," Krista testified of Nancy finding out about the affair.

She testified about her visit in the spring of 2008 to help Nancy pack and get the house ready to sell. She said, by that point, things had gotten really out of hand.

"They were screaming. They were very angry at each other. The girls were really upset," Krista testified. "It was a mess." She also recounted the story of Bella's birthday party for the jury, how Krista had offered to buy things for the party that Brad had refused to spend money on, but Nancy wouldn't let her.

"She said I got to leave and she didn't—that her life would be hell. 'You don't have to deal with the repercussions. I do, so please don't,'" Krista recalled Nancy's words.

This time Krista added a new detail to the story about Bella's birthday party. She said when they left the store and tried to put the items in Brad's trunk, they could not because it was full of sports gear and athletic clothing. This detail only added fuel to the investigators' theory that it was unusual for Brad to have a clean trunk the way it had appeared to them on July 12, 2008, the day Nancy was reported missing.

Krista said she was worried about her sister when she left North Carolina after that visit, but took solace in the fact that Nancy would soon be moving with the girls to Ontario, and they would be together again. Krista even took some of Nancy's clothes back with her to Ontario. But soon after returning to Canada, Krista got a frantic call from Nancy.

"She called me in tears," Krista remembered. "She said, 'I messed up. I gave him the key to get something out of my car and the passports are gone. I can't leave.'"

At that point, Krista said Nancy resigned herself to waiting for the separation agreement to be finalized before she could leave. She even toyed with the idea of asking her parents to buy Brad out of the house so that she and the girls could stay for a while.

"It had gotten really bad. She needed out. She was looking for any help, any idea. She just needed out," Krista said.

Krista last talked to Nancy on Friday, July 11, as she was preparing ribs for Diana Duncan's party. While Nancy tried to sound like she was in good spirits, Krista knew her sister well enough to know that she was simply putting on a brave face.

"She was angry. She was just fed up," Krista said. "She wanted it to be done." Prosecutor Howard Cummings asked her to clarify exactly what Nancy wanted to "be done" with.

"Her situation, her marriage, her life. She just wanted it to be better," Krista said.

Defense attorney Howard Kurtz, who had declined to cross-examine Donna Rentz, Nancy's mother, did not seem as concerned about the implications of cross-examining Nancy's sister. He focused at first on the trip to Hilton Head, where Nancy appeared to have no money. He said Brad had actually given Nancy seven hundred dollars for the trip, which she used to buy groceries and gas. But Krista said the money didn't go very far, and her family paid for Nancy's hotel room and her gas to return home. Plus, she added, they wanted her to have some spending money when she returned to Cary.

"I gave her some cash," Krista said. "Yes, my parents did give her some additional cash."

What Kurtz really wanted to concentrate on was the affair Nancy had had with a man in the first year of her marriage to Brad. Krista had previously testified in the custody hearing that Nancy had had a relationship with a man she met in Florida. Without telling her family, Nancy had invited the man to Krista's August 25, 2001, wedding. Krista said she was upset with her sister for doing this, but at the time, Nancy was pretty much set on staying in Canada and leaving Brad.

"Nancy hated being here. She had no car, felt stranded. She didn't have any friends. She was planning on leaving Brad," Krista said to prosecutor Howard Cummings on re-direct examination.

Kurtz kept trying to elicit from Krista whether or not she "was aware that Nancy had other relationships." But Krista wouldn't budge. Her answer was repeatedly "No."

"Nan had only had the one issue in the beginning of her marriage. When she came to my wedding, she did not plan on returning to North Carolina. That is the only relationship that she ever had," Krista said.

And then Kurtz asked the question he asked all of the witnesses who knew the couple.

"Nancy never told you Brad had so much as laid a hand on her?" Kurtz asked.

"No," Krista replied.

PILING ON

The next witness on the stand, Dr. Theresa Hackeling, met Nancy at the Triangle Academy Preschool about two years prior to her death. Hackeling didn't say anything any other witness hadn't said, but it wasn't lost on the jury that she was a *doctor*. As a result, it was likely her testimony would be weighed as more credible with the jury, a point defense attorneys made several times.

Hackeling told the same story Nancy's other friends had told on the stand about the deterioration of the Cooper marriage after Nancy found out about Brad's affair with Heather Metour.

"Heather confronted her and said, 'I have slept with your husband,'" Hackeling said. "She said she asked him outright and he denied it, and said it never happened, and said [Heather] was making it up."

Nancy soon began to suspect that Brad had been unfaithful with other women, and shared her suspicions with Hackeling.

"She did tell me she thought he had other affairs with someone at work, and then someone when he was on a trip to Europe," Hackeling testified. "She wanted to get out." When Brad admitted to the affair with Metour, "it kind of gave her peace, knowing she couldn't make the marriage work," she said.

Hackeling said perhaps the most troubling thing she could recall about the Coopers' situation was that Nancy told her she slept in her jeans, with her keys in her pocket and the girls next to her behind a locked bedroom door. When Hackeling asked her why, "She just said that maybe someday she would have to get out fast," Hackeling said, her voice laden with remorse.

PUBLIC DISPLAY

Next up were two women who also had children at the Triangle Academy Preschool, and who recalled seeing the Coopers fighting in the parking lot on May 21, 2008.

Jenipher Free said she was getting out of her car when she heard people screaming, and a woman and child crying.

"I heard Nancy yelling to give her the kids, saw Brad blocking the car, they were in separate cars, not letting Nancy get to the kids," Free testified. She said Brad was physically blocking Nancy from getting the children out of the car.

"Nancy was saying to him, 'Give me the children,'" Free said. "He said, 'You don't own the kids, I own them too.'"

Free heard Nancy say to Brad that he didn't even know the girls' teachers or what classroom they were in. "'You're just trying to be dad of the year. It is all for show,'" Free said, recalling Nancy's words. "He said, 'I don't have to fucking listen to you anymore.'"

Shirley Hull also heard and saw the Coopers arguing in the parking lot as she was carrying out her daughter. She said the altercation was so disturbing it made her daughter cry. For the most part, she just remembered screaming, crying, and profanity. But she did remember one line from Nancy that day.

"She said, 'You keep the house, I keep the girls,'" Hull testified.

FRENCH CONNECTION

Joseph D'Antoni was the first witness to take the stand on Wednesday April 6. He was a former MBA classmate of Brad's from North Carolina State University who had attended a class trip with him to Paris in February of 2007. The two men shared an interest in biking and had rooms right next door to each other during the trip, and Brad had even lent D'Antoni two hundred dollars when he lost his wallet. D'Antoni didn't know Brad well, but he knew that he was married.

"I believe it was Thursday I noticed he wasn't wearing his wedding ring, and I had noticed it on on Sunday," D'Antoni testified.

He also said that at several of the class social get-togethers during the week he'd noticed Brad getting close to one of their female French classmates. There were even photographs of the two taken arm-in-arm at several parties and at a rock-climbing outing with the group. D'Antoni said the two seemed "amorous" to him, often going off in a corner away from the group to chat with their heads close together. "They were holding hands, kind of leaning on each other," D'Antoni said. He said the class consensus was that something was going on between the two.

LEGAL AFFAIRS

In an unusual move, Alice Stubbs—Nancy's divorce attorney, as well as the custody attorney for her family—was called to the stand. Stubbs testified about Nancy coming to her in the spring of 2008 in order to draw up a separation agreement. Nancy assured her that the process would be straightforward, and that she intended to reach an amicable agreement with Brad.

"She thought that she had an agreement for she and the girls to move to Canada, but they didn't have an agreement on the financial part," Stubbs said.

Stubbs said somehow Brad had intercepted the draft agreement and became disgruntled by the contents, so much so that he changed his mind about allowing Nancy to return to Canada.

"Nancy said that the defendant would no longer agree to let the girls and her go to Canada," Stubbs said. "It was related to the money."

Stubbs continued to talk to Nancy about trying to work out a separation agreement, but she knew her client was frustrated. She told Nancy, however, that she needed to stay in the house until they could work out some kind of an agreement. Otherwise, it would look like she was abandoning the home, and there might be legal issues regarding the custody of the children.

"The defendant had taken one or both of the girls' passports, so she could not leave. She did not have a job. I think she was feeling trapped," Stubbs testified.

It was about that time that Nancy noticed issues with calls being dropped on her home phone. Stubbs urged her to find a "safe phone" to talk on, preferably a cell phone. She also told Nancy to do things to take care of herself, considering the amount of stress she was going through. This included exercising, eating well, sleeping, and minimizing her intake of alcohol.

"'Be a good mom. Do the right thing. Stay at home.' She was doing that anyway," Stubbs said.

As things continued to get worse between the Coopers, Stubbs received e-mails from Nancy detailing her concerns. She said Brad was all of a sudden "being a good dad," even buying groceries. Nancy said it wouldn't be fair if he got equal custody just because of this eleventh hour push. She was convinced this was something a lawyer had told Brad to do.

"He had not done this in four years. I have been the only caregiver. So it does not seem right that he can put on this little show and be forgiven for the past four?" Nancy wrote in her e-mail to Stubbs.

On cross-examination, defense attorney Robert Trenkle asked Stubbs whether or not Nancy had told her that Brad Cooper had been violent in any way to his wife.

"She did not send me e-mails expressing concerns for her safety," Stubbs responded.

"Nancy never complained of any violence in her marriage?" Trenkle asked.

"Not physical violence," Stubbs replied.

But on re-direct Stubbs clarified that although there was not physical violence, there was definitely emotional abuse.

"She indicated that he was mentally abusive and cruel," Stubbs said. "It was tough."

CISCO EXPERTS

Paul Giralt, a voice technology expert from Cisco, took the stand and testified about five calls Brad Cooper made the morning Nancy disappeared. At 6:37, 6:45, and 6:53 that morning Brad appeared to call his voice mail. He called Cisco's voice mail system in Ireland at 7:26 that morning and left a three second message that was sent to his North Carolina office. The voice mail said, "Testing 1,2,3." At 7:56 that morning, he called in to Cisco's conferencing call system in San Jose, California.

The testimony was highly technical and complicated, as Giralt explained how someone using Cisco technology would be able to route calls through various systems and make them appear as if they had come from a certain number. Specifically, he said it *was* possible for Brad Cooper to use Cisco technology to initiate a call remotely to his cell phone and make it appear as if it had come from his home phone.

"If that outbound call notification is programmed to use that gateway at your house and use your phone line, it will just show up as a call from your house," Giralt said.

Investigators believed that Brad used this Cisco telephone technology to make it appear that Nancy had called his cell phone from their home while he was on his way to the store the morning she disappeared. The goal—to make it appear that she was still alive.

Giralt said there was an internal invoice from a purchase Brad Cooper made for an FXO port that would have allowed him to automate calls ten different ways over the Internet from the Cooper home.

But on cross-examination, Howard Kurtz pointed out that the Cary police never actually found an FXO port in the Cooper home, and that the devices they did find were not enough to allow him to automate the call. Still, Giralt also testified that employees at Cisco had access to a variety of technical equipment at the company that they were free to bring home without a checkout system, as long as it was returned. So, if Brad did do it, he easily could have gotten rid of the evidence before the home was searched.

Another witness from Cisco, Eric Gerhardt, a security officer, said the defendant's building access key recorded Brad going into and leaving his office on July 17, 2008, around 10:00 at night for about ten minutes. *Could Brad Cooper have disposed of evidence and covered his tracks on that night?*

A FATHER'S LOSS

When Garry Rentz took the stand midmorning on Friday, April 7, he showed little emotion. As always, Garry was polite, professional, and restrained—the bedrock of the family. Unlike his wife and daughters, he was the stalwart, guiding force who always managed to lead them through each stage of the tragedy with aplomb and grace. But while he seemed calm, he also looked weary after weeks of sitting in the courtroom and listening to sterile, tedious testimony about his precious daughter's murder.

"Nancy was my third-born child," Garry said in response to prosecutor Howard Cummings's question. "I have three living children."

The word *living* rolled off Garry's tongue like it was coming out of a slingshot aimed directly at Brad Cooper. It hung in the air for a moment as everyone in the courtroom sat in stunned silence, probably wondering how they would define their own families after one of their children had died.

Garry recalled speaking to Nancy at Krista's wedding in Calgary about how unhappy she was in North Carolina. She told her father she was lonely, that she had no car and no ability to work, and that Brad was working long hours, making her feel abandoned.

"I encouraged her to carry on," Garry said. "I felt that more effort was required."

And so Nancy did carry on, returning to North Carolina and eventually having her daughters, Bella and Katie. But financial problems continued to plague the marriage. Garry said Nancy was constantly calling to ask for money for household issues. In 2007 Garry and Donna had given each of their children a gift of $23,500, which Nancy used mostly to pay off debt. A portion of that money was also used to buy the bear painting that had been a point of contention in the case. Brad had repeatedly used the purchase of the expensive painting to show that Nancy was a spendthrift. But it was actually purchased with money from Nancy's parents, not with his income.

Garry recalled the trip to Cary in late 2008 to celebrate Brad getting his MBA. At the time, Nancy suspected Brad's affair, but had not yet confirmed it. She had also told her parents about how Brad had changed after his trip to France, how he'd come back acting like the trip had been an "epiphany," and he wanted to pick up and move the family to France. After Garry and Donna returned to Canada, Nancy called them on New Year's Day and told them that Brad had admitted to the affair with Metour. Garry and Donna urged the couple to go to counseling, but what Nancy learned about Brad in counseling did not sit well with her.

"I think I'm through here. I don't know if I can get this thing to work," Nancy told her father.

In early 2008, Garry and Donna were on a cruise to China and got several disturbing e-mails from Nancy. The first one they received on February 28 at 5:00 in the evening. She wrote: "Brad seems to be going in and out of depression and things are getting a little weird. I'm not sure what to do."

Then again, that same night, several hours later, Nancy sent another e-mail to her father titled "I need help." It read in part: "Brad is going a little crazy. He had my water cut off."

Things continued to deteriorate rapidly. Garry suggested his daughter speak to a lawyer, and loaned her $7,500 to retain Alice Stubbs as her attorney. Nancy promised to pay them back as soon as the house sold. Garry said the plan was constantly changing.

In June 2008, Garry and Donna, Krista and Jim, and Nancy and the kids all went on a family vacation to Hilton Head. One day, on the beach with Bella and Katie frolicking in the waves nearby, Nancy and her father had a heart-to-heart conversation.

"Dad, I'm through. I've got to get out of here. I don't care what I have to do, but I've got to get out of this situation. It's not good for the kids, and it's not good for me," Nancy said to her father.

Garry recalled the tearful moment at the airport in Charlotte watching his wife and daughter sob and hold onto one another. He wanted more than anything for Nancy and her daughters to get on the plane with him, but he knew that Brad had taken the girls' passports, and that Nancy had no other option but to go back to Cary. But he thought surely the situation would resolve itself soon, Brad and Nancy would come to some kind of agreement, and she would be able to go on with her life. That's what he and his wife wanted, that's what Nancy wanted, and he hoped that's what Brad wanted.

On July 7, 2008, a day after returning from vacation, Nancy left her father an angry voice mail saying that she was "furious" at the disgusting state of the house when she returned home to Brad. Prosecutor Howard Cummings played the voice mail in court for the jury to hear.

"I came home and the house was so dirty. There was an ant infestation on the table. The plates the girls ate on are still in the sink with food and ants on them," Nancy said. "I'm so furious at how disgust[ing] my house was when I got there."

As the dead woman's voice emanated throughout the courtroom, several people broke down in tears, including Donna and Krista. It was almost too much for them to bear, hearing her voice right there, as if she were just a phone call away.

After hearing from Krista that Nancy was missing, Garry and his wife immediately made plans to head to North Carolina to help police find their daughter. There was no phone call from Brad, not on that day, not ever, to let them know what was going on, or even to share what should have been their mutual anxiety and grief.

Garry said he approached Brad at the vigil at the Lutheran Church in Nancy's neighborhood on Tuesday morning, July 15, the day after the body was found. "I thought he looked very drawn, there were black circles under his eyes. I thought he looked quite sad."

"I said, 'Why don't you let us get [the kids] out of here?'" But Brad said no, "he needed his kids for his diversion."

Garry then recounted the day of Nancy's memorial service, when Brad was unable to tell the girls about their mother's death. Garry said he watched Brad try and fail, because Bella was so revved up from playing in the pool with her friends that she was incapable of listening. Garry then told Brad he would handle it. As it turned out, Donna ended up telling Bella in the car on the way to the service.

"She had been lost, had been found. She was so badly hurt that she could not be mended and was now with the angels," Garry said, recalling his wife's gentle explanation to her granddaughter.

DEPOSITION

Although Brad Cooper never took the stand in his own defense, jurors still heard from him in the form of the nearly seven-hour-long videotaped deposition from the child custody case taken October 2, 2008. Brad's larger-than-life image with his cool demeanor and measured responses was projected on the big white screen in front of the jury for them to watch.

Lawyers intermittently argued about what the state had cut

out of the deposition, saying that they were taking segments out of context, making the content prejudicial to their client. The state maintained they had taken out frivolous chitchat that had nothing to do with the topic and would merely take up more of the jury's time. Both sides slung arrows at each other, questioning the other side's integrity and credibility. When defense attorney Howard Kurtz made mention of not wanting to waste the jury's time, Judge Paul Gessner said, "We're not even going to go there." Clearly, Gessner felt enough time had already been wasted.

CROSSING GARRY

After the jury finally finished watching the deposition, Garry Rentz resumed his testimony on the stand. He reiterated that a pair of women's Saucony running shoes found by the police in the Cooper home were the shoes Nancy had been using just the prior week at Hilton Head. He specifically remembered this detail because he had made fun of her in the past for not buying good running shoes, and he was happy she had finally gotten a pair.

The defense attorneys' cross-examination focused on challenging certain details of his testimony. Robert Trenkle read from an earlier interview in which Garry said Nancy had called and said she had used the money he had given her on the vacation for the exterminator, but the exterminator, Gary Beard, testified he had never been paid. Trenkle also pointed out that Garry was under the impression that Brad had withheld Nancy's allowance not because of the money she was earning for painting Jessica Adam's house, but because of the money Garry had given Nancy while on vacation. There was also the story about Brad telling the builder Nancy was critically ill and pulling out of the house deal, but Trenkle implied it was actually Nancy who had made this assertion after a benign spot was found on her lung during a bout of pneumonia.

"Brad told the builder that Nancy was seriously ill—canceled the deal," Trenkle said repeating the story. Garry said he had heard that as well, but not from Nancy, and not from the real estate agent.

But while the defense seemed to be caught up in this minutiae, Garry didn't appear one bit flustered. He simply said he could not recall those details—the details of what happened almost three years ago in the days prior to his daughter being murdered.

As usual, it all came down to one question: Was Brad Cooper ever violent to his wife?

"Physically violent, no," Garry said without skipping a beat as he emphasized the word *physically*.

FBI

When FBI agent Gregory Johnson took the stand, everyone in the courtroom held their breath. Suddenly, the gallery was packed with people who had no connection to the case. The word was out that the "smoking gun" would come from Brad Cooper's computers.

Johnson had examined the hard drive of Brad's Cisco IBM laptop that was confiscated from the Cooper home. He said there were many items located on the computer, including about a thousand e-mails. There were several heated e-mails between Brad and Nancy. In an e-mail Nancy wrote to Brad on November 21, 2007, she said: "I really did not see myself in this situation. I always thought I would be with someone like my father." Nancy went on to say how her father always helped with the housework, and how all the kids pitched in as well, because it was not her mother's sole responsibility. She said that all Brad did was work at Cisco and cut the grass, yet he was also criticizing her housekeeping abilities. "You compare me to others and tell me that I suck," Nancy wrote. "You're being unfair and ignorant."

There was also another series of e-mails between Brad and Nancy as they were trying to prepare the house for sale. In the e-mails, Brad defended the work he had done in the home, and Nancy balked at the suggestion that it was he who had been doing the work. She said the real estate agent, Tom Garrett, had recommended about $13,000 worth of upgrades that needed to happen in order to sell the house—upgrades Brad had at that point refused to pay for. She also took the opportunity to tell him how she felt about his financial control.

"The fact that I have to ask you to gas my car, buy food and buy paint is very degrading," Nancy said.

Johnson also testified about a series of e-mails in September of 2004 when Brad and Heather Metour were communicating. Metour was having problems receiving faxes and was asking for Brad's help. It was not so much *what* she was saying, but how she was saying it. Her notes were playful, even affectionate and flirtatious at times. "Brad my dear," was how she started her September 14, 2004, e-mail. She signed her September 15, 2004, e-mail "Thanks Sweets." The pair also talked about an upcoming race he was participating in where she wished him luck and said, "I believe in you." There was also talk of the two rendezvousing in San Jose, California, where they both happened to have business meetings at the same time.

Johnson also discovered a string of e-mails on Brad's computer from the French student Brad had met during his trip to France with his MBA class in February of 2007. These e-mails started shortly after the trip, in March of 2007, and had a playful, affectionate bent, though without any overtly sexual content.

The communication started off with him talking about helping her get an internship with Cisco, either in England or in the United States. It was obvious that the student was wrestling with something unresolved about their meeting in France and the subsequent state of their relationship.

"At the beginning it was hard for me," she wrote. "But now it seems to be clear. I really enjoy having a new Canadian friend."

She talked about how she looked forward to seeing him again when "it was possible."

Brad returned her affection, telling her he was constantly reminded of his trip to France and had set up a number for her in France through which she could call his mobile at a much lesser charge. He told her he was even listening to a CD in his car that was teaching him to speak French.

"It brought back vivid memories of my personal French tutor," Brad wrote. "I never would have expected my trip to have changed me so much. I spent much of my time in class last night researching relocating to France."

At one point she told him that she had taken a pretty bad fall rock climbing, but that she was going to be okay.

"Climbing with you is one of the many fond memories I have of my time with you," Brad wrote. "I want you to stay alive since I have just met you." He signed this last part with a smiley face, and then went on to say, "More confused than ever."

Johnson also discovered e-mails that were sent only to Nancy Cooper on Brad's hard drive. He explained this by saying that Brad had installed a program in the computer Nancy used that would forward her e-mails to his account, but still keep an unopened copy in her account so that she would not know Brad was intercepting her e-mails.

In April of 2008, there were a series of e-mails between Nancy and her ex-boyfriend from Edmonton, Brett Wilson. She told him "things are not well here" and that she and Brad were getting a divorce. She told him that she was "scared about the future, but also excited." In one e-mail, Wilson chillingly asked Nancy if she was safe; she said yes, but still, he warned her to "be careful."

And those weren't the only intercepted e-mails. Johnson's investigation showed that Brad received all of the e-mails from Nancy's friends, as well as all of her communications with her divorce attorney, Alice Stubbs, in the late spring of 2008.

On Tuesday, April 12, Johnson finished his direct examination, saying that Brad Cooper had logged into his computer four times between 10:00 P.M. on July 11 and midnight, a time he had previously told police he was sleeping with his daughters. It also showed that he logged into his computer on the morning Nancy disappeared, July 12, more than half a dozen times starting at 6:52 A.M.

On cross-examination Howard Kurtz stated that the defense believed "there are allegations of tampering" involving Brad's computers. Kurtz said that after Brad's computer was turned over to police, 692 files were found to have been modified. Johnson responded that that was probably due to automatic updates from Cisco.

"Nothing would stand out to me that anything had necessarily been altered," Johnson testified.

On re-direct examination Zellinger asked again if he felt the computer files had been tampered with in any way.

"It is my opinion that they were not," Johnson said.

The next witness was Detective Chris Chappell of the Durham Police Department, who worked on cyber crimes as a member of a special FBI Task Force. As part of the task force, he was asked to examine the Macintosh laptop computer that was primarily used by Nancy, and usually sat on a desk next to the Cooper's kitchen.

He found activity on the laptop up until Nancy left for her trip, and no activity until after she returned. The morning of July 12, the day Nancy was reported missing, someone—presumably Brad—logged on and did a White Pages search and then checked the weather. On July 13, there was a check of an employment website in Edmonton, as well as various news websites that had posted stories about Nancy. On July 14, the blog site Websleuths, where a whole page was dedicated to Nancy's case, was logged into.

Chappell also looked at Brad's Cisco laptop computer that he kept upstairs in his home office. Brad took this laptop to work with him as well. On Friday, July 11, the examination showed that Brad did routine things on the computer while at work like pay bills and check the weather. But at 10:17 that evening he connected to Cisco's internal site from home, and surfed various entertainment websites up until about midnight. Brad had previously told police and stated in his deposition that he was sleeping during this time, that he had gone to sleep with the girls a little after 9:00 and had only woken up briefly around midnight when he heard Nancy come in from the neighborhood party.

Chappell testified that Brad was back on his Cisco laptop early on the morning of Saturday, July 12, searching websites for information on local museums, movies, and power-washing houses. He also searched for hotel information in conjunction with the upcoming Rock 'n' Roll Marathon in Virginia Beach.

On Monday, July 14, at 11:00 in the morning, Brad searched the website bookaircanada.com. Had Brad Cooper been thinking about making a quick exit?

SMOKING GUN

As promised, the smoking gun in the state's case against Brad Cooper arrived on Wednesday, April 13. Everyone in the courtroom who had heard about it jostled impatiently in their seats wondering, *Is this it, are they going to reveal it now?*

Like a commuter train slowly pulling into the station, prosecutor Boz Zellinger slowly worked his way into the line of questioning. He had spent about thirty minutes asking Detective Chris Chappell again about all of the specific Internet content found on Brad Cooper's Cisco laptop computer. Suddenly, when they got to 1:14 on the afternoon of Friday, July 11, Zellinger pulled the train slowly up to the platform and waited there to make sure the jury was listening.

He asked Chappell what was being done on Brad Cooper's computer as it sat in his office at Cisco on that Friday, less than twenty-four hours before his wife would be reported missing. Chappell said there was a Google Maps search for the zip code 27518. The exact longitude and latitude of the search that was created fell in the middle of the zip code. The person on the computer, presumably Brad, zoomed in to get a satellite aerial view of the location. The spot was *Fielding Drive.*

"It appears to be from the area of Fielding Drive," Chappell said. "It is my understanding [that's] where Nancy Cooper's body was found."

"This is from before Nancy Cooper's body was found?" Zellinger asked, bringing the point home for the jury.

"That's correct," Chappell answered.

Brad Cooper had googled the spot where his wife's body would be dumped *before* she disappeared, *before* she was killed, three days *before* her body was found. It was an incontrovertible piece of evidence that was going to be difficult, if not impossible, for the defense to explain.

Jurors who had previously been slouching and looking weary after so many days of tedious technical testimony suddenly perked up. They sat up straight and moved to the edges of their seats. They started writing furiously in their notebooks and appeared to be reenergized by this new development in the trial.

The only other sound in the courtroom was that of people tapping away on their phones and laptops, sending the information out into cyberspace.

FORTY-ONE SECONDS

After weeks of testimony, it had all come down to this—*the forty-one seconds someone on Brad Cooper's computer searched Google Maps.*

Under cross-examination on Thursday, April 14, 2011, Detective Chris Chappell from the FBI Cybercrimes Task Force methodically explained once again how on Friday, July 11, 2008, at 1:15 P.M., Brad Cooper's computer zoomed in on the precise site where his wife's body was found several days later. Kurtz wanted him to replicate the search for the jury with a computer in the courtroom. Chappell explained that there was no way a search from July 2008 would be similar to a search in April 2011, as the area had changed drastically. "I don't want you to draw some incorrect conclusion if the test done now doesn't have the same results as it did three years ago," Chappell said.

However, he still demonstrated how the map was found, first in "satellite view," and then in a series of zooms. It was looked at as nine separate versions of the map in a forty-one second period.

"There were magnifications up to and including the area where Nancy Cooper's body was found," Chappell testified.

"Is it your theory that on July 11, Mr. Cooper was searching for a place to put his wife's body?" Howard Kurtz asked almost flippantly.

Chappell answered that this would be consistent with what he found on the computer.

"The fact remains to me the content was on the computer. The fact remains that it was at a high level of magnification," Chappell said.

Kurtz went on to question Chappell about "cookies," which are left behind on a computer when a search is run. According to the FBI's report, dozens of cookies were found on Brad's computer, but none for this particular Google Maps search. Chappell explained this by saying that it was possible that a particular cookie had been erased from the computer.

"If a file has been deleted and overwritten, it cannot be recovered," Chappell said.

"Is it your opinion that Mr. Cooper intentionally deleted a cookie off the machine?" Kurtz asked.

"I suppose that's a possibility," Chappell replied.

Kurtz went on to imply that maybe someone sat outside the Cooper home and broke into his wireless connection and planted the evidence. Chappell explained that the technical expertise, not to mention pure luck, that would be required to do this, to place this kind of evidence in precisely the right place so that it did not appear to have been planted, was highly unlikely and would require "an incredible series of coincidences."

"What traces did you find of hacking?" prosecutor Boz Zellinger asked Chappell under re-direct examination.

"None," Detective Chappell replied.

Kurtz mused as to why someone with so much computer know-how as Brad Cooper had would leave something so incriminating on his computer, and yet not leave anything else exculpatory. As Kurtz opened the door to this issue, Zellinger on re-direct examination decided it was time to try to get the information about a suicide website that Brad had bookmarked on his computer. Kurtz objected, and the jury was sent out as the lawyers argued their points in front of Judge Paul Gessner. Zellinger said it was important for the jury to understand that other damning evidence *was* found on the computer, that Brad was clearly not that careful. Gessner had previously ruled that he would not allow the information about the website called "A Practical Guide to Suicide" because it was prejudicial. Kurtz had also argued that suicide had nothing to do with homicide. "That shows what was in the defendant's head at that point," Zellinger told the judge. "Perhaps he was going to make it look like Ms. Cooper committed suicide."

At the end of the debate, Gessner agreed to allow it.

On re-cross examination, Kurtz asked Chappell if the fact that Brad surfed the Internet Saturday morning looking for activities to do with his children that day—museums, movies, parks—if that was consistent with how a killer might act?

"Is this consistent in your mind with someone who killed their wife the night before?" Kurtz asked.

"I suppose that it might be something you might do if you're trying to establish an alibi," Chappell said. "In my career as a law enforcement officer, I've had people do the strangest things."

HOMESTRETCH

While the jury may not have known it, when Detective George Daniels from the Cary Police Department took the stand in the afternoon of Thursday, April 14, there was a collective sigh of relief from those close to the state's case. He would be their last witness. As the lead investigator, Daniels would repeat what others had said, and finally connect all the dots for the jury.

A large African American man with a kind face and a gentle demeanor, Daniels had sat patiently in the back of the courtroom for weeks, watching his officers testify. By the time he got on the stand, it had all been said. Testimony about the Coopers' troubled marriage seemed painfully redundant at this point and paled in comparison to the bombshell of the Google Maps search found on

Brad's computer.

Still, Assistant District Attorney Howard Cummings took Daniels through his paces, albeit not in nearly as much detail as he had done with the previous witnesses.

Daniels described how, when he'd first met Brad Cooper on Saturday, July 12, at 6:15 P.M., he immediately noticed faint red scratches on the back of his neck.

"It looked like fingers rubbed the back of his neck, but it didn't look like there was any blood," Daniels testified. Cummings had Daniels reach around the back of his neck and show jurors the exact location where he noticed the scratches.

In that first interview with police, as Brad described his actions on the morning of July 12, 2008—Katie waking up, the two grocery store trips, Nancy going for a run—Daniels was looking for what was really going on behind the scenes of this man's life and marriage.

"He stated that they got along for the most part. They had not talked about divorce recently," Daniels said. This was in direct contradiction to what Nancy's friends had said.

Brad explained how he had taken the children home from the party the night before and fallen asleep with them around 9:30 that evening, and had only woken briefly when Nancy peeked her head in around midnight to check on the girls after returning from the party. While this piece of information had been stated many times, it was now a key inconsistency in Brad's story, as the computer examination had shown him surfing the web between 10:00 P.M. and midnight on Friday, July 11.

Another thing Daniels noticed was the complete disarray of the house, even though Brad told him he had been cleaning all morning in his wife's absence. It didn't make sense to Daniels that someone would clean, but not straighten what appeared to be chaos in every corner of the home.

"He said he was scrubbing floors, washing dishes, vacuuming and cleaning bathrooms along with laundry," Daniels said.

As they talked, Brad shared that he and Nancy did have marital problems that started with his affair.

"He explained to me that Nancy was upset about the adultery because it was with her former best friend," Daniels said.

Brad allowed the officers to take photographs of the home, and as Daniels walked through the house he noticed that the bed where Nancy had supposedly slept had no indentation in the pillow or on the mattress, and the covers were pulled way back, not like the bed of someone who'd jumped out of bed at 4:00 in the morning after a night of drinking to attend to her crying baby and do laundry.

He also noticed laundry shoved in a basket, with another laundry basket on top of it. The dress that he would eventually learn Nancy wore to the party at the Duncan's was hanging out of the lower basket with another basket on top of it. He had been told the dress was "delicate" and one of Nancy's "favorites" by Brad and her friends. Seeing it treated with such carelessness made no sense to Daniels, unless it had been placed there by someone other than Nancy.

"It appeared out of place like that," Daniels said. "It was sitting in the laundry basket hanging out like that. No care or concern with it."

On the night of Monday, July 14, Daniels informed Brad that his wife's body had been found; after that day, Brad no longer interacted with the Cary police. Daniels repeatedly asked him to come down to the station to answer questions. He even asked Brad's attorney to make him available after seeing a press conference on television in which the lawyer said his client was doing everything he could to help with the investigation. But it was to no avail. At that point, Brad was done talking. And while they continued to look at every possibility, Daniels said they could not rule out Brad as a suspect.

"We could not eliminate him as a person of interest," Daniels said. "There were things he was not giving us the full story on."

While his investigators had done a good job of laying out the circumstantial facts in the case, Daniels was the one who tied it all together. He explained why, early on in the case, suspicion was cast on Brad Cooper. Daniels testified that Brad had been watching his marriage slowly unravel since he'd admitted to the affair with Metour.

Brad admitted to police that, on the night of Diana Duncan's party, Nancy had embarrassed him by the way she'd chastised him about his lack of parenting skills in front of their friends and neighbors.

"The motive that I saw at that point was the motive of anger. A motive of pent up aggression, that at some point he just couldn't take it anymore," Daniels said. "I could tell by his statements, in the beginning, that he was hurt, that he was upset by how she treated him when she came back home from her vacation."

The day before Nancy was reported missing, the couple had fought about whether or not Brad was going to give Nancy her weekly allowance. Daniels said the conversations were heated and ugly.

"She doesn't argue with him. She argues at him, and there's tension between them," Daniels said.

"It boils down to a simple fact that this was a domestic issue, and it exploded and went to this point," Daniels said. "We were looking at the totality of the whole circumstance."

Once again, prosecutors played a part of Brad's video-taped deposition in the custody case from October 2, 2008, for the jury. It was the segment in which attorney Alice Stubbs asked him about his ability to initiate a call to a cell phone from a remote location. In the deposition, he said with the right software he could in fact initiate a call, although it wasn't something he would typically do, he added.

"Prior, he said he had a large amount of knowledge of computers, and listening to what he said, he helped our investigation understand what he does, and what he's capable of doing," Daniels said of Brad's answers in the deposition. "Basically, he was telling us he had knowledge. He had the know-how. He had the means to do it and the opportunity to do it."

But under several hours of intense cross-examination, defense attorneys were critical of Daniels' assumption about the call, saying there was no record of a remotely initiated call and that, at the time, Brad did not have the proper equipment in his home to make such a call.

"You don't have any phone records that can show that's what

happened?" Defense attorney Howard Kurtz asked.

"No," Daniels said.

"You have no expert that can show that's what happened?" Kurtz asked.

"No, I don't," Daniels replied.

But Daniels said it was precisely these inconsistencies between what Brad told investigators and what he said in his deposition that raised concerns for them. For example the constant changing of stories about what dress Nancy wore to the party.

"He's saying she wore a dress, that he couldn't tell us the color, at first, but then he tells us he washed it because it had a stain on it," he said. "As we're looking into this, from July to October, I'm thinking, 'Yes, in fact there might have been a stain from where he choked her when she came home that night.'"

Daniels said all the pieces of the puzzle pointed to an angry man who was not happy in his marriage and saw no painless way out for him. And that in some strange way, he had justified the killing by his perception of the poor way in which Nancy had treated him in the days leading up to her murder.

"In looking at all this and putting all this together, and then having the final part of knowing he knew about Fielding Drive," Daniels said. "He was still in what I say was an act of not really feeling responsible."

The tough cross-examination continued into Monday, April 18.

Kurtz hounded Daniels again about the alleged automated call.

"What specific evidence do you have that shows that phone call was automated?" Kurtz asked.

"I don't have any specific information, and I think that's one of the unusual issues here, because there were so many different ways he could have done it," Daniels said. "He had the motive. He had the means. He had the opportunity."

"Everything you're saying about the 6:40 A.M. phone call being set up, or however you want to characterize it, is pure speculation?" Kurtz asked.

"I don't believe it's pure speculation," Daniels replied. "I was shown several ways it could have been done, and that's what I was basing it off of."

Daniels was the last witness for the state. It was finally the defense's turn. No one knew for sure what Howard Kurtz and his team had in store for Brad's defense, but after the evidence of the Google Maps search, everyone speculated that he had an uphill battle. For Daniels, there was only one possible conclusion the jury could reach based on everything that had been presented by the state.

"How many times did he look you in the eye and say, 'Detective Daniels, I did not kill my wife?'" Cummings asked.

"He never did," Daniels replied.

CHAPTER TWENTY-ONE

THE OTHER SIDE OF THE STORY

Facts are stubborn things; and whatever may be our wishes,
our inclinations, or the dictates of our passion,
they cannot alter the state of facts and evidence.
—JOHN ADAMS

The defense's case got off to a fiery start on Tuesday, April 19, 2011, as Howard Kurtz tried to get his computer forensics witness, James Ward, tendered as an expert. After about two hours of voir dire from prosecutor Boz Zellinger outside the presence of the jury, Judge Paul Gessner said he would allow Ward to testify as an expert in computer security, but not as an expert in computer forensics. This prompted a volatile reaction from Kurtz. He jumped up from the table and exploded at the judge.

"I believe that your rulings have been consistently outside the bounds of prudent jurisprudence," Kurtz said, also calling the judge "biased" and asking for a mistrial. In addition, he asked that Gessner recuse himself from the case. Without discussion, Gessner denied both requests, summoned the jury back in, and told Kurtz to call his next witness.

HACKING

It was clear right away that Brad Cooper's attorneys needed to prove the Google Maps search found on his computer was either planted, or had occurred on a different date, after Nancy's body was found, and was time-stamped incorrectly. Without getting over that hurdle, little else much mattered in the case.

Howard Kurtz called Jay Ward to the stand. Ward walked the jury step-by-step through how someone would go about breaking into a computer such as Brad Cooper's.

"From a security standpoint, how effective is it to keep someone out?" Kurtz asked.

"It's like trying to keep someone out of your house using a screen door," Ward replied.

Ward testified that Brad's computer network was vulnerable to hackers, and that someone could have easily copied files onto his laptop without logging in, using free software downloaded from the Internet. Ward said this could have easily occurred in the twenty-seven hours between the time the computer was confiscated by Cary police, and when investigators eventually powered it down. Kurtz also once again implied that the Cary police could have tampered with the files on Brad's computer to make him look guilty.

On cross-examination prosecutor Boz Zellinger brought up Ward's Facebook page, where he noted his interest in "conspiracy theories." Defense attorney Kurtz said that wasn't relevant and had no bearing on his status as a computer expert, but Zellinger argued it was highly relevant, considering Kurtz's allegations that the Cary police might have conspired to frame Brad Cooper. There was also evidence that Ward had discussed the case on the blog site Websleuths and promised to "tell all" once the trial was over.

SOLE SUSPECT

A parade of witnesses testified that they believed Cary police ignored information that may have helped solve Nancy Cooper's disappearance and murder.

Sylvia Hink testified that she saw two women jogging in her neighborhood—the Oaks at Meadowridge, where Fielding Drive is located—on the morning of July 12, 2008. She also said the next morning, as she was walking in her neighborhood near a construction area, she saw two men leaning against a maroon-colored van that she said seemed out of place in her neighborhood.

Dale Kuerbitz, who lived about a mile from the Coopers, testified that he was awoken by a loud noise around 12:30 A.M. on July 12, 2008. He looked out the window and saw someone getting into a van, and then saw the van speeding down the road. Cary police came to his home and took a report, but their investigation led nowhere.

"We had a van in our neighborhood, and now, there's a missing jogger," he said.

Curtis Hodge, who'd been mentioned by name in the defense team's opening statement, testified that he had been driving north on Kildaire Farm Road on the morning of Saturday, July 12, 2008, between 6:50 and 7:10, when he saw an older Chevrolet van with two Hispanic men inside turn around and follow a jogger.

The next day, when he arrived at work at the Food Lion, he saw the missing-person flier.

"I picked it up and looked at it, and I noticed that this picture of this lady looked real similar to the lady I saw jogging Saturday morning," Hodge said. "I was a little surprised."

The defense's star witness in this group, Rosemary Zednick, had made her first appearance during the custody case. Both then and now she testified that she was sure she had seen Nancy Cooper jogging on the morning of Saturday, July 12, 2008, along Lochmere Drive. Zednick said she had tried to contact Cary police multiple times to tell them what she had seen, but they had ignored her, so she'd turned to Brad Cooper's attorneys.

"I was upset for a long time," said Zednick of Cary police not taking her seriously. "My mindset was: 'The poor girl is missing. What happened? Why don't you call me back?'"

SUPPRESSED

On Monday, April 25, defense attorney Howard Kurtz planned to offer testimony from Giovanni Masucci, another witness he offered as an expert in computer forensics. This was after Judge Paul Gessner had refused to tender Jay Ward, the witness Kurtz had called the previous week, as an expert in the same field.

Prosecutor Boz Zellinger argued that he had just received Masucci's three-page report on Saturday, inadequate time for him to prepare for cross-examination. He said he would need to consult with the FBI agents he'd previously called about Masucci's report.

"The prejudicial effect far outweighs the probative value of this evidence, at this time," Gessner ruled. Once again, the defense was making no ground proving that Brad's computer had been tampered with—their only real hope of overcoming the Google Maps search.

DIRTY LAUNDRY

Also on the stand Monday was Brad Cooper's friend, Scott Heider. Heider—Heather Metour's ex-husband—had taken Brad into his home in the days when police executed the search warrant at the Cooper house. The two had also taken a long drive one day as police followed, wondering what the men might be talking about.

"Brad was lost. Stunned. Dazed," Heider said of Brad's state of mind in the wake of Nancy's death.

Heider admitted that the relationship between the Coopers became strained after the affair between his wife and Brad became public, but said prior to that the couple had appeared to get along like a normal husband and wife, albeit with polar opposite personalities.

"Gregarious, sociable," was how Heider described Nancy, while Brad, he said, "kept his thoughts to himself."

Heider was absolutely clear about the fact that Brad, unlike what people said about Nancy, didn't talk about his marital issues.

"He never aired his dirty laundry. He was respectful. He was calm. He never said anything inappropriate in public," Heider said.

After weeks of hearing from the defense about Nancy's presumed one-night stand with neighbor John Pearson, it was finally time to hear it from the source himself. The defense called Pearson to testify late Tuesday morning.

In a strange web of infidelity, John Pearson's one-time girlfriend—and the woman being sued by his ex-wife for alienation of affection—was the same Heather Metour who had once been married to Scott Heider, and who had also had an affair with Brad Cooper.

Prosecutor Howard Kurtz immediately zeroed in on the fact that Pearson failed to tell Cary police in his first interview about his encounter with Nancy in her home in 2005 after a Halloween party.

"I did not disclose that we had a sexual encounter the night of the Halloween party, but I feel like I did fully disclose our relationship as I knew it," Pearson said of his first interview with Cary police.

Brad was out of town on the night of the Halloween party, and Pearson agreed to walk Nancy home along with Craig and Diana Duncan. Pearson said he and Nancy were both very intoxicated. But he recalled taking a shower upstairs to wash off makeup from his Halloween costume, and then joining Nancy on the couch downstairs in the den.

"She began taking her clothes off. I took my clothes off. And we, I believe, started to have sex. My memory is that we stopped and got dressed and decided to never speak about it again," Pearson testified.

He said he didn't tell police the truth at first because he didn't want to hurt his family and held back for their "privacy and protection." He also said he was fond of Nancy as a friend and didn't want to besmirch her reputation after her death, especially because he didn't feel like their encounter was relevant to the murder investigation.

"I was reluctant to do anything that would harm her memory," Pearson said.

In the weeks leading up to her death, Pearson said he and Nancy had shared several phone calls and one cup of coffee. After not having talked in about a year, she'd contacted him after his girlfriend and his ex-wife had both called Nancy to speak to her about the lawsuit, and presumably get her on their divergent sides.

Nancy was concerned that one or both of the women had learned about their Halloween encounter and might somehow try to use it to her advantage in the lawsuit—and as she was entering custody proceedings with Brad, it was not something she wanted made public.

"She sounded suspicious and uncomfortable," Pearson said when Nancy phoned him on May 8, 2008. He, too, was uncomfortable, and told Nancy he didn't want to talk about the situation on the phone, but would meet her for coffee.

"You haven't said anything to Heather about that night in 2005?" Nancy asked him when they had coffee at a bakery in downtown Cary. Nancy had come to the meeting with her youngest daughter, Katie, in tow.

"I said 'No,'" Pearson testified.

As for the allegation that Katie might be his daughter because she was born almost exactly nine months after the encounter, Pearson said the thought did cross his mind, and he had asked Nancy about it just once.

"I asked, 'Is there anything we should worry about here?'" Pearson said. "She said, 'Absolutely not,' and that was the only time we ever talked about it."

Pearson said Nancy assured him that she and Brad had been working on having a baby for some time, and that she had been undergoing fertility treatments to that end.

"We didn't believe that we had gone to that extreme where it was a possibility," Pearson said of their awkward, drunken, brief sexual encounter that he felt strongly only lasted a few seconds.

Pearson said he never imagined that he would be in a situation where someone was accusing him of murder. As a precaution, he asked his ex-wife to get a copy of her time sheet from Saturday, July 12, 2008, because she had dropped the children off at his house very early on that morning so that she could go do inventory for her job.

When he heard that "[it] was brought up by the defense that I was an alternate theory," Pearson said, "I became alarmed."

But there was no doubt that that's exactly where the defense was going.

POINT OF VIEW

Laura and Mike Hiller both took the stand on Wednesday, April 27, and testified that they never saw Brad and Nancy be anything but cordial to each other. While they knew about the marital problems the couple was having, they said that, unlike Nancy's other friends, they saw nothing publicly that indicated the marriage was in trouble.

Defense attorney Howard Kurtz had implied all along that Nancy had certain friends she shared her dirty laundry with and others she did not. He also said she was prone to hyperbole and sharing "distorted information."

After Nancy's death, it became clear that those who knew the couple were divided into "Team Brad" and "Team Nancy." There were people firmly convinced that Brad Cooper had killed his wife, and others just as firmly convinced that he did not. Mike Hiller obviously fell into the "did not" category.

"We didn't get together and disagree, but there were different beliefs," he said between the groups of friends split on Brad's guilt.

During the custody hearing for the Cooper children, Hiller had shown obvious disdain for the proceedings, as well as for Nancy Cooper herself, describing her as someone who often exaggerated and had one time bullied him in a conversation about whether or not she could afford a certain house. At the time, his distaste for a murder victim had seemed inappropriate, if not a little bit over-the-top. But at the criminal trial, he toned his ire down.

Hiller was more than just another witness with an opinion about the case; he was key to Brad Cooper's timeline alibi. Hiller said he and Brad had made plans to play tennis on Saturday morning, July 12, which Nancy certainly knew about, because he had used her phone to call Brad, and she had given her blessing to the tennis game. Therefore, Hiller then immediately assumed Jessica Adam was lying about her plans with Nancy to paint that morning, since it conflicted with the tennis match. As a result, Hiller and Adam got into an argument outside the Cooper home the day Nancy was reported missing.

"'I don't understand how you could have painting plans, because Brad and I were going to play tennis,'" Hiller said he told Adam quite forcefully.

On cross-examination, prosecutor Howard Cummings pulled out a document printed off the blog site Websleuths, in which Hiller had posted his reaction to the findings in the autopsy report in September 2008. He said he read the autopsy six times. Cummings brought up the fact that Hiller had posted a detailed conclusion of how Nancy died. He asked him to read it on the stand.

"She was attacked from behind on the Lochmere trails," Hiller read. "She fell forward to the ground and braced herself on her left knee."

"She was choked from behind by a right-hand person. I have reason for all of these statements at least in my mind," Hiller went on to say.

In great detail Hiller went on to explain in his post how Nancy had mud on her knee that he thought might have come from the trails. He also said he believed her neck was cut by a fingernail exacerbating the bug activity. Cummings asked Hiller what he did for a living. He admitted he was an engineer with no special qualifications to assess an autopsy report.

"It doesn't prove who kills her, but it supports the contention that she left that morning to jog," Hiller said, adding that he didn't think it could be a "large, enraged man" who killed Nancy because the marks on her neck were faint. In a awkward moment, he graphically demonstrated with his hands how he felt the person had choked Nancy.

"The murder was a tragic event and an unsolved crime so far and many people are still trying to reach the truth and heal in their own way," Hiller read on from his posting with growing agitation in his voice.

MAMA TRIED

After weeks of sitting quietly behind her son in the courtroom, Carol Cooper took the stand. There was no way someone could look at her and not feel sorry for the woman. While the Rentzes always had a bevy of supporters around them in the courtroom, Brad Cooper's supporters seemed to only exist in cyberspace. Most days, Carol and her husband, Terry Cooper, sat alone in the courtroom and stood alone in the hallway during breaks.

Carol was a no-nonsense-looking woman with short brown hair, brown glasses, and a drawn face. She was soft-spoken as she answered defense attorney Robert Trenkle's questions. She testified that she and her husband had arrived in Raleigh on Friday, July 18, 2008, to help their son deal with the ordeal.

"He was very sad. Very quiet," Carol Cooper said. "He couldn't believe his children had been taken and his wife, all in the same week."

At first, Brad's parents and brother stayed at a hotel, and then Carol moved into Brad's house. She opted to stay on with Brad while her husband and other son returned to Canada. She said she busied herself with organizing and cleaning the house.

Carol said instead of attending the public memorials for Nancy, their family chose instead to grieve in private.

"Bradley had bought a bouquet of flowers and he had put a

picture of Nancy at the front door—and her running cap," Carol said. "We wanted to be out of the public eye."

Throughout the trial, prosecutors had mentioned that several ornamental wooden ducks were missing from the Coopers' credenza in their front hall, implying that the ducks could have been broken during a struggle. But Carol testified that she recalled packing the ducks away in a box, and that later Brad gave them to his attorney Debbie Sandlin as part of her payment in the custody matter. Sandlin, who was hosting the Coopers at her home for the duration of the trial, told Carol that *she* had the ducks in her office. Howard Kurtz then paraded the wooden ducks out in the courtroom as if he was unveiling a smoking gun in a Lifetime television movie. This sent prosecutor Howard Cummings into a rage—he wanted to know why Carol Cooper had sat there for weeks, listening to witness after witness talk about the ducks, yet said nothing about their whereabouts.

"The state was presenting this theory that these ducks were in the foyer, and that's where a struggle was and they got busted, isn't that what you gathered from all of that?" Cummings asked.

"That's true," Carol said. "I didn't realize Miss Sandlin still had the ducks."

"But you knew where they were," Cummings retorted. "Why didn't you say something about that so we wouldn't put all these witnesses on that now look like they are a bunch of liars?"

"Nobody asked me," Carol said calmly, her arms extended and her hands palms open to the ceiling.

"Objection Your Honor, it's not her job to take care of the state's case," Trenkle said.

PRIVATE EYES

On Thursday, April 28, 2011, a private investigator, Richard McGough, took the stand for the defense. He methodically explained the route Brad Cooper took to the grocery store the morning of

July 12, 2008. He even videotaped it and showed the jury how Brad had cut through an adjacent parking lot to get to the grocery store. Defense attorneys maintained that this route was different from the one the Cary detectives had previously testified to in the trial, and that they had made Brad look like a liar when they were the ones who were wrong.

"It's a shortcut," McGough said.

"Did you see lots of people use it?" Howard Kurtz asked.

"I did," he replied.

On cross-examination, prosecutor Amy Fitzhugh asked McGough how he knew that Brad was telling the truth when he told him his route that morning.

"How do you know if anyone is telling you the truth?" McGough said with a smile.

McGough also testified about the route John Pearson said Nancy Cooper would have run that day if she were headed toward Regency Park. He looked at the time Brad said Nancy left the house, estimated her running time per mile, and placed her in the exact spots where defense witnesses Rosemary Zednick and Curtis Hodge would have seen her.

But the biggest bombshell of the day was video of Nancy shopping with her daughters the day before she disappeared. For the first time the jury got a chance to see the dead woman living, breathing, as a mother, and as a real person doing the most mundane of activities: grocery shopping. The video showed her in the self-checkout line at approximately 2:45 P.M. on Friday, July 11, 2008. She looked very thin, tired, and hurried, but clearly not aware that in just a few hours her life would be over. At first, her back was to the camera and the girls, both blond and tan, were in the seat of a shopping cart. Nancy, her hair pulled back in a messy ponytail, wore a black halter sundress tied at the neck and what appeared to be a bathing suit underneath. She rummaged in her oversized handbag, scrounging for change to pay for what most likely were the ingredients for the ribs she was making for Diana Duncan's party. Then, as she turned around and maneuvered the cart away from the checkout lane, she walked right into the frame of the camera.

Howard Kurtz stopped the video as Nancy came into close range of the camera and asked McGough what he noticed. Or more specifically, what he didn't.

"I don't see a necklace," McGough said. "Passing before the light I can see there's no necklace there."

Just three hours before she arrived at the party, Nancy Cooper clearly wasn't wearing the diamond pendant necklace that her friends had said she never took off. The state had used the fact that the necklace had been found in the Cooper home to hypothesize that Brad must have killed Nancy, taken it off her body, and kept it. But the video clearly contradicted that theory. Nancy's friend, Hannah Prichard, had been with Nancy and her children at her neighborhood pool in Apex that day. She had previously testified that Nancy was wearing the necklace at the pool. Yet, based on what she was wearing in the grocery store, it was more than likely she had just come from the pool after visiting with Prichard. And unlikely that she'd taken off the necklace in between.

DEFENSE RESTS

Late in the day Thursday came an unexpected demand from the jurors. It was clear that, like everyone else, they were getting restless and were ready to have the whole trial over with. They sent out a pointed note to the judge.

"Please encourage the attorneys to use time more wisely," read the note. "We are hoping to finish this soon! Please ask them to have their witnesses ready to go. We want our lives back."

On Friday, April 29, 2011, the defense rested. All things considered, everyone was in a good mood at the prospect of the trial coming to a close. Everyone wanted their lives back, not just the jurors, but the families, the lawyers, and the court officials—even the media. "We've come a long way," Judge Gessner told jurors. "But we still have a long way to go."

CHAPTER TWENTY-TWO

FATE

We create our fate every day we live.
—HENRY MILLER

On Monday, May 2, 2011, the state began presenting its rebuttal witnesses, starting with Cisco employee Craig Miglucci. He testified that in an instant message chat with Brad Cooper in January 2008, Brad asked to borrow one of his 3825 routers, the sort of router that could have been used to initiate a call remotely, as prosecutors believed Brad had done. Miglucci testified that he had agreed to lend Brad the router and told him it was in a shared storage unit, for which Brad had a key. Miglucci said that to date the router had never been returned.

Jessica Adam's husband, Brett Adam, then took the stand to verify his wife's claims that Nancy Cooper had planned to paint their dining room the day she disappeared. Adam testified that he moved the furniture out of the dining room at 7:00 A.M. that morning, so that Nancy would have room to paint when she arrived at 8:00. He said that, when she didn't show up, his wife became very upset. He even texted Brad himself to see if he knew where Nancy was.

"Jessie was very puzzled that Nancy wasn't there in the morning. She got very anxious," Adam said.

Next, the state called three Cary police officers to show that Rosemary Zednick's claims of being ignored by investigators was untrue, and that Zednick's theory of the case made her less than credible. Zednick had previously testified that Cary police had ignored her repeated attempts to talk to them.

On July 16, 2008, Officer Larry Arrellano was advised by detectives to contact Zednick. He interviewed her by phone and she told him she saw a woman who "looked like" Nancy Cooper jogging that day, but "she was not positive it was Nancy." She also said she thought the woman might have been wearing an iPod.

Detective Michael Lindley was approached by Zednick as she drove up to a roadblock in the Lochmere neighborhood on July 24. He said she told him she had already spoken to one Cary officer, but wanted to give him the information again. In addition, she told him she had a theory about what happened to Nancy.

"Her theory to me was that Nancy Cooper was struck by a vehicle," Lindley recalled. He said Zednick went on to say that the jogger was wearing headphones and probably didn't hear the car, and that cars often went way above the speed limit on Lochmere Drive. She hypothesized that the driver put Nancy in his or her car and then "got nervous and dumped it."

Detective Michelle Savage testified that on July 26 she also spoke to Zednick at a checkpoint. Savage testified that Zednick told her the same story she had told Detective Lindley.

"She thinks Nancy Cooper was hit by a car and [the driver] panicked," Savage said, adding that Zednick again said Nancy was wearing an iPod along the highly traveled road where drivers often sped, and mentioned her belief that "he left her along the road where she was found."

At the end of the rebuttal witnesses, it was clear that the state's goal was to discredit Zednick's testimony as much as possible. There was no evidence in the autopsy report that Nancy Cooper had been struck by a car. Also, multiple witnesses testified that Nancy never ran with an iPod, and to anyone's knowledge, didn't even own one.

To everyone's great relief, both sides then rested after defense attorney Robert Trenkle made a routine motion to dismiss the case, which Judge Paul Gessner denied. After so many weeks of passively listening and patiently waiting, the jury would finally get a chance to weigh in on the evidence.

LAST WORDS

There was a nervous energy in the air in courtroom 3C on Tuesday, May 3. After eight weeks of testimony, it had all come down to this. Attorneys would get one last chance to draw the loose ends together and to convince the jury to see it their way. Once they shared their closing arguments, Brad Cooper's fate would officially rest in the hands of ten women and two men chosen to sit in the jury box.

The defense would go first, and then the prosecution. Howard Kurtz stood anxiously at the podium in front of the jury with a bottle of water in one hand and a stack of notes in the other.

"The conclusion they jumped to was that Brad must have killed Nancy," Kurtz said of the Cary police. He said right away it was clear they were never really investigating a missing person case, but instead trying to prosecute a murder case against Brad Cooper. He accused them of having "Brad-did-it glasses" and ignoring any evidence that did not support their theory. "They considered rumor, and hearsay, and gut feelings to be evidence," he said.

"Justice was sacrificed on the altar of vengeance," Kurtz claimed, letting the flowery prose roll off his tongue and hang in the air for a moment.

He said that, while the investigation was "amazingly detailed," it amounted to "virtual justice," not real justice, because it simply went in the direction everyone expected it to go—not based upon solid evidence, but based on innuendo and conjecture that surfaced even before Nancy's body was found.

"They have not proven to you that Nancy didn't go jogging in the morning. They didn't prove it because they can't," Kurtz said, pausing to take a swig out of his water bottle.

He said they "ignored, obscured, destroyed, and withheld evidence" that could have exonerated Brad, like shoe prints, tire prints, pieces of wire, and a cigarette butt found at the body site. He also pointed out that police didn't consider Nancy's "romantic entanglements"—the sexual encounter with John Pearson or the crushes that Michael Morwick and Craig Duncan reportedly had on her—as possible motives for the murder.

Kurtz was especially fired up over Detective Jim Young erasing the data from Nancy's cell phone. Kurtz said there was no excuse for this in a murder investigation, and he didn't buy the officer's explanation that this was accidental.

"It was destroyed intentionally to prevent any of that information from that BlackBerry from getting out," Kurtz claimed.

Kurtz said the police tried to use "absurd items masquerading as evidence." For example, Brad cleaning the house, which he said was simply a husband in the doghouse trying to get back into his wife's good graces. On the other hand, Kurtz accused the police of colluding with Nancy Cooper's friends to persuade everyone in her inner circle to come up with consistent evidence and stories to build the case against Brad—that Jessica Adam attempted to coerce friends into submitting damaging affidavits in the custody case, and that Hannah Prichard tried to get friends to send police photographs of Nancy wearing the diamond pendant necklace to prove that she never took it off.

Kurtz said it was clear that Nancy was not controlled, that three hundred dollars a week was a respectable allowance, and that she was free to go out with friends and vacation with her family.

"She was able to come and go as she pleased," Kurtz said.

Kurtz also pointed out that all of the witnesses, including the state's witnesses, testified that they never saw Brad act violently toward Nancy or the children.

"You've heard Brad never reacted in anger, that he simply ignored it, that he was not aggressive in any way," Kurtz recalled.

As for the alleged automated phone call that Brad made to his cell phone the morning Nancy disappeared to prove she was still alive—Kurtz said there was no evidence this happened, and that Brad did not have the proper router in the house to make this call.

"If Nancy calls Brad at 6:40 in the morning, then Nancy's alive at 6:40 in the morning and their theory falls apart," Kurtz said.

Everything he had said up to this point was information that had been hashed and rehashed throughout the trial. But the evidence Kurtz really needed to address was the Google Maps search that Brad allegedly did on his computer the day before Nancy disappeared. He once again pointed to the fact that Cary police had left the computer on for twenty-seven hours after it was confiscated from the Cooper home, and that during that time, 692 files were modified in some way.

"FBI did nothing to eliminate the possibility of tampering," Kurtz said.

He said that after June 22, 2008, the majority of the timestamps were invalid on the computer.

"This indicates that the computer was tampered with," Kurtz said.

Plus, there was no cookie found on the computer for the search, something Kurtz said was impossible to plant.

"If you know where you want to drop a body, you don't do a Google Map search," he said incredulously. "It is simply inconsistent with what anyone would logically do."

In closing, Kurtz said Cary police had an agenda, that they wanted people in the community to feel safe, so they zeroed in on Brad Cooper because "it was easy." He asked the jury not to act on their emotion but "to seek justice for both Brad and Nancy Cooper" because the killer or killers were still out there. He said if they convicted Brad Cooper, an innocent man would be sent "to rot in a dungeon" because of the "shoddy and unprofessional work" of the Cary Police Department.

After a short break, Brad's other defense attorney, Robert Trenkle, was up. He immediately honed in on the fact that none of the physical evidence the state presented ever linked Brad to his wife's murder.

"There is physical evidence," he said, "just no physical evidence that indicates Brad Cooper."

He started by talking about the trunk of Brad's BMW, which prosecutors alleged was used to transport Nancy's body to Fielding Drive.

"No evidence that body was ever in the trunk," Trenkle said. "It was negative for blood, negative for bodily fluids." Even the dress Nancy wore to the party the night before had no traces of blood or any other bodily fluids on it.

"The house, the car, everywhere they tested—no blood, no bodily fluids, no evidence. Are you entirely convinced? Or do you have a reasonable doubt?" Trenkle said, the last line a mantra he repeated every few moments in his closing argument.

Trenkle also talked about the autopsy, noting that Nancy's blood alcohol level was .06, inconsistent with someone killed just after drinking heavily. He also said the fact that her stomach was empty, following a party where she had been eating, was another red flag. Instead, he suggested that she was killed the next morning while out jogging, and dragged into the woods by her sports bra.

He talked about the hoops Brad would have had to go through to make all of the things police say happened come together. He would have to kill her, drive across town, dump the body, go the grocery store, clean the house, get rid of the mysterious router used to make the phony phone call and the shoes he wore on Fielding Drive, all in just a few short hours. And yet no one saw him, no one at all. They did, however, see a mysterious van.

Trenkle said three separate witnesses saw a similar van in the vicinity of Lochmere: One man saw a van speeding down his street late on the night of July 11, 2008. Another man saw a van following a jogger on the morning of July 12. A woman in the neighborhood where Nancy's body was found also saw a similar van on the morning of Sunday, July 13.

"Maybe that was an incredible coincidence, but it was a coincidence that should have been investigated," Trenkle said.

He closed by asking the jury to "hold the prosecution to the law." He reminded them of the seriousness of their responsibility, that they held a man's life in their hands, and that the only standard they could use to find Brad Cooper guilty was "beyond a reasonable doubt."

"They can't meet that burden," Trenkle said of the prosecutors.

BURDEN OF PROOF

Prosecutor Boz Zellinger argued first for the state. He immediately put the case into perspective.

"The defendant googled where he was going to put his wife's body. He lied to police," Zellinger said passionately. "Those two little girls will never see their mother again because of his actions that day."

Zellinger showed the jury a photograph of the front yard of the Cooper home, so perfectly manicured, the picture of the all-American dream. Then he showed a photograph of their backyard—all dirt and weeds, and no grass. He suggested that, like the photographs, the Coopers' relationship had a public face that appeared to be well groomed and manicured, and a private face that was much uglier, "the backyard of their relationship."

Zellinger focused in on the key piece of evidence—the Google Maps search of the body site on Brad Cooper's laptop computer. It was clear from the activity on Brad's computer that day at Cisco that he was the one who was logging in and accessing different websites. He said that, as far as experts in computer forensics, the FBI agents were the only experts in this field who testified in the trial. He said the opinion that the computer was tampered with came only from the defense attorneys, and no one else.

"There was no tampering," Zellinger said definitively. "You cannot explain that away. Twelve hours before his wife was murdered and he is zooming in on where his wife's body was ultimately found."

And there were other things found on Brad's computer, like the bookmarked suicide website that Zellinger suggested might walk someone through asphyxiation, the manner in which Nancy died.

Zellinger also talked about the phone call from the Cooper home to Brad's cell phone on the morning of July 12, 2008.

"He faked the 6:40 phone call," Zellinger asserted.

Zellinger said all of the calls to Brad's voice mail the following morning were evidence that he was doing something strange. The fact that he drove the long way to the grocery store on the second run was so that he could test the system, to make sure the call would go through, Zellinger said. Brad had the know-how, the access to the equipment, and the ability to use numbers all over the world to route calls through.

The only missing ingredient was the router, a router Brad had clear access to from Cisco, a router that had since disappeared. Zellinger showed a photograph of a dusty bookshelf near where Nancy Cooper's computer sat. There was a clean square with no dust. Something had been in that square. Zellinger asked, *Could it have been the missing router?*

Zellinger said that on the afternoon of July 12, 2008, Brad continually failed to return calls made to his cell phone from Cary police and Nancy's friends. They went to voice mail, voice mail that he did not check in the afternoon, despite the fact that he had been checking it all morning. Zellinger asked, *Wouldn't a man whose wife was missing pick up calls and check his voice mail?*

As for no one ever seeing Brad be violent with Nancy, Zellinger said that was an old-school argument; domestic abuse does not always come in the form of obvious injuries, and that clearly the Coopers' was not a normal relationship.

"The defendant controlled Nancy Cooper. He controlled her finances. He controlled her communications. He controlled her travel," Zellinger said.

Just as Zellinger finished his argument by noting that Nancy's family had been waiting two years for justice, Donna Rentz broke down in tears and had to leave the courtroom. For so many weeks she had been holding her emotions inside, but now it was all coming to a head. She knew that as soon as the state finished and the judge gave jurors instructions on the law, the future would be in their hands.

But the jury still had to hear from Wake County's Assistant District Attorney Howard Cummings. Cummings had shared the prosecution of the case with his younger colleagues, Boz Zellinger and Amy Fitzhugh, but the veteran litigator took the reins to bring the case home.

He started by asking the jury to use common sense when examining the case. Cummings pointed out that none of the other men the defense had thrown under the bus were viable suspects, because none of them had any motive to kill Nancy. But Brad Cooper did.

Cummings asked the jury to use common sense in evaluating what Brad did after the murder. Did he communicate with Nancy's family or friends? No, he didn't. In fact, he didn't have any conversation with Nancy's mother until her deposition on October 10, 2008, when he cornered her in the law firm's kitchen and told her that everything Jessica Adam, Hannah Prichard, and Diana Duncan had said were lies.

"First thing he says to her since her daughter was murdered," Cummings said incredulously.

Despite what his attorneys had claimed, Brad only talked to Cary police in the beginning, when Nancy was missing; but Cummings said his stories were inconsistent, and didn't make sense. Once his wife's body was found, Brad ignored repeated attempts from investigators to have him come down to the police station and answer their questions.

"If I keep telling the police the same thing over and over again, will they go away?" Cummings said, imagining Brad's thoughts at the time.

Cummings asked the jury to use common sense in evaluating the evidence. As for the assertion that Cary police somehow planted evidence, "If Cary was going to fabricate something, wouldn't they have done more with physical evidence?" Cummings asked the jurors.

When Cary police came to the home, they asked Brad for an item of Nancy's to give the canine officer. He told them the sneakers he gave them were her newest ones, the ones she ran in. Yet, if that was the case, why wasn't she wearing them if she disappeared while jogging?

"Perhaps that is a mistake—he hasn't committed the perfect murder quite yet," Cummings said, his words dripping with sarcasm.

On her body was a red and black sports bra, the same sports bra Cummings pointed out that Brad coincidentally told police she was probably wearing, even though he never saw her leave that morning and, being an avid runner, she probably owned at least half a dozen.

"That's the one he tried to get on her to make it look like she was going for a jog," Cummings said.

Use common sense, Cummings urged, when looking at Brad Cooper's statements. For example, examine the phone call when he said Nancy asked him to get Naked Green Juice for Bella. Witnesses had testified for the state that they never knew Bella to drink that juice, that it was actually Brad's favorite, as evidenced by shopping records showing him buying it multiple times after his children went to Canada. Nancy wouldn't have asked him to buy the juice for Bella. And she couldn't have called him, Cummings said, because she was already dead.

Cummings asked the jury to use common sense in evaluating what Nancy's friends said—how Susan Crook called a domestic violence organization on her behalf, how Nancy slept behind a locked door with her keys and phone, how Brad had taken the children's passports. Think about what she told them, Cummings said, that she hated him and that he was "breaking her."

And then he asked them to think about what defense witnesses had said about Nancy Cooper, about how they had tried to trash the memory of a dead woman, as if having been unfaithful and prone to exaggeration made her life less valuable.

"Was there some reason to rub Nancy's memory in the dirt?" Cummings asked of the defense case.

As Cummings entered the home stretch, he talked about

how it only took a short time to make someone pass out from strangulation, but it took at least three minutes of constant pressure to kill a person.

"When Mr. Cooper is holding his wife's throat, the mother of his kids, he has to hold it long enough, between three and four minutes," Cummings said.

He then took out a stopwatch and stood silently in the courtroom as he held a hand to his neck.

"When he assaulted her, he began, to strangle her—right handed," Cummings said clutching his own neck.

He announced that a minute had passed, then two.

"She's not dead yet," Cummings said. And then he announced three minutes had passed. He paused, and then spoke in a very quiet voice. "Now she's dead. I ask you to find him guilty of first degree murder."

DELIBERATIONS

After Judge Paul Gessner read the instructions to the jury, which explained that they would be able to consider first or second degree murder, they went out to choose a foreman and begin their deliberations. Almost immediately, the jury had requests: a 2008 calendar, a witness list, and an evidence log, among other items. It was clear they were prepared to hit the ground running.

Deliberations continued into Wednesday, May 4, 2011. After about five hours, the jurors came out and asked to see specific pieces of evidence again. They wanted to see two photographs of Nancy's body from behind, three photographs taken by police of the Coopers' master bathroom, cell phone records from both of the Coopers' phones, customer records from two grocery stores, and the videotaped deposition of Brad Cooper from October 2008. The requests signaled to everyone sitting in the courtroom that the jury was struggling, and that more evidence was needed to sway some members into agreeing to a unanimous verdict.

As Thursday, May 5, 2011, dawned, the anxiety was growing. Garry and Donna Rentz huddled together in the courtroom with their attorney, Alice Stubbs, as well as Nancy's sister, Krista, and her husband, Jim, and her friends, including Hannah Prichard and Jennifer Fetterolf. It was clear that they could not escape the tension that swirled around them. Although no one said it out loud, it was becoming increasingly obvious there was a chance Brad could walk out of the courtroom a free man. Terry and Carol Cooper sat quietly, sometimes reading, sometimes chatting with their son's legal team. Occasional smiles crossed their faces as the attorneys must have shared the positive news with them that the longer a jury was out, the more likely there was to be an acquittal.

Donna had been growing increasingly emotional in the past week. By mid-afternoon that Thursday, she had broken down and run out of the courtroom. Krista chased her to a back hallway, where Donna closed herself in a room and refused to come out, preferring to cry in private. Krista stood on the other side of the wooden door, her cheek, ear, and palm pressed to the flat surface, speaking quietly to her grieving mother, asking her to let her in to comfort her.

Little did Donna and Krista know that at that very moment the jury was putting a mark on the verdict sheet, and in just a few minutes the waiting would be over. After a little more than nine hours of deliberations, the jury had reached a unanimous decision.

DECISION DAY

Judge Paul Gessner notified the attorneys that the jury had a verdict. Within minutes, the courtroom was packed, as those who had been in the hallway, including Donna and Krista, rushed in. Security personnel lined the hallway outside the courtroom in case there was an outburst from anyone in the audience.

"The verdict of the jury reads, 'We the jury by unanimous verdict find the defendant, Bradley Graham Cooper, to be guilty of first degree murder,'" Gessner read from the verdict sheet.

Brad and his attorney, Howard Kurtz, had no visible reaction to the verdict. As he had done for most of the trial, Brad sat stone-faced, staring straight ahead. Not even a muscle appeared to twitch in his face. His parents also stared straight ahead without expression. On the other side of the courtroom, Krista quietly wept, and then pulled her mother in and kissed her on the forehead. Jeff Rentz leaned in between the two women from the row behind them and they all put their heads together and arms around one another. When they pulled back, Krista was smiling through her tears. She reached over gently to wipe tears off her mother's cheek.

Several of the jurors also wiped tears from their faces—possibly from relief at the end of their ten weeks of service, which included intense and emotional deliberations, or possibly because they sat ten feet from the family of a dead woman to whom they had just delivered a gift. It was not a gift that would bring their daughter back, but it was a gift that would allow them to go on with their lives.

Even Judge Gessner appeared choked up, weary, and emotionally drained from the epic and contentious trial. He stated that "The court makes no findings on sentencing points and prescribes the sentence prescribed by law and that is an order that the defendant be sentenced to a term of life in prison without parole in the North Carolina Department of Corrections."

Kurtz notified the judge in open court he intended to appeal the case. He put his hand on Brad's shoulder and spoke a few quiet words to him as Brad nodded. They then stood together, Kurtz's hand still on Brad's shoulder, as two deputies stood on either side of Brad and led him away for the last time.

"We have asked, and expected, and demanded an extreme sacrifice from each of you," Gessner said addressing the jury. "You have placed your lives on hold and have devoted your full attention to this trial,"

"You deserve to be commended. I cannot say thank you enough," Gessner went on to say. "I know this was an emotional strain on each of you, and I suspect this matter will weigh heavily on you in the days and the weeks to come."

"If you're bothered by what you experienced in this case, I can assure you, you are not alone."

Gessner told the jury they were now free to talk to anyone they wanted to about the case, and to read the newspaper or watch television news. But he cautioned them not to "second-guess" their verdict or "question the process" based on what they heard in the media in the days and weeks to come.

"And certainly, don't concern yourself with the opinions of the bloggers and the comments to the news stories. You heard all this evidence. You had the opportunity to judge the credibility of each witness firsthand. Your opinion is the only opinion that counts. The anonymous uninformed opinions of others are completely irrelevant," Gessner said.

He said that he would allow the sheriff's deputies to escort the jurors from the building so that they could avoid having to deal with the media as they had collectively decided not to talk at that point.

"May God bless each of you as you get back to your lives, and thank you for sharing your time with us. The jury is excused," Gessner said in closing.

AFTERMATH

As soon as court was adjourned, the Rentzes were up on their feet and heading in the direction of Terry and Carol Cooper. Garry Rentz put a hand on Terry's shoulder from behind and told him he was sorry for his loss. Garry said Terry didn't react to his sympathetic gesture. Donna Rentz reached out for Carol's arm as Carol awkwardly backed away from Donna, quickly gathering her belongings from her seat. Donna told Carol that she was sorry, and that she knew it would be difficult, but when she felt up to it, she wanted Carol to call her to discuss seeing the grandchildren.

"I'll try," Carol said just above a whisper to Donna.

It was clear that the Coopers were not ready for overtures of kindness from Nancy's family—not now, maybe never. But still, the

Rentzes felt that it was the right thing to do at the time.

"You feel like a parent. It's a child and someone else's child that's on trial. So you feel for them as I'm sure they felt for us," Garry said with his trademark graciousness. "The message we wanted to give to them was you're the other half of the grandparent role for two young women, and we need that communication to be open," Garry said to the media assembled in the courtroom.

As they left the courtroom, the Coopers briefly hugged members of their son's legal team. They then rushed out the doors and down the stairs, shielded from the media by Howard Kurtz and Robert Trenkle, who looked shell-shocked and had no comment. In the days to come, Kurtz would say his client was innocent, was framed, and that the Google Maps search was definitely planted. He would say that had his computer experts been allowed to testify, his client would have been exonerated.

Nancy's family stayed behind in the courtroom and shared tearful embraces with prosecutors and friends. Donna stood on her tiptoes and hung onto Howard Cummings's neck and cried. Fitzhugh patted Donna's back during their embrace as she spoke quietly in her ear and cried. Boz Zellinger, the youngest member of the state's team had not tears, but a huge smile on his face as he reached in for a hug from Krista.

"The relief is palpable," Garry said as the family gathered for a brief press conference in the courtroom. He and the family focused on Bella and Katie. "Today we feel that the love and nurturing and care that we've given Bella and Katie has been rewarded, and we're going to be blessed with being able to continue the care for those wonderful children."

"I just felt her presence," Donna said about believing Nancy was with her when the verdict was read. "I was happy that this day finally came. I am happy for the little girls and happy for our family."

But their joy was bittersweet, as it came on the heels of their darkest hour.

"The tragedy is that you have two young lives that were wasted. Nancy, who is no longer with us, and Brad, who now faces an elongated period of incarceration, and I just feel sad for both of those. There's no particular joy in either of those for us," Garry said.

"I'm quite proud of how Jim and I have come through, have raised and continued on Nancy's legacy with Bella and Katie, it's going to be, it is going to be bittersweet," Krista said.

As far as Brad not taking the stand and not even making a statement before sentencing, the family said they never really expected anything from him. All but Krista said they didn't even know what they would ask him given the chance.

"I've always wanted to know why," Krista said with conviction. "I've always wanted to know why."

The prosecutors also weighed in on the verdict.

"If you want to say, 'What is wrong with this picture?' then you have to put in every part of that picture," Assistant District Attorney Howard Cummings said of the sheer length of the trial. "You look at a man who doesn't go to his wife's memorials. When you look at a case when he doesn't ever talk to the police, 'What's going on with my wife's case, why haven't you arrested anybody?' He didn't care because he knew what the answer was."

Cummings also responded to criticism regarding the lack of forensic evidence linking Brad Cooper to the crime.

"When everything is washed and cleaned, there's nothing left, and so you have to be able to say to the jury, 'This is what happened and the reason we don't have any blood and the reason we don't have any body fluids is because he's been cleaning up for hours,'" he said.

Cummings also defended the Cary police from the attacks that the defense lobbed at them continually throughout the trial. "All the allegations against them were never proven. They were false and obviously the jury was not concerned about that," he said.

"I think that the defendant googled where he was going to place his wife's body twelve hours before she was murdered was as close to a smoking gun as we could get in this case," Boz Zellinger said. He praised the FBI, members of Cisco Systems, and all those who helped him simplify the technical aspects of the case into layman's terms for the jury.

"At the end of the day, those folks from all those different agencies really helped us break it down so that anyone could understand the sort of universal theme of someone controlling their wife's communications and other aspects of their life," Zellinger said.

He said the case was really always about domestic abuse—and not just about what people can see, like black eyes and broken arms.

"In today's day and age, people understand that domestic violence is far past that ... It involves strained relationships, emotional abuse and issues of control, and that's exactly what you could see in this case," Zellinger said.

Nancy's family agreed. "We've come through the loss of a child. We know that loss is a result of domestic violence. We'd like to do what we can to solve the problem or to save some other family from the journey we've just gone through," Garry said. He likened his feelings to that of a runner who had just run up a very steep hill and was now standing at the top. Looking back down the hill, he couldn't believe how far he's come, and how difficult it really was. Garry said that's what the past three years were like for his family.

"We, as a family, I think a long time ago made our mind up that we would not deal with ourselves as victims, but rather deal with ourselves as survivors. We're going to go home and pick our lives up," Garry said. "It's been a long run for us."

CHAPTER TWENTY-THREE

THE REST OF THE STORY

There is a higher court than courts of justice and that is the court of conscience. It supersedes all other courts.
—Mahatma Gandhi

"Brad Cooper had no chance," his attorney, Ann Peterson, said referring to his 2011 murder trial. It was April 9, 2013—the day the North Carolina Court of Appeals was hearing oral arguments concerning the 39-year-old's bid for a new trial. Many court watchers thought it was a long shot that the judges would grant an appeal and overturn Cooper's conviction; others thought there was a very good chance.

"There's so much evidence in this case against the defendant," Dan O'Brien, the assistant attorney general, insisted when it was his turn to speak in front of the three-judge panel. He slipped this last thought in just as his court-dictated time limit on arguments was almost up, as if to leave the judges with a blanket overriding statement that might cancel out Peterson's claims in their minds.

Almost two years after his conviction, Cooper's appellate attorney finally got the chance to tell the court why she believed her client deserved a new trial. Primarily, her arguments centered around the contention that the superior court judge who presided over the case, Judge Paul Gessner, made a mistake when he disallowed certain testimony that Peterson believed might have swayed the jury to find Cooper not guilty.

At issue, was the testimony of two witnesses, Jay Ward and Giovanni Masucci. Peterson argued that Gessner violated Cooper's right to a fair trial when he limited the scope of Ward's testimony and would not let Masucci testify at all. Specifically, they intended to testify that they believed a Google Maps search of the location where Nancy Cooper's body was found had been planted on Brad Cooper's laptop. Throughout the trial, the defense contended that the computer had been tampered with. Defense attorneys implied the tampering was done either by the Cary police, the FBI or some third party, possibly a disgruntled ex-lover.

"The defendant has the constitutional right to present his defense. The Google Maps was his defense. Mr. Ward and Mr. Masucci were his defense, and the jury heard none of it," Peterson told the judges, adding that she was not aware of any other similar case where the defense was denied the right to call these types of experts to testify, barring some type of bad faith intentions or agenda on the part of the attorneys.

At trial, defense attorneys offered Ward as a computer network security expert and their goal was to have him testify as to his opinion regarding whether not the Google Maps search retrieved from Cooper's laptop could have been planted. The forty-five-second search, done the day before Nancy Cooper disappeared, basically pinpointed the exact location where her body was found.

But by Ward's own admission, he was not trained or certified as a forensic analyst even though he had been conducting computer examinations for nearly two decades. As a result of what the judge deemed was a lack of qualifications, Gessner limited the scope of Ward's testimony saying he was not qualified as an expert in this area, and therefore, could not testify to this specific point about the search possibly being planted with any real credibility.

"There's no question Mr. Ward was not certified, but he worked with that data for twenty years. He knew computers inside and out.

He was a super expert," Peterson argued to the appellate judges on Cooper's behalf.

But when it was the state's turn to argue in front of the appellate panel, Assistant Attorney General Latoya Powell pointed out that Ward had managed to testify to much of what the defense was trying to get on the record despite the judge's ruling. Ward told the jury that the time stamps for the 507 files related to the Google Maps search were invalid, and that during the investigation police had left the computer on for twenty-seven hours during which it may have been susceptible to hacking.

The appellate judges pressed the state's attorneys, asking them what makes someone qualified as a "forensic analyst," pointing out that Ward seemed to have decades of hands-on experience in the area of computer examination which appeared to be relevant to the testimony he was being asked to give.

"What is a forensic analyst? That was the basis of Gessner's ruling. What is it?" Judge Martha Geer peered down from the bench, briefly interrupting Powell's argument.

"To give an expert opinion you must be qualified by knowledge, skill, education, or experience. Mr. Ward testified he'd only conducted two forensic examinations ever in his career," Powell pointed out. "Jay Ward specifically said he was not one."

Masucci had planned to share the same belief with the jury—that the Google Maps search was planted in an effort to frame Brad Cooper. Gessner ruled that Masucci could not take the stand in any capacity. The basis for this ruling centered on the fact that Masucci was a last-minute addition to the defense witness list. They had two other computer experts on their list, but instead, chose to call Masucci. This, the state implied, was because their other experts must not have bought into the defense theory of the case. Given the eleventh-hour notice, prosecutors said they did not have time to vet Masucci or prepare for his testimony. Gessner also deemed that Masucci was not prepared to testify given the last-minute circumstances and that his preliminary findings would unfairly prejudice the jury.

"By his own admission, he only had forty-eight hours to investigate the computer, wasn't finished with the investigation and hadn't even written a complete report," Powell told the appellate panel.

"The court said, 'Too late, so sad, his name is not on the list,'" Peterson woefully told the panel regarding Masucci. Her staccato voice was dismissive, as if to suggest the decision not to allow his testimony was off-the-cuff and flippant.

Because the Google Maps search—according to Peterson's written request for the appeal—was "the only evidence presented by the State directly linking Defendant to the murder," she maintained that not allowing this testimony from these two men was not only prejudicial to Cooper, but denied him his constitutional right to a fair trial.

Peterson further argued that Gessner erred during the trial in not allowing the defense access to the FBI's standard operating procedures on how it handles computer forensic examinations. At trial, prosecutors argued the FBI's tactics could not be revealed because the revelation might compromise national security. But Peterson said that keeping these procedures secret in the name of protecting national security was not a legitimate argument.

After the hearing, Peterson spoke briefly outside on the sidewalk in front of the courthouse.

"I think the fact that those experts didn't get to testify is what allowed that jury to come back guilty. It was critical," Peterson said to the small crowd of reporters and photographers assembled in front of her. "I believe the jury should hear both sides, and they only heard one side."

Unlike her complex legal arguments in the courtroom, Peterson spoke simply on the sidewalk, reminding the journalists that she was fighting for her client, Brad Cooper, not for a reprieve based on a legal technicality.

"He has lost his entire family. He lost his job. He lost his career. Think about it. It's been horrible. It's a nightmare," Peterson said. "I think he's pretty down. You would be too if you lost your wife and your kids and were sitting in jail."

WRAL-TV Reporter Julia Sims followed up, asking whether or not Cooper was optimistic about his chances for getting a new trial.

"It's hope, that's all," Peterson replied.

For Nancy Cooper's family, there was a different kind of hope—a hope that the verdict would remain intact, a hope that they would not have to bear another painful trial and a hope that the Cooper children, Bella and Katie, who were still in elementary school, would not be wrenched from the loving arms of Nancy's twin sister, Krista Lister, and her husband, Jim, and returned to their father.

Maybe it was weariness after so many hours spent in the courtroom over the years, or maybe just a notion that the appeals court judges would not be swayed by their presence, but Nancy Cooper's family did not travel from Canada for the hearing. Instead, her close friend, Hannah Prichard, came to represent the family. It was clear that she, like Nancy Cooper's family, never expected to be back in a courtroom again dealing with this case.

"She will always be remembered by her loved ones," Prichard said solemnly before hustling away from the cameras.

And then the clock started ticking. With new eyes on the case, Brad Cooper was finally getting the chance Peterson said he was owed.

DECISION DAY

The wheels of justice turn slowly whether you are the defendant or the victim. During the appeals process, everyone involved in a case is at the mercy of the judges making the decision. For Brad Cooper, every day without a decision presented the possibility that things would go his way, that he would be granted a new trial. For Nancy Cooper's family, the waiting meant just the opposite—that the court was considering the possibility of a new trial very carefully.

On September 3, 2013, five months after the North Carolina

Court of Appeals heard oral arguments in the Cooper case, the judges handed down a detailed 56-page ruling, finding that "the trial court did err in limiting (Jay) Ward's testimony." In its unanimous decision, the three-judge panel overturned Cooper's first-degree murder conviction and ordered that he be granted a new trial.

"The Google Maps files recovered from the defendant's laptop were perhaps the most important evidence admitted in this trial," the court opinion read. "We hold that the trial court abused its discretion in excluding Ward from testifying, relying on the state's own evidence, to his opinion that the Google Maps files recovered from the defendant's laptop had been tampered with."

The court also addressed Judge Paul Gessner's decision not to allow Giovanni Masucci to testify on April 25, 2011.

"We hold that imposing the harsh sanction of excluding (Giovanni) Masucci from testifying constituted an abuse of discretion," the appeals court ruling stated. "We hold that excluding Masucci's testimony as a sanction for a discovery rules violation violated Defendant's rights under constitutions of the United States and North Carolina."

Finally, the court addressed the issue of not allowing the defense to have access to how the FBI went about analyzing Brad Cooper's computer. At trial, prosecutors told the judge that the FBI didn't share this information because it could compromise national security.

"It was an error for the trial court to shut down this line of questioning without ascertaining how, or if, national security of some other legitimate interest outweighed the probative value of this information to Defendant."

At the bottom of page fifty-six there were two simple typed words that would irrefutably change the course of the case: "New trial."

FALLOUT

While it was clear to all of the stakeholders in the case that the conclusion rendered by the Appeals Court was a possibility, it rocked the very foundation of what prosecutors and Nancy Cooper's family believed, that with or without the experts' testimony Brad Cooper was a guilty man.

"We're clearly disappointed with the court's decision," Wake County District Attorney Colon Willoughby told the media. "Ordinarily in cases like this where there are some issues about the admissibility or non-admissibility of evidence, the courts tend to look at the whole of the case and see what the evidence was, that the other evidence was so strong that the err was harmless, and I would have expected that in this case."

Willoughby said he would be consulting with the North Carolina Attorney General's Office in asking the North Carolina Supreme Court for a discretionary review of the Appeals Court decision. Because the ruling was unanimous, there was not an automatic right to appeal the case to the highest court in the state. But the Supreme Court could opt to review it at its discretion if the Attorney General asked it to do so.

"The Court of Appeals spent a lot of time talking about constitutional issues which ordinarily are of interest to the Supreme Court," said Willoughby.

However, for Brad Cooper's trial attorney, Howard Kurtz, the ruling was a vindication that his defense strategy and his strenuous objections to the original court rulings, which denied his witnesses the ability to testify, had been correct all along.

"I had utter confidence that our Court of Appeals was going to do the right thing in this case," Kurtz said reacting to the ruling. "I'm thrilled. I'm really happy that Brad is going to get another day in court.

"The evidence that drove the conviction was the map, so the fact that I had not only one, but two witnesses prepared to say that these maps were planted on that computer would have made all the difference."

But Kurtz's relief and joy was tempered by the regret that it had taken this long to get to this point in the case.

"It's hard to be completely happy when something like this happens because we shouldn't have had to have gone through an appeal," he said.

FULL STEAM AHEAD

On September 20, 2013, the state of North Carolina asked the North Carolina Supreme Court to review the Appeals Court's decision. As part of the petition, the state asked the court to grant a stay temporarily blocking the ability of Brad Cooper and his defense team from moving forward with a new trial. The court agreed to grant the temporary stay while it considered the request for discretionary review.

Four months later, on January 24, 2014, the North Carolina Supreme Court ruled it would not review the case, which meant, in effect, it was allowing the ball to begin rolling on a new trial.

Howard Kurtz posted a statement on his website in response to what he saw as another victory for his client.

"As criminal defense lawyers, it was excruciating to be prepared to defend our client with strong expert testimony that was unreasonably concealed from the jury," Kurtz said. "Our only relief comes now as we learn that Brad Cooper will be entitled to a full defense and the jury will now be entitled to hear it."

For Nancy Cooper's family, this was the final step standing between hope and possible devastation. With his typical diplomacy and aplomb, Nancy Cooper's father, Garry Rentz, chose his words very carefully, but the subtext was an underlying sense of fear, fear that if Cooper were freed he would try to regain custody of the couple's two children.

"The matter is for the court to decide. It is not a decision we make. We will honor the court's decision. It is honestly beyond our control," said in a telephone interview. The Cooper children, Bella and Katie, were flourishing with Krista, Nancy's twin sister, and her husband, Jim. The last thing the family wanted was for their world to be upended again.

"We would be concerned, because we don't want any more issues in their lives than they've already had," Rentz said solemnly with the tone of a man reluctantly resigned to go back into a battle he thought was far behind him.

District Attorney Colon Willoughby was also a reluctant warrior. He said the case would most likely be retried in what promised to be another long journey to justice.

TURNING THE WHEELS

When the case returned to Wake County Superior Court on January 30, 2014, the courtroom was packed with curious court watchers eager to see how Brad Cooper had fared in prison since his conviction in the spring of 2011. Huskier and with less hair, Cooper appeared to have aged from the sleek triathlete he once was to a larger, softer version of himself as an inmate. But one thing hadn't changed since 2011; Cooper's stoic courtroom demeanor remained intact as the legal process swirled in every direction around him. He looked straight ahead, devoid of any expression as the judge explained that he was basically at square one again, a man simply charged with a crime, innocent until proven guilty, entitled to all of the protections under the law.

Attorneys from the North Carolina Capital Defender's Office were appointed to represent Cooper—James Freeman and Laura Meyer. Prosecutors and Judge Donald Stephens discussed the calendar for the case, acknowledging it would require a large chunk of the court's time to re-try. Stephens said he intended to set a bond at some point and that Cooper would be eligible for pre-trial release. In a way, it was all routine court business, yet to the onlookers, absolutely nothing was routine about the Cooper case.

MAKING DEALS

On August 14, 2014, Brad Cooper's case was on a list of pending murder cases to be discussed during the quarterly homicide status hearing in Wake County's superior court. The day involved checking in with attorneys on both sides in every pending murder case in the county. The cases were heard in chronological order—older cases first, followed by the most recent.

The original prosecution team, led by First Assistant District Attorney Howard Cummings, had signed on to prosecute Cooper again. The team also included assistant district attorneys Boz Zellinger and Amy Fitzhugh.

Complicating matters, Willoughby had just retired from his post to go back into private practice after nearly thirty years in office, and several assistant district attorneys representing both parties had thrown their hats into the ring for what had become a very contentious race. Zellinger vied unsuccessfully for the Democratic nomination and lost to the current Clerk of Superior Court, Lorrin Freeman. Defense attorney John Bryant was the Republican nominee after a runoff with longtime assistant district attorney Jeff Cruden. The election had divided the office down party lines and created alliances that left veteran Cummings, who had always been Willoughby's partner and the person who ran the day-to-day operations of the office, uncertain about his future. In short, until Cummings knew who his new boss was going to be, he wasn't making any promises about staying.

"I'm not sure I will stay here just to try this case," Cummings told Judge Stephens candidly as they again looked at the calendar trying to clear a date for what promised to be a long, drawn-out affair.

But Cummings added a caveat, inferring there was another possibility. He said that during the original trial the state had offered Cooper the opportunity to plead guilty to second-degree murder, which carried a much shorter sentence than life in prison. Cummings said this plea offer was clearly expressed to Cooper's attorney, but he had no knowledge as to whether the deal had ever been communicated to Cooper.

In a way, it was an odd non-sequitur for Cummings to bring up the earlier plea deal. But as his words lingered in the courtroom above the din of the routine legal speak, it became clear that the state was ready to make a deal.

COMING TO THE TABLE

Word spread quickly among the courthouse insiders and select members of the media that something big was about to happen in the Cooper case. On September 8, 2014, WRAL-TV was able to confirm that Brad Cooper was getting ready to plead guilty to second-degree murder. Garry Rentz, Nancy's father, in a telephone interview that day, acknowledged the plea offer and said that the family was okay with it because it would finally put the case to rest for the Coopers' two daughters.

"It's a matter of getting closure for them and not having to wonder. They worry about what their future is until it gets solidified," Rentz said.

The local media was told to be in court on September 22, with cameras ready to go. Even though a plea offer had been confirmed by several news outlets, pleas were never set in stone. A defendant could change his mind at the last moment, sometimes derailing weeks, or even months, of tense negotiations between the two sides. Especially in a case like this one where there had been so many twists and turns, there was always a chance Brad Cooper could change his mind.

The anticipation in the courtroom was palpable as Nancy Cooper's family and a handful of friends assembled in the front row behind the prosecutor's table. The media occupied the back right corner of the courtroom, while the rest of the seats were full of curious court watchers, many who had no connection to the case, but simply wanted to see its conclusion. Everyone spoke quietly, but frenetically, creating a throbbing, nervous din in the courtroom as they waited for the hearing to begin.

For Garry and Donna Rentz, hearing their former son-in-law take responsibility for their daughter's death was much more important than him spending the rest of his life in prison. After years of wondering how and why their daughter was killed, they shared that it had become critical for them to them to hear Brad admit he had killed his wife. Beyond that, their main concern was keeping the Coopers' children safe and happy. They were not people who harbored revenge against Brad or wallowed in their anger over Nancy's death; they simply wanted their tragic story to end peacefully.

A hush fell over the courtroom as Judge Paul Gessner approached the bench. He asked the attorneys if they had agreed upon a plea deal, and when they said yes, he read the terms of the agreement. Brad Cooper would plead guilty to second-degree murder and be sentenced to a range of twelve to fifteen years in prison with credit for the time he had already served. This meant, potentially, he could be a free man in six to seven years. Also part of the deal, he agreed to give up his parental rights to Bella and Katie, clearing the way for Nancy's sister, Krista Lister, and her husband Jim, to legally adopt the girls.

Prosecutor Howard Cummings gave a brief synopsis of the case to the judge. They were details that Gessner knew intimately after having presided over the trial, but the recitation of the factual basis for the agreement was an important part of documenting the plea for the court record. Cummings said that Nancy's death was the culmination of years of "mental and psychological domestic violence."

Cummings reiterated what the state had presented at trial as the motive in the case, that Brad didn't want the expense of a divorce and a child custody battle.

"What he did was prevent her from leaving, for among other reasons, because it was going to cost too much," Cummings said.

As to the contention that someone may have hacked into Brad's computer and planted the Google Maps search, Cummings said this would have been an impossible task given the time and expertise required to achieve something like this. And who would have done that or made that possible? Certainly not the Cary Police. Cummings defended them after the beating they took from defense attorneys at trial.

"They got run through the mill the likes I've never seen," he said. "They are very professional. They did things exactly the way they needed to be done."

When it was time, Gessner asked Brad Cooper to stand so that he could review the terms of the plea agreement with him and ask him questions. After the usual questions about entering into the plea agreement willingly and of sound mind, Gessner asked the question Nancy's family had been waiting six years to hear the answer to.

"Do you now personally plead guilty to the charge that I have just described?" Gessner asked the defendant.

"Yes," Brad Cooper replied without hesitation.

"Did you in fact kill Nancy Cooper and dump her body on Fielding Drive?" Gessner asked pointedly.

This time he hesitated. It was obvious from the stunned look on his face that Brad Cooper was thrown off by the specificity of the question, one that he was clearly not anticipating. He leaned over and whispered something to his attorneys. They then asked to approach the bench and speak with the judge privately. After a few minutes of hushed conversation, all of the parties returned to their places, and he answered the question with no elaboration.

"Yes," he replied without elaboration.

It was then Gessner's turn to speak his mind before pronouncing the final sentence, a sentence that was already agreed upon and clearly defined by the plea agreement. Like the Cary Police, Gessner had been a punching bag for defense attorneys during the trial as they consistently accused him of a pro-state bias. Adding further insult, Gessner's rulings about the defense witnesses prompted the Appeals Court to overturn the guilty verdict. Now was his opportunity to have the last word.

"It just bothers me that you have an individual who will,

apparently, bargain away their rights as a parent," Gessner said referring to the defendant's willingness to allow his children to be adopted by Nancy Cooper's sister in return for a shorter sentence. "I find that repulsive."

When it was all over, Nancy's family gathered in front of the TV cameras in the empty courtroom to share their feelings about the long-awaited day. Donna and Garry stood flanked by their son, Jeff Rentz, to Donna's right, and their daughter, Krista Lister, to Garry's left. The only person absent was their youngest daughter, Jill Dean, who they said was too emotional to speak to the media. Jill had missed the trial because she had just given birth, so this was her first experience in the courtroom with Brad. It was also her first experience listening in person to the facts about her sister's murder recounted out loud for everyone to hear. But despite her absence, the family displayed their trademark grace and diplomacy in front of the hungry crowd of reporters.

"First of all, when we started this process years ago, one of the first things I said that I wished was that the person that was responsible for this crime would come forward and acknowledge guilt and own up to their behavior. That's happened today. So, I feel very satisfied that we're now at the spot that there's closure to something that started all those years ago," Garry Rentz said confidently. "It brings closure to us as a family and we feel like we can move forward."

"It's nice to get the guilty plea because it acknowledges that he in fact did do what we all felt he did all along," Jeff Rentz said solemnly. "It's tough to keep ripping off that Band-Aid and expect the wound to heal. So, now, that it's complete, and we've got the guilty plea, and we can move forward, we can close this chapter and move on."

Donna Rentz stood silently in between her husband and her son looking weary, and appeared to be constantly on the verge of saying something. Finally, it was her turn.

"I think it would have been nice to hear him say himself what he did and why he did it," Donna Rentz said putting the day in perspective. The grieving mother had gotten some, but not all, of what she had come for that that day. Her heart still ached at the thought of living the rest of her life without knowing exactly what happened to her daughter and why. In her mind, only one person held the key to that information, Brad Cooper. And after his plea, it was clear she would probably never get those answers.

"I don't know if justice is something I really thought about. We were more interested in making sure the kids' futures were secure. And we're satisfied with the outcome, and I think that's what counts for us," Garry Rentz said, bringing the focus back to what appeared to be the family's desire in the plea negotiation.

"We're just very happy with what happened for Bella and Katie Lister, to move on with their lives with the knowledge and certainty of what their father did to their mother, and that certainty will be very important in the years to come."

"They know what happened with Nancy," Krista Lister said bitterly, "especially Bella, and it destroyed her for many years. She's gotten over it, she's moved past. Thankfully, I've got an amazing family to help, and they got through it."

Krista told the reporters Brad was now out of the girls' lives forever.

"It's amazing, it's total relief," said Krista of having the way cleared to allow her and her husband Jim Lister to adopt the girls they had been raising for six years. "He (Brad Cooper) doesn't deserve them. He doesn't deserve to know them. And I'm very happy about that."

But even with the apparent finality of the case, "happy" didn't describe the looks on the faces of Nancy Cooper's family members, nor did it describe the look on Brad Cooper's face as he made a bargain that would allow him to get his life back at a relatively young age. The truth was that no one was happy at the outcome of this case. Nancy Cooper was dead. Bella and Katie had lost both their parents. There was no happy ending, and in a way, there was no real ending, not the "closure" that Nancy's family longed for. Brad will eventually get out of prison and have to figure out how to assimilate back into the world as an admitted murderer. He is scheduled to be released on November 23, 2020, just after his forty-seventh birthday. Bella and Katie will eventually grow up, and even surrounded by a loving family, they will still have questions and struggles dealing with their tragic past.

"Happy" was definitely not the word to describe the ending to this story.

It's a cautionary tale, a tragic tale; a tale that leaves more questions than answers. It's a trail of broken hearts and a litany of secrets. Only two people know the truth. One is dead, and the other won't gamble his silence for freedom.

EPILOGUE

REFLECTIONS

Life is not so much about beginnings and endings
as it is about going on and on and on. It is about
muddling through the middle.
—Anna Quindlen

On Monday morning, July 14, 2008, two days after Nancy Cooper was reported missing, I stood in my bathrobe and drank coffee on my back porch. I was enjoying a few minutes of solitude before getting ready for another busy day. The early-morning sunlight sprinkled the lush green forest just beyond the edge of my overgrown yard with a diamond-like pattern, and a warm breeze rustled the leaves above the persistent hum of the cicada bugs. As I looked into the thick green brush, I had a strong sense that Nancy Cooper was not far away, that, despite the diligent searching, she was still probably nearby.

As I approached the search headquarters at the local coffee shop, Java Jive, I immediately recalled seeing Nancy at this very coffee shop, wearing a pretty green sundress and sitting at the same table that was now littered with maps and fliers with her picture on them. I stood at the edge of that table doing a live shot for the noon news and thinking about how many times my path had probably crossed with Nancy's. I felt a sudden rush of sadness that it had taken her disappearance for me to get to know her.

Later that day, I left the first press conference at the Cary Police Department feeling even more convinced that Nancy, despite what Chief Pat Bazemore had said, was probably not coming home alive. That night her body was found discarded in a drainage ditch just a few miles as the crow flies from the very spot where I had sipped my morning coffee fifteen hours earlier.

Tuesday, July 15, 2008, was a typical beautiful North Carolina summer day with blue skies and sunshine for miles. The sunlight glimmered across the surface of the local pool. Young children threw rubber toys into the water, then dove down to retrieve them, bursting back up to the surface with shouts of victory. On the far side of the pool women bounced up and down in a water aerobics class in bright, flowered swim caps. But beneath the warm feeling of the perfect summer day was an undercurrent of sadness. I couldn't help but imagine that Nancy and her young daughters, Bella and Katie, would probably have been here on a beautiful day like this, frolicking in the pool, laughing and carrying on with friends.

The truth was that the summer of 2008 was anything but normal for people who lived in Lochmere. The tree-lined streets that formerly boasted crowds of walkers and runners every morning were less traveled. The freedom and innocence everyone had once enjoyed in the community was stolen when Nancy was murdered.

As the investigation dragged on, there were whispers. *What if it is never solved?*

I tried to ignore the voices, but I heard them everywhere—at the pool, at the grocery store, at the gym, at the ballet school. Everywhere I went, people asked me about the case—what I thought about it, what I thought might happen. But in reality, I was asking myself the very same questions. As I passed the Cooper home every night on my way home from work, I couldn't help but slow down and peer into the lit windows and wonder, *What happened in there?*

After Brad Cooper was arrested on October 27, 2008, the black cloud that had hung over the neighborhood that summer started to dissipate. The crisp fall mornings were full of sunshine and the promise of balmy afternoons that perfectly embodied the phrase "Indian summer" in North Carolina. As I passed the Cooper house, I no longer looked. I knew it was empty now.

But the months of waiting for the case to go to court after Nancy's death turned into years. And when it was finally time to go to trial, the anxiety that people in the community had felt surrounding the crime was fresh again, like old wounds torn open and doused with salt. The trial took an emotional toll on everyone connected to it—the families, the friends, the lawyers, the court officials, the jury, and, yes, even the media. Once again, it was a hot topic of conversation everywhere I went in Cary. They talked about it in the grocery store, at restaurants, and in low voices as they jogged past me in the morning. The black cloud was back, and it was darker than ever. While the arrest gave some resolution to the case, a conviction was needed to close this painful chapter.

The day the verdict came down was a relief to so many people—it was over. After years of wondering how the story would end, there was finally an answer to the questions and the speculation. But little did everyone know their relief would be short-lived. The overturned conviction would ultimately return the case square one again, and throw the stakeholders into legal and emotional limbo. It wasn't until Brad Cooper pleaded guilty, six years after his wife's murder, on September 22, 2014, that the conclusion became real.

I didn't know Nancy Cooper personally, but I had the privilege of meeting her through the detailed memories of her family and friends. They didn't saint her—instead, they made her a real, tangible person to me, someone with great attributes and human frailties. Someone, like the rest of us, who was not perfect, but was the perfect Nancy to those who loved her—her children, her parents, her siblings and many, many friends. From what I learned, I know I would have liked her and related to her, especially as the mother of two girls. I think about her often—the missed opportunities in a life cut tragically short, the missed opportunities for her daughters who are growing up without her.

I think about Nancy the most when I am running, a pastime that was one of her passions. There is nothing but the sounds of my shoes hitting the pavement and heavy breath exhaling. It's in these moments that I enjoy a quiet slice of peace away from the chaos of the courtroom, and say a silent prayer that just maybe, Nancy has found peace too.

CPSIA information can be obtained
at www.ICGtesting.com
Printed in the USA
BVHW081502090719
552977BV00001B/1/P